MEDICAL IMAGING

AND RADIATION PROTEC

FOR MEDICAL STUDENTS AND CLINICAL STAFF

Edited by

Colin J Martin

Philip P Dendy

Robert H Corbett

Published by The British Institute of Radiology

Editors

Dr Colin J Martin
Health Physics
West House
Gartnavel Royal Hospital
GLASGOW
G12 0XH
UK

Dr Philip P Dendy
c/o The British Institute of Radiology
36 Portland Place
LONDON
W1B 1AT
UK

Dr Robert H Corbett
Department of Diagnostic Radiology
Hairmyres Hospital
Lanarkshire Acute Hospitals NHS Trust
East Kilbride
GLASGOW
G75 8RG
UK

Contents

Preface

The use of diagnostic imaging has increased dramatically in the last 10–15 years. It is now a routine part of the clinical investigation of many patients and is often crucial in determining their management. The majority of techniques use ionising radiation, *i.e.* X-rays, and radioactive tracers. Other techniques, notably ultrasound and magnetic resonance imaging (MRI), do not use ionising radiation. Medical exposures are, by far, the largest contributor to the average radiation dose to the population from man-made sources.

To promote and encourage the prudent use of ionising radiation, the European Commission published a revised version of an earlier Directive relating to medical exposures in 1996. Member States are required to introduce legislation that incorporates the Articles of the Directive. This should lead to standardisation of radiation protection principles and practices as applied to medicine throughout the European Union. All doctors have a duty to choose the most effective investigation or investigation strategy. Hence, one of the recommendations of the Directive is that the fundamentals of radiation protection should be included in the basic medical school curriculum.

The dual purpose of this book is to provide an update, at the appropriate level, on diagnostic imaging techniques and to present information for medical students and doctors in training on the prudent use of ionising radiation in medicine.

The first two chapters give an overview of radiation in the environment and the use of radiation in medicine. These are followed by five chapters that provide a simple introduction to the main imaging techniques; conventional X-rays, X-ray computed tomography (CT), nuclear medicine, ultrasound and MRI. The emphasis is on clinical situations where each is appropriate.

Chapters 8–12 focus on the principles of radiation protection. Starting from basic radiobiology and radiotherapy, a framework for risk estimation is developed and the risks associated with a wide range of radiological examinations are presented in a way that doctors can readily explain to their patients. Chapter 12 summarises the relevant legislation.

Chapter 13 is perhaps the most important for many readers, since it deals with the subject of "Requesting an X-ray". Unnecessary or badly formulated requests give an avoidable radiation dose to the patient, waste scarce health service resources and may actually result in illegal procedures.

Chapters 14–16 deal with more specialised issues — personal protection for staff and patients, research projects involving radiation and radiation protection implications of screening.

Finally, Chapter 17 considers the overall diagnostic strategy and draws together many of the issues considered earlier. These include the choice and sequence of investigation, good clinical practice and risks relating to the use of ionising radiation.

The principal target readership is medical students and doctors in training. However, the book has been written with a range of other readers in mind, including house doctors starting their careers and those beginning to use fluoroscopic techniques. Senior members of the medical profession who wish to brush up on these matters, radiographers in training, and nurses working in radiology departments, on wards or in theatres where X-rays are used will find much to interest them.

To assist the reader to navigate through the book, extensive use has been made of "boxes" in the page layout. There are three types of box:

(a)   At the start of each chapter there is a small box summarising the content.
(b)   The most important boxes, containing key information, are highlighted by a bolder outline and contain bullet points.
(c)   "Insight" boxes provide greater detail. They may not be of interest to all readers and can be omitted without losing the main thrust of the chapter.

Philip Dendy
September 2003

Acknowledgments

The Editors wish to acknowledge the helpful comments during preparation of the manuscript given by Ian Brock McHardy, David Gentle and Mark Whitby.

Abbreviations

ADH	Antidiuretic hormone
ALARA	As low as reasonably achievable
ALARP	As low as reasonably practicable
A-mode	Amplitude mode (ultrasound display)
AP	Anteroposterior
ARSAC	Administration of Radioactive Substances Advisory Committee
AXR	Abdominal radiograph
B-mode	Brightness mode (ultrasound display)
Bq (and MBq)	Becquerel (and megabecquerel)
CCTV	Closed circuit television
CHART	Continuous hyperfractionated accelerated radiotherapy
CR	Computed radiography
CSF	Cerebrospinal fluid
CT	Computed tomography
CTDI	Computed tomography dose index
CTPA	Computed tomography pulmonary angiography
CTV	Clinical target volume (radiotherapy)
CXR	Chest radiograph
D/C	Double contrast
DICOM	Digital communication in medicine
DNA	Deoxyribonucleic acid
DR	Direct (digital) radiography
DRL	Diagnostic reference level
DSA	Digital subtraction angiography
DSI	Digital subtraction imaging
ECG	Electrocardiogram
ENT	Ear, nose and throat
ERCP	Endoscopic retrograde cholangiopancreatography
EU	European Union
eV	Electron volt
FDG	Fluorodeoxyglucose
GI	Gastrointestinal
GP	General practitioner
GSD	Genetically significant dose
Gy (and mGy)	Gray (unit of absorbed dose) (and milligray)
HDR	High dose rate
HIS	Hospital information system
HL7	High level 7 (language used by RIS and HIS)
HSE	Health and Safety Executive
Hz	Hertz (cycles per second)
IAEA	International Atomic Energy Agency
ICRP	International Commission on Radiological Protection
IMRT	Intensity modulated radiotherapy

IQ	Intelligence quotient
IR(ME)R	Ionising Radiation (Medical Exposure) Regulations
IRR	Ionising Radiations Regulations
IT	Information technology
ITU	Intensive therapy unit (Intensive Care)
IVU	Intravenous urogram
kV(p)	Kilovoltage (peak)
Lat	Lateral
LDR	Low dose rate
LMP	Last menstrual period
LNT	Linear no-threshold
MAA	Human albumin macroaggregates (nuclear medicine)
MAG3	Benzoylmercaptoacetyltriglycerine (nuclear medicine)
MARS	Medicines (Administration of Radioactive Substances) Regulations
mA(s)	Milliamp (× seconds) (X-ray exposure factor)
MHz	Megahertz
MIBG	Meta-iodobenzyl guanidine (nuclear medicine)
MLC	Multileaf collimator (radiotherapy)
M-mode	Motion mode (ultrasound display)
MPE	Medical physics expert
MR	Magnetic resonance
MRCP	Magnetic resonance cholangiopancreatography
MRI	Magnetic resonance imaging
MRPA	Magnetic resonance pulmonary angiography
MU	Monitor units (radiotherapy)
NHS	National Health Service
NHSBSP	NHS Breast Screening Programme
NM	Nuclear medicine
NRPB	National Radiological Protection Board
PA	Posteroanterior
PACS	Picture archiving and communication system
PE	Pulmonary embolus
PET	Positron emission tomography
PM	Photomultiplier
PTC	Percutaneous transhepatic cholangiography
PTV	Planning target volume (radiotherapy)
PVE	Partial volume effect
RBC	Red blood cell
RBE	Relative biological effectiveness
RCR	Royal College of Radiologists
REPPIR	Radiation (Emergency Preparedness and Public Information) Regulations
RIS	Radiology information system
RNI	Radionuclide imaging
RPA	Radiation Protection Adviser
RSA	Radioactive Substances Act
SHO	Senior house officer
SPF	Sun protection factor

Sv (and mSv)	Sievert (unit of effective and equivalent dose) (and millisievert)
T_1 and T_2	MRI relaxation times
TB	Tuberculosis
TIPS	Transjugular intrahepatic portosystemic shunt
TLD	Thermoluminescent dosemeter
TGC	Time gain compensation (ultrasound)
TPS	Treatment planning system
UNSCEAR	United Nations Scientific Committee on the Effects of Atomic Radiation
US	Ultrasound
UV	Ultraviolet
VQ	Ventilation/perfusion scintigraphy (nuclear medicine)
w_R	Radiation weighting factor
w_T	Tissue weighting factor

Chapter 1

Radiation is all around us

CJ Martin

This introductory chapter explains the differences between ionising and non-ionising radiations and presents some basic information on radiation properties that impact on radiation harm and radiation safety.

Radiation is all around us in the natural environment and in some manufactured articles. This chapter describes some of the sources of which you may or may not be aware.

1.1 Radiation

Ionising radiation has played an important role in medicine ever since the discovery of X-rays and radioactivity at the end of the nineteenth century. The benefits that it has brought are innumerable, but there is also a risk of harm from any exposure. The aim of this book is to present information about the range of imaging modalities and treatments using both ionising and non-ionising radiations and how these techniques can best be utilised with minimal risk in patient management.

This chapter attempts to explain something about the different types of ionising radiation and looks at some applications outside medicine. Before proceeding further, the first question to answer is "What is radiation?" Radiation is a means by which energy is transported through space or through matter. Light, X-rays and radio waves are all electromagnetic radiations. They all behave like waves and carry energy in small "packets" called *photons*. Sound is another form of radiation, as it also has the properties of a wave and conveys energy. The types of radiation described so far do not have any mass, but small *particles* are also considered as radiations, as they carry energy in the same way.

One purpose of the book is to consider the harm that radiation might cause. A major distinction is made between two categories, ionising and non-ionising radiations, based on the amount of energy carried. Photons or particles that have sufficient energy to separate an electron from an atom are called ionising radiations. Such an interaction produces a positive ion and a free electron (Figure 1.1).

- **Ionising radiations**
X-rays, γ-rays, α-particles, β-particles, neutrons, cosmic rays
- **Non-ionising radiations**
light, ultraviolet, infra-red, radio waves, microwaves, ultrasound

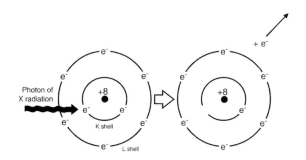

Figure 1.1 Ionisation of an oxygen atom. An oxygen atom with 8 protons and 8 electrons on the left is converted to an ionised oxygen atom (O^+) with 8 protons and 7 electrons. An energetic electron e⁻ is released.

Single photons or particles of ionising radiation have the potential to affect biological cells (see Chapter 8). The same is not true for non-ionising radiations. Non-ionising radiations will be considered later in this chapter, but first the properties and varied uses of ionising radiations will be explored.

1.2 Radioactivity

This section will remind you of some basic things about radioactivity that you may have forgotten.

An atomic nucleus that is unstable may change spontaneously to a more stable nucleus by emitting a small particle with a positive or negative charge. Such spontaneous nuclear transformations are called radioactive decay and may also be accompanied by the release of energy in the form of γ-ray photons (see box, page 3).

The activity of a sample containing radioactive atoms that are decaying will gradually decline. A simple law governs the change in activity with time for any radioactive decay process. A time or *half-life* can be defined in which the activity will fall to one-half. Every radionuclide has its own characteristic half-life. For some radionuclides this is a fraction of a second, while for others it is billions of years. The half-life is one of the properties that determine the choice of radionuclide for different clinical investigations (see §5.3). For example, a radionuclide with a half-life of a few minutes could not be used for a metabolic study scheduled to last for several days.

Different pathways through which radioactive decay can occur are by emission of α-particles, β⁻-particles or positrons (β⁺-particles). The hazards from radiation exposure depend on the type of radiation emitted and on whether the exposure is from an external source or from radioactive material inside the body. These hazards are discussed in more detail in Chapter 8.

Radioactive atoms or radionuclides

- An atom has a tiny nucleus made up from protons, which have positive charges, and neutrons.
- The space around the nucleus contains electrons, which have negative charges.
- Atoms with many different combinations of protons and neutrons in their nucleus can exist and each combination is called a nuclide. Some are stable, but others are not and these are called *radionuclides*.

Insight: The becquerel

Radioactivity is measured in terms of the number of radioactive atoms that are decaying or the activity. The basic unit is the becquerel, which is the amount of radioactive material in which, on average, one atomic nucleus disintegrates every second. Prefixes are: kBq, kiloBq (×10³); MBq, megaBq (×10⁶); GBq, gigaBq (×10⁹); and TBq, teraBq (×10¹²). An older unit, the curie (Ci) is still occasionally used [1 Ci = 37 GBq].

Insight: Atomic symbols

Atoms with the same number of protons have a similar chemical form and are represented by the same chemical symbol. The family of different nuclides for a particular element are known as the **isotopes** *of that element. A particular nuclide is represented by the chemical name or symbol and the number of protons plus neutrons in the nucleus (e.g. carbon-14 or ¹⁴C). All isotopes of carbon have 6 protons, but as shown below the number of neutrons can vary from 4 to 9.*

Isotopes of carbon: Stable nuclides ¹²C, ¹³C
Radionuclides ¹⁰C, ¹¹C, ¹⁴C, ¹⁵C

1.3 Properties of ionising radiations

There are a few important properties of ionising radiations that it is useful to know in order to understand more about their uses and hazards.

1.3.1 Inverse-square law

Radiation intensity decreases quickly as you move further from a source. This is because the same amount of radiation energy is spread over a larger area (Figure 1.2). The intensity incident on a surface is proportional to the square of the distance between the source and the surface. This type of law applies provided that the distance from the source is much larger than its size. Thus, it would apply to radiation from an X-ray tube

---

Insight: Ionising radiations

α-particles: *α-particles consist of two protons and two neutrons. They interact strongly with matter and are more damaging to biological cells than other types of radiation, if taken into the body (see §8.11).*

β⁻-particles: *A β⁻-particle is a high energy electron emitted from the nucleus. β⁻-particles can cause an external radiation hazard to the skin or an internal hazard if atoms that emit β⁻-particles are ingested.*

Positrons: *A positron (β⁺-particle) is like an electron holding a positive charge. Positrons have a very transitory existence. They combine with electrons and the mass of the two particles is converted to energy and emitted as a pair of γ-ray photons.*

Neutrons: *Neutrons are produced in copious numbers in reactors and can be obtained from artificial sources. Since neutrons have a similar mass to hydrogen nuclei (protons) they can transfer their energy readily to any material containing hydrogen and so are particularly damaging to tissue.*

γ-rays: *γ-rays are high energy electromagnetic wave photons emitted by some atomic nuclei during radioactive decay. The γ-rays are usually emitted effectively at the same time as the nuclear transformations. However, the excited state of the radionuclide technetium-99 following the decay of molybdenum-99 has a half-life of 6 h in making the transition to the ground state. A nuclear excited state with a long half-life is termed metastable and is given the symbol "m", e.g. ⁹⁹ᵐTc used extensively in nuclear medicine.*

X-rays: *X-rays, like γ-rays, are high energy electromagnetic radiations, but result from interactions with electrons surrounding the nuclei of atoms rather than being emitted from the nucleus as part of the decay process. When a high energy electron strikes a metal target it loses energy, which may be emitted in the form of an X-ray. This is the mechanism involved in the production of X-rays in an X-ray tube (see §3.2).*

---

or small radioactive source. However, the dose rate will not fall as rapidly when you move away from a patient containing radioactivity, because you are being exposed to radiation emitted from various parts of the body, rather than a single point.

1.3.2 Attenuation of X-rays and γ-rays

X-ray and γ-ray photons can penetrate substantial thickness of material, as they only interact with occasional atoms. That is one of the reasons why they are useful for imaging.

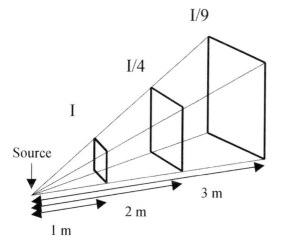

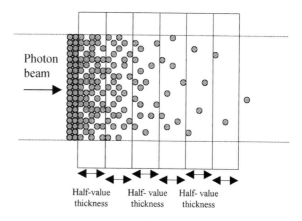

Figure 1.2 Inverse-square law: intensity decreases as the square of the distance from the source.

Figure 1.3 Attenuation of a beam of γ-rays by six half-value thicknesses.

As a beam passes through thicker and thicker layers of material, the intensity is gradually reduced. This reduction in intensity is referred to as *attenuation*. For a beam of γ-rays all with the same energy, there will be a particular thickness of any given material that will reduce the beam intensity by half. This is called the *half-value thickness* (HVT). Further layers of the same thickness will reduce the transmitted intensity by further factors of two (Figure 1.3). However, the intensity will never fall to zero, no matter how thick the layer.

1.3.3 Absorption and scatter

Two mechanisms contribute to attenuation of X-rays as they pass through matter (Figure 1.4). Some of the energy of the photons is transferred to electrons, which go on to ionise other atoms. This transfer of energy is called *absorption*. It is the absorption of energy in tissue that gives the radiation dose. This will be discussed in more depth in Chapter 8. Some photons may be completely destroyed and all the energy absorbed in the medium.

Other photons are diverted in random directions and only part of the energy or even none at all is absorbed by the medium. The photons that are changed in direction are said to be *scattered*. Both absorption and scatter reduce the intensity of an X-ray beam. Since denser materials attenuate X-rays more than lighter ones, it is the attenuation process that helps to form the image seen on an X-ray film (see §3.2). In an X-ray imaging system, some of the scattered photons may reach the film or other image receptor and these produce a random variation in the background, or "noise", which degrades the image.

X-ray photons are scattered in all directions. Therefore, staff who must stand near to a patient being X-rayed, for example in theatre, must take special care.

1.4 Radiation in the environment

Ionising radiation is not a new phenomenon. Most radioactive materials on earth were produced in cataclysmic events far back in the history of the universe. Most of the radiation dose that everyone receives is from natural radiation rather than from artificial sources. The sources that give the main contributions to the dose received by an average person in the UK are shown in Table 1.1. 14% of our radiation dose is from man-made sources, and the majority of this is from medical uses of radiation.

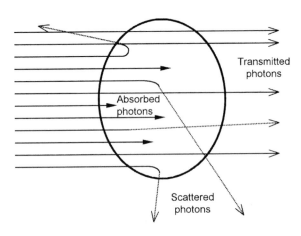

Figure 1.4 Transmission, absorption and scattering of X-rays by an object. Scattered photons are marked by dotted lines and absorbed photons by termination at a solid arrow.

Insight: Implications of different half-value thicknesses

Shielding
*Half-value thicknesses of materials used for **shielding** to provide protection against X-rays and γ-rays vary drastically with photon energy. Whereas a quarter of a millimetre of lead in a lead/rubber apron may provide protection against diagnostic X-rays, many centimetres of lead or a metre or two of concrete may be required to shield against high energy X-rays or γ-rays used in radiotherapy. A knowledge of the shielding efficiency of different materials is essential when working with ionising radiations (see §14.2.3 and §14.4). The interactions of particle radiations differ from those of X-rays and γ-rays in that there is a limited range within which all particles will be stopped.*

X-ray filtration
*An X-ray beam contains photons with a range of energies that are attenuated by different amounts. Thus, the distribution of photon energies in a beam transmitted through a patient is different from that in the incident beam. Thin metal **filters** are placed in the beams from medical X-ray equipment to remove lower energy photons that are heavily attenuated in the patient and so would not contribute to the final image (see §14.3.2).*

Table 1.1 Average annual dose in the UK at the start of the 21st century

Type	Source		Average dose in UK (mSv[a])
Natural background	Cosmic rays		0.26
	Terrestrial γ-rays		0.35
	Internal radionuclides (*e.g.* ^{40}K)		0.3
Domestic and social	Radon		1.3
	Air travel		0.01–1
	Household products		<0.001
Medical	Diagnostic X-ray		0.34
	Nuclear medicine		0.03
Nuclear power	Nuclear power discharges		0.0002
Nuclear weapons	Fallout from tests in 1950s and 60s		0.005
Occupational exposures	Aircrew		2.0
	Defence		0.8
	Nuclear power workers		0.7
	General industry		0.4
	Health professionals		0.1
	Average for whole population		0.007

[a] mSv is a unit used in radiological protection as a measure of radiation dose. It will be discussed further in §8.11, but at this stage it is only the relative magnitudes of doses from different sources that are relevant.

Diagrammatic display of relative magnitudes.

1.4.1 Terrestrial radioactivity

There are significant quantities of natural radionuclides in rocks and soils, because a few of these radionuclides have extremely long half-lives. For example, uranium-238 has a half-life of four and a half billion years. Radioactivity in rocks usually comprises a radioactive atom with a very long half-life mixed with a series of radionuclides with shorter half-lives produced from decay, called "daughter" products. Such a chain of disintegrations is referred to as a radioactive series.

1.4.2 Radon

The uranium-238 decay series includes radon-222, which is a gas and has a half-life of 4 days. If radon or its daughter products decay while in the lungs they will deliver a radiation dose from α- and β⁻-particles to the lung tissue. Radon is given off from soil where the underlying geology has high levels of the uranium decay series, in particular granite. Radon gas produced deep below the ground may reach the surface through fissures in rock. Radon levels in Cornwall and Devon, where the granite rock is fractured, are the highest in the UK, but levels in Aberdeen, where the granite rock is more solid, are relatively low. Radon gas is concentrated in buildings, as the higher indoor temperature causes air to rise and draws the radon from the soil. Radon delivers approximately 50% on average of the radiation dose to the population in the UK and more than this in other parts of Europe.

1.4.3 Cosmic radiation

Atomic nuclei with a wide range of energies are incident on the earth's outer atmosphere where they interact with air molecules to produce a mixture of particle and γ-radiation. At the earth's surface the general public receive a small dose each year from cosmic radiation, but doses are much greater at high altitudes because there is less attenuation by the atmosphere. Thus, persons travelling by plane are exposed to higher levels of cosmic radiation. Pilots and cabin crew receive on average higher radiation doses than workers in the nuclear industry (Table 1.1).

1.4.4 Other natural radionuclides

There are other natural radionuclides with lower atomic numbers that are important. Potassium-40 (^{40}K) has a long half-life (1250 million years) and, as a result, 0.012% of all potassium is radioactive. The body contains 0.03 g of ^{40}K, the highest level of radioactivity in the body. A bag of garden fertiliser contains enough ^{40}K to be readily detectable with a hand-held monitor.

Carbon-14 (^{14}C) has a shorter half-life (6000 years), but the levels are constantly renewed by transformation of nitrogen-14 in the atmosphere, induced by cosmic ray bombardment. This process has maintained the level of ^{14}C in the atmosphere at roughly the same level for tens of thousands of years. The carbon that forms living matter all contains a similar proportion of ^{14}C. However, when living matter dies, the ^{14}C gradually decays, so the properties can be used to date ancient artefacts.

1.5 Industrial uses of ionising radiation

The range of applications of ionising radiation in industry is wide and varied. Most natural radionuclides are not suitable for industrial or medical applications, but it is possible to manufacture artificial radionuclides. Sources are constructed so that the radioactive material is either sealed within a solid matrix or encapsulated, wherever possible, so that radioactive material is unlikely to be released. The risk to workers associated with different applications varies considerably from trivial to moderate.

Gamma irradiation systems

High doses of radiation kill biological cells and provide an efficient method for ensuring equipment is free from micro-organisms. Industrial irradiation plants with arrays of high activity γ-ray sources are employed in the sterilisation of needles and syringes for hospital use as well as in the food industry to kill bacteria and so increase the shelf-lives for a range of products. Small-scale γ-ray irradiators are used in hospitals to irradiate blood.

X-ray radiography

Radiography is the recording of X-ray or γ-ray images, usually on film. Fixed X-ray devices are used for examination of luggage at airports and high security establishments. Portable X-ray units are used by security firms for radiography of suspicious packages or incoming trucks at ports. There is a risk of exposure for persons standing close to any object being X-rayed with a portable unit that does not have a shielded enclosure.

Veterinary radiography

Vets use portable X-ray units to image animals of all sizes, from cats to horses. Small animals are frequently anaesthetised to avoid the animal having to be held or restrained. This may not always be possible and particular care is needed when an animal has to be held while it is being X-rayed, to minimise exposure from scattered radiation by shielding the body and to avoid placing any part of the hands in the beam.

Industrial radiography

Portable γ-ray sources are used to produce images of welds in metal objects such as pipes to check for cracks and to assess the uniformity of concrete. The γ-ray sources are housed in shielded containers and are connected to wires to enable them to be manoeuvred remotely. A number of incidents have resulted from mishandling of these sources.

Measuring gauges

The attenuation of radiation is used in a wide range of applications. Sources emitting β⁻-particles are employed in paper and plastics industries for thickness measurement; γ-ray and neutron sources are used for gauging thickness of coatings in road construction. Sources are used in the oil and gas industry in logging to assess the strata density from measurement of attenuation or scatter.

Smoke detectors

The α-particle emitter americium-241 is used in smoke detectors, and other sources are employed in monitoring gas or dust levels in various industries.

Luminous signs

Since radioactive materials may continue to emit energy for long periods of time, they have been used to make low-level light sources in which the radioactive material is mixed with a phosphor. The ionising radiation excites atoms in the phosphor, which subsequently emit the excitation energy as light. This technique provides a low-level light source that is permanently "on". It has been used in luminous dials of watches and clocks, and in luminous exit signs.

Cardiac pacemakers

Nuclear-powered cardiac pacemakers were fitted to patients in the UK during the 1970s and there are members of the public with such pacemakers. Although the casing was designed to withstand the high temperatures encountered during possible cremation, there is a potential risk. Any person with such a pacemaker should be identified so that the power pack can be removed at post-mortem and disposed of safely.

Unsealed radioactive materials

There are some applications for which radioactive material is incorporated into a liquid or gas. Radionuclides that are chosen for use in this unsealed form have a relatively short half-life, so that the risks are small if any material is taken into the body. Major users of unsealed radioactive materials are hospitals, universities, research institutes and pharmaceutical companies.

Nuclear-powered satellites

Nuclear energy is used to power some satellites. There are two types of system: in one, the heat associated with decay is used as the power source, while in the second a small nuclear reactor provides a higher power level. There is a risk when a satellite returns to earth that the radioactive material will not be burnt up in the atmosphere and may contaminate the ground around where it lands. However, only minor traces have been found from satellites that have returned to earth.

1.6 Nuclear power

Nuclear power produces about 25% of the electric power generated in the UK. The main source of energy is from fission of uranium-235 (^{235}U) nuclei. The ^{235}U nuclei absorb low energy thermal neutrons, split into pairs of smaller nuclei called fission products and release more neutrons. These neutrons in turn go on to induce further reactions. The difference in mass between the ^{235}U and the product nuclei is released as energy.

New nuclear reactor fuel is only slightly radioactive, but once it has been in a reactor, the creation of fission products makes it highly radioactive. If an accident occurs in a reactor core, a cocktail of highly active fission products could be released. Fear of the consequences of a nuclear accident has meant that no nuclear reactors have been built in the UK since the accident at Chernobyl in 1986.

Nuclear power does not involve the burning of fossil fuel and so does not produce carbon dioxide and contribute to global warming. Thus, the arguments in favour of the use of nuclear power may outweigh those

> **Insight: The Chernobyl accident**
>
> *The accident happened at the Chernobyl reactor near Kiev, Russia, on 25 April 1986. Operators overrode safety systems and this led to the nuclear reaction going out of control. The resulting explosion blew off the roof of the reactor building and released 4 million TBq of fission products into the atmosphere. The remains of the reactor have been entombed in a sarcophagus. The radionuclides released that had the most significant radiological consequences were caesium-137 and iodine-131 (^{131}I). The health consequences included both short- and long-term effects. 134 of the emergency personnel involved in controlling the accident suffered acute radiation sickness, from which 28 died. ^{131}I was responsible for a large increase in childhood thyroid cancer in nearby Russian states.*

against if the consequences of global warming are perceived to be more catastrophic than those of radioactive waste disposal and potential nuclear accidents.

1.7 Non-ionising radiations

Radiations with photon energies less than 12 eV are called non-ionising radiations. The non-ionising part of the electro-magnetic spectrum can be divided into optical radiations and electromagnetic fields. The electromagnetic field part comprises radio waves and low frequency fields, but only radio waves will be considered here. Non-ionising radiations may be absorbed and so may heat any object on which they are incident or may be reflected from the surface.

> ### Insight: Radiation energy (eV)
>
> *Energies of electromagnetic and particle radiations are measured in electron volts (eV). 1 eV is the energy that an electron will gain if it is accelerated through a potential difference of 1 volt.*

1.7.1 Optical radiations

Optical radiations are ultraviolet, visible and infra-red radiations. They do not penetrate far into the human body, so the eyes and skin are the only organs at risk from exposure.

We are all exposed to ultraviolet (UV) radiation from the sun and this is the most important source of exposure. Artificial sources (see Table 1.2) include arc welding and sun beds for cosmetic purposes. UV radiation induces photochemical reactions in the skin that produce erythema and tanning. Prolonged repeated exposure will, in the long-term, cause premature ageing of the skin with deep wrinkles and a leathery texture. UV exposure also gives an increased risk of skin cancer. Outdoor workers have a high incidence of basal and squamous cell skin cancers on exposed areas such as the head and neck. These make up 90% of all skin cancers, but are rarely fatal. Malignant melanoma, the most lethal form of skin cancer, occurs most frequently on the trunk and legs of Caucasians. It is linked to intermittent exposure from recreational activities. The

> ### Insight: Sun, shade and sunscreen
>
> *   **Protect your skin** *from too much UV exposure from the sun on summer holidays and at summer weekends.*
> *   **Shade, hats and clothing** *provide better UV protection than sunscreen.*
> *   **Sunscreen** *use helps to prevent squamous cell carcinoma. However, use of sunscreen is linked to an increased risk of malignant melanoma. This is probably partly because sunscreen users spend longer in the sun.*
> *   **Sun protection factors** *(SPFs) for a typical application of sunscreen are about a third of the SPF given on the bottle. Thus, a SPF of 5 will reduce the exposure to 50% and a SPF of 15 will reduce it to 20%.*
> *   **You need sun exposure** *in the autumn and winter to maintain your vitamin D status.*

Table 1.2 Optical radiation sources and hazards (energies less than 12 eV)

Type		Wavelength	Artificial sources	Hazard
Ultraviolet	UVC	100–280 nm	Sterilization	
	UVB	280–315 nm	Arc welding	Sunburn
				Photokeratitis
	UVA	315–400 nm	Sun beds	*Skin cancer*
				Photo-aging
Visible		400–770 nm	Incandescent lamps	Retinal injury
			Diode lasers	
Infrared	Near	770 nm–1.4 μm	Nd:YAG laser	Retinal injury
			Furnaces	Skin burn
	Far	1.4 μm–1 mm	CO_2 laser	Corneal burn
				Thermal cataract
				Heating of body

Effects in *italic* are long-term.

incidence of malignant melanoma is rising in the UK, almost certainly due to increased UV exposure during holidays in sunnier climates. UV exposure of the eyes produces photokeratitis (snow blindness) and, in the long-term, a risk of cataract.

The most intense sources of visible light and infra-red radiation are the sun, lasers and high temperature sources such as furnaces and molten metal. High power lasers are used to etch, weld and even cut metals, while low power ones are used in a wide variety of applications including printers, CD players, bar code readers, pointers and light displays for entertainment. The power level of lasers in everyday devices should be below that at which there is a hazard to the eye, or protective features should be incorporated into the equipment in which they are used. Engineering and procedural controls must be in place for higher power lasers to ensure that people cannot be exposed to the laser beams.

1.7.2 Radio waves

Radio waves are even lower photon energy electromagnetic waves, usually characterised by their frequencies (between 30 kHz and 300 GHz). They are used extensively in communications devices and some applications of different frequency ranges are given in Table 1.3. TV, radio and mobile phone signals are transmitted from masts of varying height, while longer range communication signals are transmitted via satellite or bounced off the ionosphere. In all cases the transmitter is either some distance above the ground or is directed up into the sky, so that field strengths on the ground are low.

The energy from radio waves is absorbed by tissue. The only known harmful effect is heating, but a variety of other harmful effects, including malignant disease, have been postulated. However, experimental data are equivocal and no convincing mechanism for any of these effects has yet been suggested. The levels where members of the public have access are well below the level at which any hazard has been confirmed.

Radiocommunication handsets have the potential to interfere with the operation of certain electromedical equipment and their use is restricted in hospitals where patient-connected equipment is used, such as intensive care units.

What is a laser and what are the risks?

• Laser stands for **L**ight **A**mplification by **S**timulated **E**mission of **R**adiation and is a way in which energy can be converted into high intensity light.

• Light is reflected backwards and forwards within a laser cavity to build up an intense, well collimated beam of photons, all with the same wavelength.

• The main hazard from intense sources of visible light or infra-red radiation is to the eye.

• The eye has a natural aversion mechanism in the blink response to intense visible light, but this will not necessarily protect against the intensity levels from high power lasers.

• Visible light and near infra-red radiation can damage the retina, while far infra-red is absorbed in the cornea and lens.

Insight: Medical equipment that may be affected by radiocommunication devices

Ventilators   Infusion pumps   Monitors
Defibrillators   External pacemakers

Table 1.3 Radio wave sources and hazards (wavelengths 1 mm–100 km)

Radiation	Frequency (Hz)	Sources	Biological effects
Microwaves	300 GHz	Microwave telecommunications	Heating of body surface
	30 GHz	Radar	
		Satellite communications	
Microwaves	3 GHz	Mobile phones	Heating to depth of 10 mm
		TV transmitters	
		Microwave ovens	
Very high frequency	300 MHz	FM radio	Raised body temperature
		Emergency service radios	
High frequency	30 MHz	International radio	
Medium frequency	3 MHz	AM radio	
Low frequency	300 kHz	Shop/airport security	Cumulation of charge on body surface
	30 kHz	Visual display units	
		Television sets	

1.7.3 Sound

Sound waves or mechanical vibrations are a form of non-ionising radiation. Sound can travel through matter, but since it relies on the transfer of energy through movement of atoms and molecules, it cannot propagate through empty space. The technique of transmitting pulses of sound and listening for echoes to find structures or objects that are hidden from view has many different applications, including geological surveys, location of shoals of fish and detection of cracks in metal. Ultrasound, which is high frequency sound, can be propagated through the body and techniques based on the same principle of echo location are used in medicine. The ear, being the organ designed to pick up sound, can be damaged by high intensity sound.

1.8 Summary

- Radiations can be divided into ionising and non-ionising. Ionising radiations have sufficient energy to separate an electron from an atom.
- Radioactive atoms or radionuclides are atoms that are unstable and will decay by emitting ionising radiation in the form of particles and γ-rays.
- Each radionuclide has a particular half-life governing its decay.
- X-rays are produced by the interaction of electrons with atoms.
- The further you go away from a source of radiation, the lower the intensity and radiation dose rate.
- X-rays and γ-rays are attenuated by matter.
- X-ray and γ-ray photons may be absorbed by matter, losing their energy, or may be scattered and change direction.
- For γ-rays of a particular energy, a half-value thickness (HVT) of a material can be specified that will transmit half of the radiation. Further HVTs will each reduce the intensity by half, but the intensity will never fall to zero.
- Attenuation depends on the photon energy and the material. A fraction of a millimetre of lead will provide protection against diagnostic X-rays, but tens of centimetres would be required for high energy X-rays used in radiotherapy.
- Particle radiations have a definite range in which they will be stopped, depending on the particle energy and the material.
- Over 80% of the radiation dose received by the average person in the UK is from natural sources. Most of the rest is from medical exposures.
- Artificial sources of ionising radiation are used for a wide range of applications by society.
- Non-ionising electromagnetic radiations can be divided into optical radiations, which are ultraviolet, visible light and infra-red, radio waves and low frequency waves.
- Ultraviolet radiation exposure is associated with an increased incidence of skin cancer, especially malignant melanoma, and skin ageing.
- Lasers have the potential to damage the eye and controls must be in place to restrict the potential for exposure to beams from high power lasers.

Further reading

Hughes JS. *Ionising radiation exposure of the UK population: 1999 review*, NRPB Report R311. Chilton, Didcot, UK: National Radiological Protection Board, 1999.

National Radiological Protection Board. *Living with radiation*. Chilton, Didcot: NRPB, 1998.

Information leaflets on the uses of ionising and non-ionising radiation can be obtained from the National Radiological Protection Board, Chilton, Didcot, Oxon OX11 0RQ, UK.

Chapter 2

Radiation in medicine

CJ Martin and RH Corbett

This is the second introductory chapter and complements Chapter 1 by reviewing the wide range of diagnostic imaging and therapy techniques that now use radiation, both ionising and non-ionising.

2.1 Introduction

Ionising radiation has provided physicians with techniques to look inside the living body and see changes in internal organs and body systems that will assist their investigation of disease. The potential value of ionising radiation for medical diagnosis was realised as soon as X-rays were discovered in 1895. Radiology departments were established in major hospitals throughout the developed World within a few years of Roentgen's discovery. There have since been numerous developments in the use of X-rays and there is a continuing search for ways in which other types of radiation can be used for imaging the body. This research and development has provided clinicians with a comprehensive armoury of imaging modalities to aid in the fight against disease (Table 2.1). The techniques provide detailed images of anatomy and physiology, which can be used to diagnose a wide range of pathological diseases. Early detection of an abnormality enables appropriate clinical management of the

Table 2.1 Techniques available for medical imaging (in chronological order of use)

Technique	First used	Cost $(1–5)^a$	Hazard $(1–5)^b$	Properties visualised	Main organs investigated
Endoscopy	1879	1	3	Visual appearance	Gastrointestinal system, bronchus
X-ray, radiography	1896	1	2	Heavier atoms in tissue	Skeleton, lungs, breast, abdominal organs, joints
X-ray, fluoroscopy	1896	2	3	Heavier atoms in contrast media	Gastrointestinal system
Nuclear medicine	1950	3	2–5	Biochemical function	Heart, lung, kidneys, bone lesions, brain, thyroid
Ultrasound imaging	1950	2	1	Elastic and inertial properties	Fetus, heart, abdominal organs, vascular system
X-ray, CT	1972	4	4–5	Tissue density	Soft tissue, brain, abdominal organs
X-ray, digital imaging	1977	4–5	4–5	Heavier atoms in contrast media	Heart and vascular system
MRI	1980	5	1*	Hydrogen atoms and environment	Brain and central nervous system, abdominal organs

^{a}Cost per examination: 1, <£100; 2, £100–200; 3, £200–300; 4, £300–400; 5, >£400. These costs are given as indicative relative costs at the time of publication. They will depend on the equipment and type of service provided at individual hospitals.
^{b}Hazard: Long-term effects: 1, negligible; 2, minimal; 3, very low; 4, low; 5, moderate (see Chapter 11).
Short-term effects: 1*, possible effects during exposure.

patient. New methods have contributed different types of information, many of which complement existing ones. The aim of this chapter is to give a brief overview of all the techniques available using both ionising and non-ionising radiations in order to provide an initial perspective. Therapeutic uses of radiations are also mentioned briefly at the end of the chapter. Each imaging modality is dealt with in more detail in subsequent chapters.

2.2 Conventional X-rays

Conventional X-rays are "shadow" images of organs within the body and portray variations in density or tissue composition (Figure 2.1). Heavier atoms attenuate X-rays more, so bones and other structures that contain calcium show up readily, while the more subtle variations in soft tissue are more difficult to image. Image contrast for visualisation of vessels, ducts or hollow organs can be improved by introducing liquids, called *contrast media*, which contain heavier atoms. For example, drinks and enemas containing inert barium sulphate are used for investigating the gastrointestinal tract, and iodine compounds are employed to image vessels.

The techniques used today to produce X-rays and to display images are similar in principle to those used in the early years of radiology, but they have been improved and refined to increase safety and efficiency (see §3.2). The most significant change in conventional radiology in recent times has been the application of digital technology.

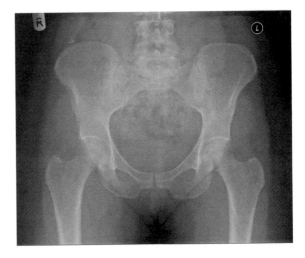

Figure 2.1 Radiograph of a pelvis, clearly demonstrating the differences in attenuation between bone and soft tissues.

Insight: Risks from conventional radiology

All procedures involving X-rays have an associated risk. The main risks are long-term effects, either cancer of radiosensitive organs or hereditary effects in future offspring of the patient (Chapter 10). The risks of effects occurring from exposure of a fetus are greater, so particular care is required for examinations carried out during pregnancy (§11.4). The radiation dose and thus the level of risk are related to the complexity of the procedure. An indication of the hazard associated with different techniques is given in Table 2.1. Risks from ionising radiation are discussed in more depth in Chapter 11. A balance has to be maintained between the benefit of a procedure, the risk from the procedure and the danger of not doing the procedure at all.

Radiography

A photographic film is used to record the radiation that has passed through the patient, hence the "negative" image produced. Efficiency is improved by placing the film in contact with fluorescent screens, which improve X-ray absorption, contained inside a light-tight cassette. Each X-ray photon produces large numbers of light photons when it interacts with a fluorescent screen, so the amount of radiation needed to form an image is reduced by about a factor of a hundred (see §3.3.1).

Fluoroscopy

X-ray images of moving structures can be viewed in real-time with fluoroscopy, often known as "screening". The image, which is formed on a fluorescent screen, is enhanced using an image intensifier and the final image is observed using a television camera and displayed on a monitor. The intensifier greatly reduces the amount of radiation required, but the image quality is still adequate for diagnosis. Fluoroscopy is used extensively for investigations employing contrast media (see §3.3.2).

Digital images

New technology enables images to be converted to digital form, wherein the image data are reduced to a matrix of numbers. This has advantages for storage, transfer and manipulation of images. Digital images are normally displayed on a monitor. The contrast and brightness can be adjusted to show up features required for diagnosis. Digital images are obtained in various ways, such as *computed radiography* (CR), where the image is stored on a phosphor plate contained in a cassette, or *direct radiography* (DR), where image data are recorded directly for static images (see §3.3.3).

In modern fluoroscopy systems, images are recorded from the image intensifier screen in digital form. For imaging the vasculature, timed sequences of images are recorded as a contrast medium is introduced. The vessels themselves are radiolucent and abnormalities in vessels are shown up by the contrast medium. *Interventional radiology* is keyhole surgery with X-ray vision. The improvements in digital imaging systems, coupled with developments in catheter techniques, have enabled interventional radiology to replace surgical intervention in many situations. This has advantages in reduced patient morbidity, mortality and cost.

2.3 Computed tomography

The most significant step forward in the application of X-rays in medicine was the development of computed tomography (CT) in 1972 by Sir Godfrey Hounsfield. This is a different type of imaging and, because of its importance, is treated in a separate chapter in this book. CT allows cross-sectional images of the body to be reconstructed from X-ray data collected in digital form (Figure 2.2). This only became feasible with the development of computer processing technology. The basic hardware consists of an X-ray tube with an array of detectors positioned on the opposite side of the body. The X-ray tube and detectors are contained within a doughnut-shaped gantry and the patient lies on a table that passes through the centre. The X-rays are collimated so that a narrow beam passes through a slice of the patient's body to give a one-dimensional set of X-ray attenuation data. (For more detail on the processes involved in X-ray attenuation see §1.3.2 and §8.3.) The X-ray tube and detectors can be rotated within the gantry to determine the attenuation by the body from many different angles, and large numbers of one-dimensional data sets are recorded from different directions. An image of a transverse slice through the body, showing differences in tissue

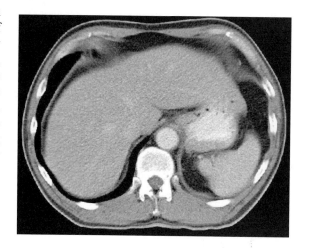

Figure 2.2 CT image of a transverse section through the abdomen. Soft tissues of the liver and spleen appear grey, the vertebrae show up as white because of their high density, and the fat surrounding the liver is dark. Blood within the aorta has a similar density to that of soft tissue and can be enhanced, as here, by contrast media. CT images are capable of much manipulation on review monitors, hence reversal of black and white may give very different clinical information.

Insight: New CT technology

CT technology continues to develop rapidly. **Helical scanning**, *sometimes called spiral scanning, in which the X-ray beam is operated continuously as the patient is moved through the X-ray tube gantry, is now routine. New systems with increased rotation speeds, detector arrays able to produce multiple slices from each rotation, and increased detector efficiency have allowed improvements in scanner speed and image quality. Developments in processing techniques have enabled visualisation of three-dimensional image data sets in many different formats. The flexibility that these developments allow facilitates use of the technique for many different applications.*

---

densities, is reconstructed from these data. CT provides high resolution diagnostic information about tissues that is not available from other techniques and enables abnormal lesions with sizes as small as a few millimetres to be detected. (For a more detailed treatment see Chapter 4.)

Insight: Risks associated with CT examinations

The radiation doses from CT examinations are relatively high and, with the steady increase in the number of examinations performed, CT contributes 40% of the collective (overall) radiation dose from medical exposures in the UK.

2.4 Nuclear medicine

Nuclear medicine involves the administration of radioactive materials to patients for diagnosis or treatment. This section deals only with diagnostic tests. Pharmaceuticals, which will be taken up by a particular organ, are labelled with a radioactive atom or radionuclide. The radiopharmaceutical is injected into a vein or sometimes administered through another route such as inhalation. The radioactive atoms act as a tracer and the distribution of radioactivity in the body can be determined by forming an image from the radiation emitted using a gamma camera. The role of the radionuclide is completely passive. Uptake in the organs depends solely on the properties of the pharmaceutical. Since uptake depends on the physiological processes occurring in the organ, nuclear medicine enables functional changes to be measured and imaged rather than simply portraying anatomical structure. Nuclear medicine images have inherently poor resolution, so this information complements the higher resolution structural data obtained from X-ray and other imaging modalities. The physiological processes of any organ may be studied if there is a suitable radiopharmaceutical available. As well as imaging, radioactivity levels may be measured in samples of blood, urine or exhaled breath taken following administration of a radiopharmaceutical to investigate various conditions.

The most important developments in nuclear medicine imaging were the invention of the *gamma camera* and the introduction of the radionuclide *technetium-99m* (^{99m}Tc), which has ideal properties for imaging, especially in terms of half-life and the type of radiation emitted. (For more information see Chapter 5.)

There are many key biochemical compounds into which ^{99m}Tc atoms cannot readily be incorporated, *e.g.* glucose. Radionuclides of more physiological

---

Insight: Risks from radionuclide imaging

The risks from nuclear medicine are of a similar type to those from X-rays, the main difference being that radioactive material is inside the body and cannot be switched off. The distribution within the body determines the organs exposed. There is a wide range in the radiation dose levels and risk from use of different radiopharmaceuticals, depending on the activity administered, the radiation emitted, the physical half-life and the residence time in the body (see §5.2).

---

elements (*e.g.* C, N and O) emit positrons (positive electrons) that rapidly combine with electrons and emit pairs of γ-ray photons. This has allowed the development of *positron emission tomography* (PET) scanners. Coincidence counting techniques are employed to register the pairs of γ-ray photons from which images are reconstructed. These are proving useful in a variety of applications in oncology, cardiology and neurology. Unfortunately, the radionuclides all have very short half-lives. They can only be produced in specialised facilities with a cyclotron, so this places limitations on the number of centres able to use this modality.

2.5 Ultrasound imaging

The techniques described in the early sections of this chapter all use ionising radiation, but there are several methods that employ non-ionising radiation. Ultrasound is the most widely used. In concept and execution, the technique is relatively simple. *Pulses* of high frequency sound are transmitted into the body and *echoes* are detected from organ boundaries and inhomogeneities within the tissues. Since the speed of sound in most soft tissues is similar, it is relatively simple to determine the position of the boundaries producing the echoes. This information can be used to form an ultrasound image of organs in a section through the body in the direction in

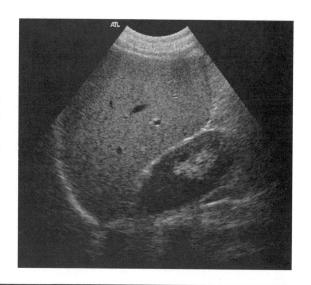

Figure 2.3 Ultrasound scan of a longitudinal section through the abdomen. The speckle echo pattern from the liver tissue is brighter than that from the kidney that lies behind it. The organ boundaries and the calyces of the kidney show up as more intense echoes. Vessels within the liver appear as dark spaces.

Insight: Risks from ultrasound

Ultrasound is a non-ionising radiation. There is no epidemiological evidence to suggest that levels of ultrasound used in diagnosis produce any harmful effects on the body. Thus, ultrasound is used widely for routine assessments during pregnancy as well as in a wide range of abdominal and cardiac investigations. The relative safety of the technique also means that the restrictions on length of exposure that are applied to imaging with ionising radiations need not be employed for ultrasound, although there are guidelines on maximum permitted intensity levels, which are kept under review (see §6.5).

---

which the ultrasound beam is pointed (Figure 2.3). The major limitation is the inability to penetrate structures containing gas or bone, which will reflect almost all of the ultrasound. Probes containing arrays of ultrasound transducer elements, together with digital processing of signals received by individual elements, enable the sensitivity and resolution of the technique to be optimised to provide good quality images. Ultrasound interactions depend on the mechanical nature of tissue, which involves elastic and inertial properties that are different from those imaged by X-rays. Real-time imaging is used to view movement of tissues, which enhances the diagnostic capability. This is particularly useful in *echocardiography* in which heart movement can be studied either in two-dimensional images or through the temporal change in position of heart valves and chamber walls.

As well as providing images based on the straight mechanical properties of tissues, it is also possible to look at changes in ultrasound frequencies relating to the velocity with which an object is moving. This is the well known *Doppler effect* and can provide information on blood flow, which can be used to characterise changes in arteries and even solid lesions. Movement of blood within the heart is assessed in the diagnosis of cardiac disease. (For more information see Chapter 6.)

2.6 Magnetic resonance imaging

Magnetic resonance imaging (MRI) is another non-ionising radiation technique used for imaging organs within the body. MRI enables images to be produced from the *hydrogen nuclei* in water, soft tissue and fat molecules. The hydrogen nuclei each have an electric charge and a spin, which causes them to behave like small magnets and thus tend to align with a strong magnetic field, producing a resultant magnetisation M. The orientation of M can be tipped away from the aligned position through excitation by a pulse of radio waves. When the pulse is turned off, the spins return to the equilibrium position and give off the excitation energy in the form of radio waves through interactions with neighbouring molecules. It is these radio waves that are used to produce an

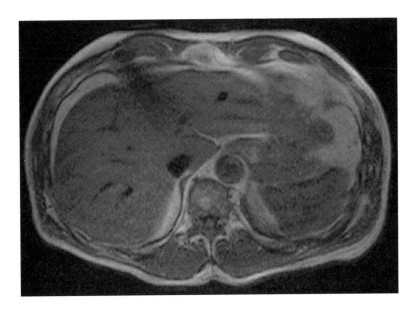

Figure 2.4 MRI image of a transverse section through the abdomen. The liver and spleen appear as dark grey, while the fat surrounding the liver is lighter. Blood within the aorta is darker. The image presentation will vary considerably depending on the MR image acquisition sequence used.

image. The frequency of the radio waves needed to excite the spins is dependent on the local magnetic field strength. If a field gradient is applied, so that the magnetic field varies with position along the body, the frequency of the radio waves required to excite molecules will change with position along the body. This can be used to select a particular slice for imaging. Magnetic gradients are applied in the other dimensions to enable full positional information within the slice to be derived. The data are reconstructed in the form of sectional images (Figure 2.4).

MRI systems are built around large magnets. In most cases, these are cooled by liquid helium to –263°C, at which temperature the current-carrying wires become "superconducting" and so have no resistance. Therefore, once current is flowing, no electrical power is required. The imager incorporates sets of coils in three orthogonal directions to create the magnetic field gradients. Various surface, body or intracavity coils are used to transmit and receive the pulses of radio waves.

The magnetic resonance signals obtained from the hydrogen atoms are strongly influenced by their *biochemical environment*. Magnetic resonance properties are sensitive to alterations in soft tissue and so can provide information not obtained from other imaging modalities. Different sequences of radio-frequency pulses can be designed to maximise contrast mechanisms that are required for particular applications. These give MRI the potential for greater flexibility than CT. MRI has proved to be the most sensitive technique for diagnosis of diseases of the central nervous and musculoskeletal systems. It has replaced CT as the technique of choice for these regions, but scanners are expensive and up to now have only been available in larger hospitals, although many general hospitals are now being equipped with both CT and MRI. (For more information see Chapter 7.)

Insight: Risks associated with MRI

The radiations used in MRI are non-ionising. There is little evidence for harmful effects of MRI and all recognised effects are only present during a scan, provided that recommended exposure advice is adhered to. The radio waves used are typically in the frequency range employed for radio broadcasting and are quite low level, although localised fields close to coils will be greater. The high static magnetic field will exert a force on any magnetic object either implanted inside the body, such as an aneurysm clip, or external to the body. This may cause significant hazard and must be taken into account. The rates of change of the magnetic fields are maintained below recommended safe levels to prevent effects such as nerve stimulation or significant heating of the body (see §7.4).

2.7 Endoscopy

Another route by which it is possible to view inside the body is direct observation using a fibre optic endoscope introduced via a natural or specially created access port. This technique can identify abnormalities inside hollow organs, for example an endoscope can be used to investigate the oesophagus, stomach and duodenum and so provides an alternative method of diagnosis to barium investigations for upper gastrointestinal tract problems without ionising radiation exposure. Endoscopes can be used for investigation of any accessible natural cavity and can provide an important tool for gynaecology, urology and ENT. Endoscopes are also used in endoscopic retrograde cholangiopancreatography (ERCP) for imaging the bile and pancreatic ducts. X-ray images of the ducts are taken using retrograde injection of contrast medium. Instruments may also be passed down the endoscope to allow biopsies and stenting to be carried out.

> ### *Insight: Risks from endoscopy*
>
> *Risks from endoscopy are small and arise from the actual procedure itself, such as risk from damage and penetration of the wall of the vessel under investigation.*

Diagnostic strategy

- It is important that those responsible for the use of medical exposures keep up to date with current trends to ensure that each patient receives the best diagnosis and treatment available at the time. The whole question of diagnostic strategy when a range of investigations is available is considered in Chapter 17.

2.8 Radiotherapy

In addition to its role in diagnosis, ionising radiation also plays an important part in the treatment of malignant disease. X-rays were used to treat cancer as early as 1896. A volume of tissue containing a tumour as well as surrounding tissues where infiltration of malignant cells may have occurred is treated with radiation. Ideally, the radiation dose should be high enough to kill all the tumour cells, but the dose to the surrounding healthy tissue must not be too high in order to minimise the risk of any serious damage. The dose that can be tolerated by nearby critical organs generally limits the dose that can be delivered to the tumour.

Radiation treatment can be given in a variety of ways and the choice will depend on the tumour type, position and accessibility. The tumour can be irradiated by external radiation. In this method, radiation beams from several different directions are often used to deliver a high dose to the tumour while keeping the dose to surrounding tissue at an acceptable level. Alternatively, a radioactive source can be introduced at the tumour site (brachytherapy), for example for treatment of the cervix, a source is introduced *per vaginum*. The radiation dose rate will be highest near the source and will decline with distance, so giving a higher dose to the tumour. A third method of treatment is to use radiopharmaceuticals in liquid or tablet form. For example, radioactive iodine is an accepted treatment for hyperthyroidism and thyroid cancer, since most of the radioactive iodine will be concentrated within the thyroid and so will provide an effective method of killing thyroid cells. The volume of tissue to be irradiated, the radiation dose delivered and the time period over which treatment is given are chosen to provide the best chance of success. More information on radiotherapy is given in Chapter 9.

Early detection is an important requirement in combating cancer. The imaging techniques described in this book play an important part both in detection of disease and in treatment planning. Different techniques may contribute complementary evidence to the final diagnosis. Organs for which each technique is suitable, together with an indication of the relative risk, are given in Table 2.1 at the start of the chapter.

2.9 Other non-ionising radiation techniques

Non-ionising radiations are used for therapeutic and other diagnostic purposes in addition to those discussed in §2.5–§2.7. Some of the applications of optical radiations are summarised in Table 2.2. Visible lasers have an important role in ophthalmic surgery, allowing treatment of the retina without damage to the anterior of the eye. Other lasers are used to carry out surgery through endoscopes and bronchoscopes with minimal trauma or to treat skin lesions such as birthmarks. Drugs that are activated by light are used together with lasers or other intense light sources in the treatment of cancer by photodynamic therapy. Large area ultraviolet phototherapy sources comprising banks of fluorescent lamps are used for treatment of skin conditions such as psoriasis, and blue lamps are used to aid in the breakdown of bilirubin for neonates with hyperbilirubinaemia.

Electromagnetic fields are employed in some areas in medicine, examples of which are given in Table 2.3. High frequency (short wave) diathermy (27 MHz) is applied widely by physiotherapists for heating tissue to aid healing of injuries. Ultrasound is also used by physiotherapists to encourage healing of injuries.

Table 2.2 Optical radiations in medicine

Radiation	Wavelength range	Applications
Ultraviolet	190–260 nm	Corneal surgery lasers
	310–315 nm	UVB phototherapy
	320–400 nm	PUVA phototherapy
		UV fluorescence
Visible	425–475 nm	Neonate phototherapy
	500–700 nm	Ophthalmic lasers
		Photodynamic therapy
Infra-red	600 nm–1 μm	Surgical and therapy lasers
		Physiotherapy heat lamps
		Diaphanography
	1 μm	Nd:YAG surgical laser
	1–8 μm	*Thermographic imaging*
	10 μm	CO_2 surgical laser

Diagnostic applications are given in *italics*.

Table 2.3 Applications of radiofrequency electromagnetic radiation in medicine

Frequency range	Applications
300 MHz –3 GHz	Microwave hyperthermia
27 MHz	Therapeutic diathermy
8–100 MHz	MRI pulses
300–500 kHz	Surgical diathermy

2.10 Summary

- Conventional X-rays produce shadow images of organs, showing up differences in tissue composition and density.
- X-ray images of moving structures are produced using image intensifiers. These use a low dose rate, but give a level of image quality that is adequate for diagnosis.
- Digital radiology allows manipulation, transfer and storage of image data.
- Visualisation of vessels using contrast media and image subtraction coupled with keyhole surgery has allowed interventional radiology to replace surgical intervention in a range of situations.
- CT allows cross-sectional images of the body related to tissue density to be reconstructed from data on X-ray transmission.
- CT scans contribute 40% of the radiation dose from medical exposures in the UK.
- Nuclear medicine involves the administration of radioactive materials to patients for diagnosis and treatment.
- Nuclear medicine enables functional changes to be measured and imaged.
- Ultrasound is used to image the mechanical structure of soft tissue organs, the fetus and the heart.
- Changes in ultrasound frequency resulting from the Doppler effect are used to determine blood flow velocities and to image flow patterns.
- MRI displays properties of tissue related to the biochemical environment of the molecules.
- MRI has a particular role in diagnosis of diseases of the central nervous and musculoskeletal systems.
- Endoscopy provides a method for investigation of hollow organs.
- Radiotherapy plays an important role in the treatment of malignant disease.
- Different techniques may contribute complementary evidence to a diagnosis (Table 2.1).

- There are small risks associated with most imaging techniques, with risks for the more complex ionising radiation techniques being greatest.
- For some diseases one imaging modality may be obviously superior.
- For other diseases the information required may be obtained from several different modalities, of which one has a much lower risk and so provides the best option.
- For yet other diseases, different techniques may provide complementary evidence and all will contribute to the final diagnosis.
- Recommended techniques for investigating particular organs change with time, so radiologists and others must keep up with current trends.

Further reading

International Commission on Radiological Protection. *ICRP Supporting Guidance 2, Radiation and your patient: a guide for medical practitioners*. Ann ICRP 31 (No. 4). Exeter, UK: Pergamon, 2001.

Chapter 3
Diagnostic radiology

J Shand and CJ Martin

This chapter looks at the traditional method of obtaining diagnostic information using X-rays and some situations in which this is the most appropriate investigation. The way in which the properties of different tissues affect the contrast seen in the image and how this contrast can be enhanced is explained. A brief look into the future explores how a filmless radiology department might change the work of a referring physician.

3.1 Introduction

X-rays have been used in clinical medicine for over 100 years and the uses to which they have been put have been constantly increasing in number and complexity as technology has progressed. Change in technology has never been faster than at the current time. This has created a counterpoint whereby the method of X-ray production is essentially unchanged from when X-rays were first discovered by Wilhelm Roentgen in 1895, but the method of image capture has evolved enormously. In fact, while Roentgen would probably recognise a modern X-ray tube for what it is and understand how it works, modern methods of image production would be totally beyond his ability to comprehend with the levels of scientific understanding available at the end of the 19th century. This chapter describes how X-ray images are produced, examines the type of information that they provide and discusses how this can affect the clinical management of patients. A basic description of how the technique works is given in the text and additional explanations of the physics and other aspects are given in "Insight" boxes for those wishing to understand the factors involved in more depth.

3.2 How X-ray imaging works

Production of X-rays

X-rays are produced from an X-ray tube (Figure 3.1). The tube contains a heated filament from which electrons are drawn off and accelerated to a high velocity. The electrons are then made to collide with a metal target and in some of the collisions X-rays are produced. Because electrons would collide with air molecules, the filament (cathode) and the metal target (anode) are held within an evacuated glass tube.

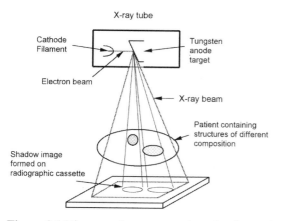

Figure 3.1 Diagramatic representation of radiography of a patient, showing the beam of X-rays produced by bombardment of the X-ray tube anode and the formation of an image.

The voltage applied between the cathode and the anode, measured in kilovolts (kV), determines the velocity of the electrons and in turn the energy of the X-rays produced. An X-ray beam contains photons with a broad range of energies up to the maximum determined by the kilovoltage, *e.g.* 80 keV for an 80 kV setting (see §1.7 for definition of eV). Different kilovoltages are used for different applications, with 70–90 kV being used for the trunk and 28–30 kV for the breast (mammography).

Formation of the image

The information in an X-ray image is created by the interaction of X-ray photons as they pass through the patient. In the patient the X-ray beam will pass through different structures such as skin, soft tissue, solid organs, lungs and bone. As the beam strikes these structures, some photons will pass straight through without being affected and some will interact with the tissues (see §1.3.3). The part of the beam that passes through without interacting forms the image (Figure 3.2). An X-ray image can therefore be thought of as a shadow image.

The proportion of the X-ray beam that passes through the patient to produce an image will depend on factors such as the number of heavier atoms within tissue, the densities of the various structures and their thickness. Whilst there are many types of interaction between X-rays and matter, the photoelectric effect and Compton scattering are the dominant ones, and more information about these is given in the box on page 23 for those interested. Photoelectric interactions are much more likely to occur with heavier atoms than with lighter ones. These interactions give the greater difference in attenuation between the various structures and so are the more useful in creating an image.

X-ray images show:

- an X-ray shadow of structure inside the body;
- differences in atomic composition, densities and thicknesses of tissue components.

Insight: Patient dose and image quality — the trade-off

*Absorption of energy from the X-ray beam reduces its penetration and gives the radiation dose to the tissue. A high kilovoltage X-ray beam, containing higher energy photons, will have greater penetration and therefore will tend to give a lower radiation dose. However, the reduction in penetration occurs because there are fewer photoelectric interactions. As a result the differences in the numbers of X-rays penetrating different tissue structures, and so the **image contrast** (see §3.3), will be smaller, and this determines how well the structures can be seen in the image. Thus, choice of X-ray beam kilovoltage is a trade-off between image quality and dose. 70–80 kV is often used for X-rays of the trunk as representing the best compromise.*

The balance between image quality and dose

• Lower kV, 50–60 kVp	• Higher kV, 90–100 kVp
• Better contrast	• Poorer contrast
• Less beam penetration	• More beam penetration
• Higher radiation dose	• Lower radiation dose
• Used for thinner or less attenuating regions, such as arms and legs	• Used for thicker, more attenuating parts, such as lateral views of the spine

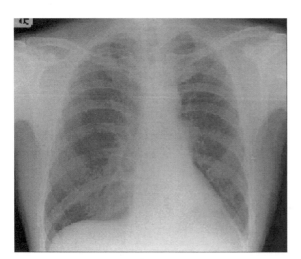

Figure 3.2 Plain film chest radiograph showing the darker lungs where X-ray attenuation is low and the lighter mediastinum where attenuation is high.

Insight: Interaction of X-rays with matter

Photoelectric effect
The interaction of X-ray photons with tightly bound electrons.
An electron absorbs all the energy of the X-ray photon.
There are large differences in the probabilities of interaction for heavier and lighter atoms.
Photoelectric interactions are more likely for lower energy X-ray photons.

Compton scattering
The interaction of X-ray photons with loosely bound electrons.
The X-ray photons lose some energy and are deflected or scattered.
The probability of interaction does not vary much with the atoms present in the tissue, only with tissue density.
Similar numbers of interactions occur at all X-ray photon energies.

Differences in attenuation between tissues relate primarily to the photoelectric effect. As the energy of an X-ray beam is increased, there is a reduction in the proportion of interactions by the photoelectric effect. At high kilovoltage, when the Compton effect dominates, image contrast is due to density differences.

3.3 X-ray techniques

X-rays are used in several imaging techniques:

- Plain film radiography
- Fluoroscopy
  - Barium studies
  - Angiography (including digital subtraction angiography (DSA))
  - Interventional radiology
- Computed tomography (CT)

CT involves a different method of image production and will be discussed separately in Chapter 4. Plain film radiography and fluoroscopy have, for many years, relied on the properties of photographic emulsion and fluorescent screens to visualise X-ray images. These are now being joined by digital acquisition methods, which allow the development of filmless radiology departments.

3.3.1 X-ray film

X-ray film is an acetate or polyester base coated with light-sensitive emulsions. A negative image is produced, with the darker areas being where the greatest number of photons passed through the patient, such as in the lungs (Figure 3.2). Efficiency is improved by using *intensifying screens*, which convert the X-ray photons to UV or light photons. So many of these photons are produced from one X-ray photon that, collectively, they are about a hundred times as effective in forming an image. The intensifying screens are held in contact with the film in a cassette and the sensitivity of the X-ray film is matched to the light emitted by the screen to provide a suitable *film–screen combination.*

Image contrast

The relationship between the degree of blackening of the film and the amount of radiation striking it is highly non-linear, with only a small optimal linear portion that will produce a diagnostic image (Figure 3.3). Therefore, the amount of radiation or *radiation exposure* used to produce a film radiograph of a patient must lie within a

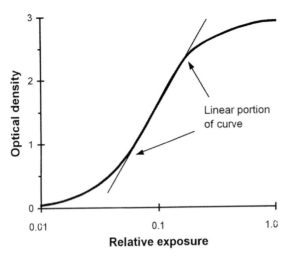

Figure 3.3 Interaction of X-rays with film shown in the characteristic curve. This is a plot of the optical density on the film against the relative exposure on a logarithmic scale.

narrow range. However, because film blackening or *optical density* varies rapidly with exposure within this range, small differences in X-ray attenuation can be detected in an image. The difference between the optical densities in different parts of an image that have received different exposures is related to the slope of the curve in Figure 3.3 and is referred to as *image contrast*. For practical purposes, the optical densities in a plain film radiograph can be broken down into four categories: black, gas; dark grey, fat; light grey, water/ soft tissue; and white, bone. The difference between the darkest and lightest parts of the usable image is referred to as the *dynamic range*.

3.3.2 Fluoroscopy

The other conventional type of X-ray image visualisation, called fluoroscopy, produces images in real-time using an image intensifier. The real-time capability of fluoroscopy allows organ and tissue movement to be portrayed as well as the guidance of both diagnostic and therapeutic procedures in interventional radiology. A mobile image intensifier unit typical of those used in theatres is shown in Figure 3.4.

3.3.3 Digital image capture

Conventional images produced by film–screen combinations are known as *analogue images*, with the interaction of each X-ray photon faithfully recorded where it strikes the film–screen. In a *digital image*, the image space

> ***Insight: What affects image sharpness?***
>
> *An X-ray image is not perfectly sharp. Factors that contribute to the amount of blurring or "unsharpness" are:*
> ***The X-ray source****: the source (known as the focal spot) has a finite size.*
> ***Fluorescent screens****: the many light photons produced from an X-ray interaction radiate in all directions and expose a larger area of the film.*
> ***Movement****: no matter how co-operative a patient is, they cannot control involuntary movements such as those related to the cardiac cycle.*
>
> ***Interplay of factors***
> *Thicker layers of phosphor in the screen give greater sensitivity but a more blurred image. Different film–screen combinations are used for different applications. "Detail" cassettes with thinner screens are used for the extremities where the dose is already small and fine detail such as the trabeculae in the bone is crucial. Thicker screens are used for imaging the trunk, where it is important that the dose is low.*

> ***Insight: How an image intensifier works***
>
> *An image intensifier works by forming a light image of the X-rays that passed through the patient by means of a phosphor screen, analogous to an intensifying screen in a film cassette. The light photons are then converted into electrons, which are accelerated and focused, both amplification processes, and converted back into light. This produces a smaller, brighter image that is captured by a video camera and can then be further processed and displayed on a monitor.*

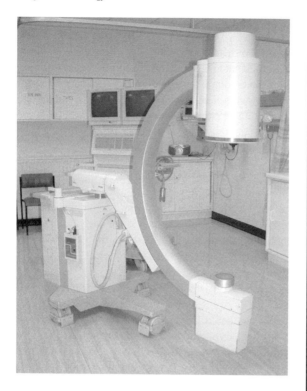

Figure 3.4 Mobile fluoroscopic unit with the image intensifier above and the X-ray tube below. Fluoroscopic units are used in this orientation to avoid the upper body of the operator being exposed to radiation scattered from the surface of the patient.

Insight: Digital radiology devices

There are several methods of converting the X-rays that have passed through a patient into a usable digital image.

Phosphor plates *are referred to commercially as* ***computed radiography*** *(CR). The plates simply replace the film–screen combination in a cassette. They are able to store an image and when the plate is scanned by a laser in a CR reader the stored energy is released as light, which is converted to digital form.*

Semi-conductor devices *are direct digital devices that are hard wired into the X-ray unit couch and generate images virtually instantaneously, with no handling of a cassette required. This technique is referred to as* ***direct radiography*** *(DR).*

Film digitisers *take an image from an X-ray film and scan it. This method may be required for hospitals running digital picture archiving systems in order to digitise important historical data and films from elsewhere.*

---

is divided up into a large number of discrete picture elements or *pixels* and the number of photons interacting with the image receptor is recorded for each pixel. Thus, the digitised image is essentially a matrix of numbers. When the image is reconstructed, a certain brightness or grey level is assigned to all pixels with numbers within a particular range and a grey-scale image is generated.

To make up images with good enough resolution to ensure that little of the diagnostic information imaged on plain films is lost, the number of pixels along each side of the image is usually one to two thousand, so each image may contain several million pixels. Present generation computers are able to handle the large amounts of data involved.

A digital image can be viewed and manipulated on a monitor. This is referred to as *soft copy*, the printed image being *hard copy*. A digital image is not constrained by the viewing requirements of an image on a film. First of all the image capture systems have a wider dynamic range. If a film radiograph is recorded at a much higher or lower dose it will be too dark or too light and information will be lost, whereas the grey level settings in a digital image can be adjusted to allow optimal display of the data recorded. The rate at which the blackness increases with dose, *i.e.* the slope of the graph equivalent to that in Figure 3.3, can be changed on the monitor after the image has been recorded to provide the most favourable viewing conditions. This technique of adjusting contrast and brightness, known as "*windowing*", allows far more information to be gleaned from the image data by displaying it in different ways. Other processing options such as edge enhancement can be used to improve the appearance of the image or the visibility of certain features. Different display options may be appropriate for images of different parts of the body and these are included in display software provided by the manufacturer and tailored to the requirements of the user.

3.4 Contrast media

So far in this chapter we have used the term contrast to refer to differences in density or darkness between different structures in an X-ray image. The term is also used, somewhat loosely, to refer to substances of differing density, often containing heavier atoms, that are used to enhance contrast artificially in a radiograph. These contrast media can be introduced into a patient to alter the patient's natural or inherent contrast, aiding and enhancing visualisation of certain structures. The changes in density resulting from use of a contrast medium can be either positive or negative with reference to the structure being demonstrated and the contrast medium can be introduced by a variety of routes depending on the information required (see Table 3.1).

3.4.1 Positive contrast media

The most flexible contrast media are iodine based, also referred to as water-soluble contrast media. There are many proprietary makes, which are all variations on a tri-iodinated benzene ring. When introduced into a tissue, *e.g.* blood, CSF, or a solid organ, the average atomic number of that tissue will increase, thereby causing a greater number of photoelectric interactions to occur. This will produce greater attenuation of the X-ray beam and will alter the contrast of that tissue relative to adjacent tissues (Figure 3.5). This alteration is not constant but will vary depending on how the contrast medium has been administered, the speed at which it is administered and the time after administration at which imaging is performed. A contrast medium is normally administered through a peripheral vein using a pre-programmed pump that can control the volume, rate and time interval between the injection and the scan acquisition. Movement of iodine through the vasculature can be tracked in a series of digital images. If a sequence of images is recorded of the same area, an early image before the iodine passed through can be used as a mask and subtracted from later images, so that the only contrast in the image is related to flow through the vessel. This technique is called *digital subtraction imaging* (DSI) or *digital subtraction angiography* (DSA). If the arterial phase of enhancement is desired, the delay time is short, of the order of 20 s, but if the venous phase is desired, the delay will be longer, possibly closer to 60 s. Sometimes images are acquired in more than one phase to detect changes in vascularity between normal and pathological tissue. An example of this time effect would be in the use of contrast media in triple phase CT of the liver. A rapid series of images is acquired prior to the intravenous injection of contrast medium followed by two further series at 20 s and 60 s. The images are then examined for alterations in vascularity. This is very useful in the detection of metastases, as normal liver parenchyma receives most of its blood supply from the portal venous system whereas metastases are mainly supplied by the hepatic artery. Metastases therefore enhance with contrast medium in the 20 s images to a greater extent than the surrounding liver tissue and can be identified more easily. Contrast media

Table 3.1 Positive and negative contrast media

Contrast medium	Route of administration	Investigation
Positive		
Iodine-based	Intravenous	Venography, IVUs, vessel enhancement for CT
	Intra-arterial	Angiography
	Oral	Water-soluble meal
	Rectal	Water-soluble enema
	Intrathecal	Myelogram or radiculogram
	Intra-articular	Arthrography
	Virtually any other body cavity	Examinations such as PTC, ERCP, nephrostograms, sinograms
Barium	Oral	D/C barium meal
	Rectal	D/C barium enema
Negative		
Air	Oral	D/C barium meal
	Rectal	D/C barium enema
CO_2	Rectal	D/C barium enema
	Intra-arterial	CO_2 angiography
Fat	Oral	CT (to outline GI tract)

D/C, double contrast.

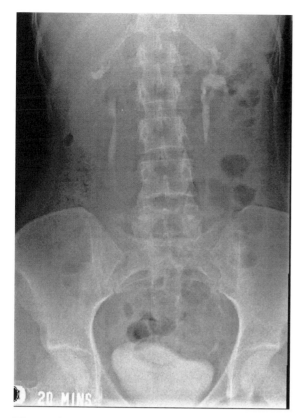

Figure 3.5 Image recorded during an intravenous urogram with iodine contrast medium showing the ureters, kidneys and bladder.

are also used in other investigations, including intravenous urograms (Figure 3.5). In this investigation the contrast medium is injected intravenously and the image is obtained immediately following the injection, termed the nephrogram phase where there is enhancement of renal parenchyma. The contrast medium is excreted by the kidneys into the collecting system, this being termed the pyelogram phase, which is optimally seen after about 10 min.

As with all drugs that are administered to patients, complications may occur when iodinated compounds are used as contrast media. While some of these are due to direct haemotoxicity and the hyperosmolar nature of contrast media, those that cause most concern are the allergic reactions. These vary from minor, such as urticaria, to severe, including hypotension, bronchospasm, anaphylaxis and occasionally death! The risk of allergic reaction is raised in atopic and, especially, in asthmatic patients in addition to those with a history of previous reaction to contrast media. If a patient has any of these conditions it is important that this is mentioned along with the clinical details on the request. The importance of this is discussed in more detail in §13.5.

Barium sulphate, conversely, is not soluble in water but is administered as a suspension, either orally or rectally, to outline the gastrointestinal (GI) tract. Investigations in which it is used include barium swallows, barium meals, follow-through examinations (to demonstrate small bowel), small bowel enemas and barium enemas (Figure 3.6). In the first three examinations it is swallowed, in the latter two it is given via a catheter. Radiographically, barium is very dense because of its high atomic number. Barium sulphate is pharmacologically relatively inert. If it inadvertently gets into the peritoneal cavity it can cause formation of granulomas and should therefore be avoided if there is a risk of perforation of the GI tract.

3.4.2 Negative contrast media

The most commonly used negative contrast agents are air and carbon dioxide. They are referred to as negative contrast media because they attenuate the X-ray beam less than tissue and therefore appear dark on a conventional X-ray image. While they are occasionally used in digital subtraction angiography, their most widespread use is in double contrast examinations of the GI tract, together with barium. In the case of barium swallows and meals, carbon dioxide is introduced into the stomach before the barium using effervescent granules. The barium is then swallowed and coats the mucosa of the distended viscerae. The X-ray image is therefore of the mucosal detail. This increases the sensitivity of the examination in disease detection compared with simply filling the viscera with barium and studying the outline. With barium enemas the barium is instilled first, again to coat the mucosa. Insufflated air then distends the colon and helps to demonstrate the mucosal detail (Figure 3.6).

3.5 What do images show?

Having discussed how plain film images are produced in diagnostic radiology, what can they show and how can they be of benefit to patients?

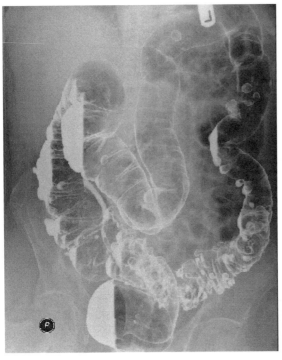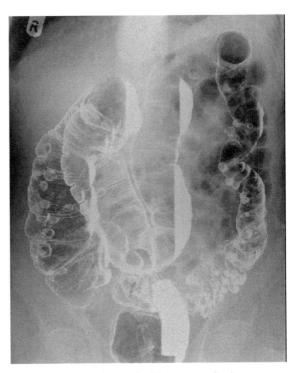

Figure 3.6 Images of the colon with barium contrast medium recorded during a double contrast barium enema examination in the decubitus position.

First, we have to know what information we can gain from X-rays. The densities that produce a plain film image in a patient can be divided into four broad categories, which can be translated into densities or separate contrasts on the film:

- Black (gas)
- Dark grey (fat)
- Light grey (water/soft tissue)
- White (bone)

This short list is vital to the interpretation of plain films. No matter how large a mass within a patient, if there is no difference in contrast between it and the adjacent structures, its edges will not be identified. Thus, if a pathological process fails to cause a change in thickness, density or atomic number, X-rays will not detect it. A useful analogy is that of a black cat. Put it in a coal cellar and it will be virtually impossible to see, whereas if it is moved to a snowfield it will stand out very clearly.

An important consideration in X-ray interpretation is to remember that X-ray films are shadows produced by structures, both anatomical and pathological, within the patient. Therefore a sound understanding of three subjects is required for interpretation of images. These are anatomy, pathological anatomy and the physical basis of the interaction of X-rays to form an image on the image receptor. Anatomy and pathology are covered elsewhere in the undergraduate medical curriculum and this book goes some way to covering the physical basis of image formation. Once all three elements are in place it should be possible to understand what the specialist is saying. You should not be overawed when confronted with a film, but attempt to identify for yourself what the specialist has indicated. Although in the absence of specialist training and experience some of the subtleties may elude you, this should not prevent you using X-ray images as a diagnostic tool.

In addition to contrast between structures, it is important to note displacement of normal structures by pathology. In this way it is sometimes possible to infer the presence of a mass with no surrounding or adjacent structures of differing density to provide contrast.

3.6 Uses of radiology

Radiology, as with any test or investigation carried out on the patient, should only be performed if two criteria are met:

- What information do I expect to gain and will the test answer my clinical question?
- Having gained this information, will it affect the management of my patient?

If these criteria are not satisfied, the examination should not be performed. The second criterion can be expanded into four categories as laid out in the box.

Uses of radiology

- Confirm or refute a provisional diagnosis.
- Detect a previously unsuspected diagnosis.
- Monitor a patient's progress.
- Screen for a treatable condition.

Confirm or refute a provisional diagnosis
This is fairly obvious and needs no further explanation.

Detect a previously unsuspected diagnosis
This arises where an appropriate examination for the patient's differential diagnosis, constructed on the basis of the patient's history, physical examination and any other tests, has been performed. Even the best clinician will occasionally be surprised by the radiological examination turning up something completely unexpected. It should be stressed that this is not a reason for random examinations in the hope of detecting some pathological process.

Monitor a patient's progress
This is well established, with a common example being serial chest films on patients in intensive care. However, the basic tenet of an examination only being performed if it will affect management still holds. If the patient has been in the ITU for a long time and is in a relatively stable condition, daily chest X-rays are almost certainly not justified.

Screen for a treatable condition
Screening for a treatable condition is a far more complex area and is dealt with in detail in Chapter 16.

3.7 Making the diagnosis

Probably the most important single fact that can be gleaned from an X-ray image is whether or not it is normal. This can often be the most difficult decision to make in X-ray interpretation. A useful analogy is the wide variation in human facial features. Similar variation occurs within the body, which can be demonstrated radiologically, and as a result a normal variant may masquerade as pathology. One consequence of this is that no radiology reporting room is complete without several books demonstrating and describing normal variants.

All investigations have limitations, with measurable statistical sensitivities and specificities. These create disadvantages for both symptomatic and screening investigations using any imaging technique.

- *Sensitivity* is how reliable a technique is at detecting the pathology that is being looked for, *i.e.* the proportion of people with the disease who are identified (true positive fraction).
- *Specificity* measures how accurate the technique is at detecting what is really the pathology being looked for, *i.e.* the proportion of people free from the disease who react negatively (true negative fraction).

The positive predictive value of a test is the percentage of true positives among the total number of positives identified by the test, *i.e.* the proportion of those identified that are really abnormal. It depends on the sensitivity, specificity and proportion of the group examined who have the disease. In an investigation of a patient with symptoms that could be due to one of only a few causes, there is a significant chance that the disease will be present, so the positive predictive value for the technique will be high. However, if the chance of the disease being present is low, the number of normal individuals that might be wrongly identified as having the disease will be greater, so the positive predictive value will be low. If patients are not fully examined and a full history taken prior to requesting investigations, there will be a large number of inappropriate referrals. This will lead to a reduction in disease incidence in the group referred and thus a reduction in the reliance the referring clinician can place on the radiology report. A veritable example of shooting oneself in the foot!

Another important consideration is that a normal X-ray does not exclude pathology. This is true even for disease processes that are routinely demonstrated on X-rays such as lung cancer. The tumour may be too small to be recognised amongst the blood vessels that are represented amongst normal lung markings. It may be lying in a position where it is masked, such as behind the heart or in the lung apex behind the clavicle. It may be hidden in an area of surrounding infection. Finally, the lesion may simply be missed on the film. No matter how much care is taken in image interpretation, there will always be the occasional lesion that is not recognised for what it really is. These are all reasons why it is important to follow up chest pathology to ensure that it resolves completely and that there is no underlying abnormality.

Once an abnormality has been identified on an X-ray, the next problem is to reach a diagnosis. Lesions that are pathognomonic, that is have a sign that is unique to the particular disease, are unfortunately rare. An example of a pathognomonic abnormality is the presence of calcified pleural plaques involving the hemi-diaphragms indicating that the patient had been exposed to asbestos at some time in the past. For most abnormalities detected there will be a differential diagnosis. Sometimes this may be quite a short list but often it can stretch into double figures. In such cases it is important to combine the differential diagnosis from the X-ray image with the patient's history, examination and other test results. If this does not produce a definitive answer, it will hopefully produce a shorter list that can be further refined with another test, not necessarily radiological.

Always consider carefully what information you will gain from an X-ray and consider whether this will affect the management of the patient. Remember that X-ray images are one part of an investigative jigsaw and should **never** be interpreted in isolation.

> ## Insight: The effect of disease incidence on positive predictive values
>
> *A high test sensitivity is always important. If no more than 1 or 2 in 100 positive cases is to be missed, the sensitivity must be 98–99%. It is more difficult to predict the desirable or necessary specificity since this also depends on the prevalence of disease in the population examined.*
>
> *Looking at two extreme cases, if the prevalence was 50% and 200 patients were examined (100 true positive and 100 true negative), a sensitivity of 98% and a specificity of 95% would result in only 5 false positives, a positive predictive value of 95%. If, however, the prevalence were low, say 0.5%, analogous to a screening situation, detection of 100 true positive cases would require 20,000 persons to be tested and would result in 1000 false positives, a positive predictive value of only 9%.*
>
> *The value of the test then depends on the method of follow-up for the false positives. If the definitive diagnosis required a more expensive but non-invasive test, the initial test would be well worthwhile. However, if it required a more expensive and invasive examination, e.g. surgery, the initial test would have subjected a large number of healthy patients to unnecessary trauma.*

3.8 Filmless radiology departments

Since images can now be obtained in digital form, it is now possible to run a radiology department without recourse to film or any other medium that may be held in the hand. The term PACS (Picture Archiving and Communication System) is used to refer to an entirely filmless environment, where images are captured digitally, interpreted on monitors and stored electronically. There are many benefits of such a system, including:
- **Speed:** both the requests coming into the department and the images leaving the department are passed electronically. Compare e-mail to conventional (snail) mail.

- **Access to images**: they can be viewed simultaneously at multiple locations; previous images are instantly available, sorted in the correct order. If the archiving system is robust, they cannot be lost.
- **Image manipulation** and viewing options can be selected. For example, one image can be compared with another, possibly from a different modality, either side-by-side or superimposed.
- **Teleradiology:** this is the logical extension of PACS, whereby images can be transmitted to sites that are geographically remote; for reporting by a radiologist (either routinely or at home after hours); for a specialist opinion (*e.g.* a neuroradiologist); or if the patient has been transferred to another site.
- **Linkage to reports:** when the images are viewed by clinicians, the X-ray report will be available concurrently.

But there are some disadvantages:
- **Cost:** these systems require fast computers networked together with access to a huge amount of memory.
- **Resolution:** as with digital photography, it is difficult to match the spatial resolution that is achieved by film.
- **Reliability:** even in a total power cut a conventional film can be viewed, albeit suboptimally, by holding it up to daylight. (It should be stressed that this is not to be recommended. It is a recipe for missing abnormalities and is only to be used in extreme situations.) Any downtime in a digital imaging system could jeopardise patients' lives, and reliability or uptime has to be well in excess of 99%.
- **System incompatibility:** while efforts at harmonisation are being made through industry standards such as DICOM and HL7, there have been differences in manufacturers' interpretation that can prevent systems "speaking" to each other.
- **Security:** electronic networks containing confidential patient details can be hacked into.

For a PACS system to function in a hospital it must be linked with other IT systems, the two important ones being:
- **RIS** (Radiology Information System), which handles the non-imaging data in an X-ray department such as requests, appointments, reports and exposure details.
- **HIS** (Hospital Information System), which can handle patient demographics and interface with all the other patient-related IT systems in the hospital to produce an Electronic Patient Record.

The impact of a fully electronic Imaging Department on working practices cannot be overemphasised. The main advantages and disadvantages have already been described, but in order to attempt to stress the relevance to all doctors, a futuristic scenario involving an A&E senior house officer (SHO) will be described.
- Patient arrives in A&E out of normal working hours with a head injury.
- Demographic details are checked with the HIS.
- Patient examined by SHO who makes his clinical notes onto the HIS using voice recognition and decides CT is indicated.
- This is requested electronically with the system already knowing the patient details, history, location and physical state. None of this information needs to be duplicated on paper.
- The request is e-mailed to the Radiology Department, justified (§11.6) and scheduled. This automatically creates a portering request in the HIS, again removing a lot of duplicate information recording.
- The patient is moved from A&E to the CT suite by a porter and is scanned.
- The images are sent using teleradiology to the radiologist, either at home or at another site, who reports them using voice recognition. The report is sent back to the PACS system via e-mail and linked with the CT images.
- The images are made available with the report to the SHO in A&E who then decides the patient needs a neurosurgical opinion at a remote site.
- The neurosurgeon receives not only the CT images using teleradiology but all the patient information in a similar manner (telemedicine).
- The patient is then transferred by ambulance, the request having been passed electronically to Ambulance Control.

The only part of this scenario not affected by an electronic environment, compared with conventional paper and film systems, is the physical movement of the patient. In all other areas there is an increase in the speed of data transfer and a reduction in potential errors from transcription of information. All the individual parts of this scenario are currently available, but the linkage into a seamless electronic environment for patient management is yet to be achieved.

3.9 Summary

- X-rays are produced by the interaction of a beam of high speed electrons with a metal target.
- X-rays with a range of energies are produced. The kilovoltage (kV) applied to the X-ray tube determines the upper limit of the X-ray energies.
- X-rays give a shadow image of organs within the body.
- X-ray interactions with tissue are by the photoelectric effect (energy absorption) and by Compton scattering.
- Photoelectric interactions are the main source of contrast in an X-ray image.
- A radiographic image is produced on a film sandwiched between fluorescent screens. It is light emitted from the screens that darkens the film.
- Fluoroscopy provides images of moving structures in real-time at low dose with the aid of an image intensifier.
- X-ray images in digital form are produced in a variety of ways and provide the means for enhancement and manipulation.
- Contrast media containing high atomic number elements such as iodine and barium are used to enhance visualisation of certain structures.
- On a plain film, any gas appears black, fat appears dark grey, water or soft tissue as light grey and bone as white.
- Reasons to request an X-ray examination are to confirm or refute a diagnosis or to monitor a patient's progress. An examination should not be requested if the outcome will not influence patient management.
- The reliance that can be placed on a technique relates to the sensitivity and specificity of the test as well as the incidence of disease in the group examined. Inappropriate referrals reduce the predictive value of the test.
- Radiology is moving towards a filmless environment where images are captured digitally, interpreted on monitors and stored electronically.

Further reading

Ansell G, Betterman MA, Kaufman JA, Wilkins RA. *Complications in diagnostic imaging and interventional radiology*. Oxford, UK: Blackwell, 1996.

Dendy PP, Heaton B. *Physics for diagnostic radiology* (2nd edn). Bristol, UK and Philadelphia, PA: Institute of Physics Publishing, 1999.

Farr RF, Roberts PJ. *Physics for medical imaging*. Philadelphia, PA: WB Saunders, 1997.

Chapter 4

Computed tomography

SJ Golding

X-ray computed tomography (CT) is now such an important diagnostic imaging technique that a complete chapter is devoted to it. The technique is explained briefly and there is information on recent technical developments such as helical CT and multislice CT.

CT is a relatively high radiation dose technique but there is now a wide range of clinical investigations in which its use is justified, so the chapter also contains a broad introduction to CT in clinical practice.

4.1 Introduction

The invention of computed tomography (CT) by Sir Godfrey Hounsfield at the laboratories of EMI Limited was a revolution in medical investigation. Hounsfield developed a method of using X-rays to produce cross-sectional images of the body, and the first CT scanner was unveiled at the British Institute of Radiology in 1972. It was immediately clear that an important medical advance had taken place.

The earliest systems could only examine the head, but a body scanner followed in 1975 and, before the end of the decade, most large hospitals had a CT scanner (Figure 4.1a). Technical advances since that time, both in engineering and computing, have been dramatic. Image resolution has increased and scan times have reduced from around a minute per slice to a matter of seconds. Advanced computer processing offers new reconstructional methods to produce three-dimensional (3D) imaging and other options. CT now provides a highly flexible clinical tool, applicable over a wide range of conditions, but this extreme utility is also its challenge in terms of radiation protection.

4.2 How CT works

CT is a specialised form of radiography. The beam of X-rays has the shape of a fan that is broad enough to irradiate the whole diameter of the body, but only 1–10 mm wide (Figure 4.1b). This beam irradiates a narrow section, or *slice*, within the body. The transmitted radiation is recorded by an array of detectors positioned on the far side of the patient. Each detector measures the attenuation in one direction, or *projection*, through the body. Many sets of attenuation data are acquired at different angles by moving the X-ray tube and detectors to different positions around the body. A two-dimensional image of a section through the body is reconstructed from mathematical analysis of these data sets. Computer reconstruction produces an image composed of a matrix of numbers each of which represents the mean attenuation of the tissues at that position (Figure 4.2).

CT images are:

- cross-sectional;
- a matrix of individual elements;
- based on attenuation of X-rays;
- amenable to further processing.

Figure 4.1 (a) CT scanner. (b) The principle of CT, with the X-ray tube rotating around the patient opposite an array of detectors.

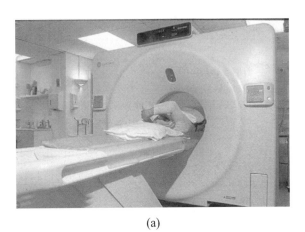

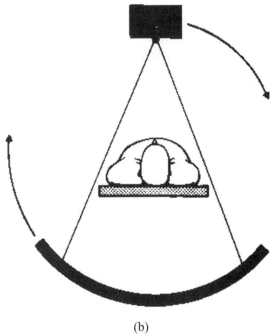

(a)   (b)

There are two types of scanner, *axial* and *helical*. The initial description given in this section relates to the axial type. Differences in the more recent helical scanners will be discussed in §4.4. An examination in an axial scanner is built up of sequential cross-sections by moving the patient on a couch in small increments, usually equal to one slice width, and repeating the scan at the new location to obtain an image of a new slice.

The attenuation scale is expressed in *CT numbers*, which describe the attenuation coefficient for each tissue relative to that for water, with high values indicating dense structures. The CT number in each element or pixel in the image matrix represents the attenuation coefficient for a volume of tissue, known as a *voxel*, and the image formed reflects the attenuation coefficients of all the tissues within it. CT images are usually obtained with high X-ray tube voltages (120–140 kV) and variations in CT number and image contrast are due primarily to differences in tissue density.

Insight: Patient dose and image quality — the trade-off in CT

*The number of X-ray photons is an important factor in determining the level of image quality. If a smaller number of photons is employed, then the random variation in pixel values, or **noise**, may be too large to allow small variations in contrast to be seen. The number of photons is determined by the X-ray tube output, the scan time and the width of the slice being imaged. The output will be increased for imaging thinner slices and decreased for thicker ones if noise levels are to be similar. The choice of output for a particular **slice width** is a balance between achieving the necessary level of image quality and keeping the radiation dose to the minimum.*

Resolution in CT is closely linked to voxel size. However, detection of low contrast lesions in thinner slices may be inferior to that for thicker ones because the output is often not increased proportionately to allow for the narrower beam width and this results in higher noise levels. In practice these parameters are set according to clinical indication. The choice of settings used will have important implications for the absorbed radiation dose.

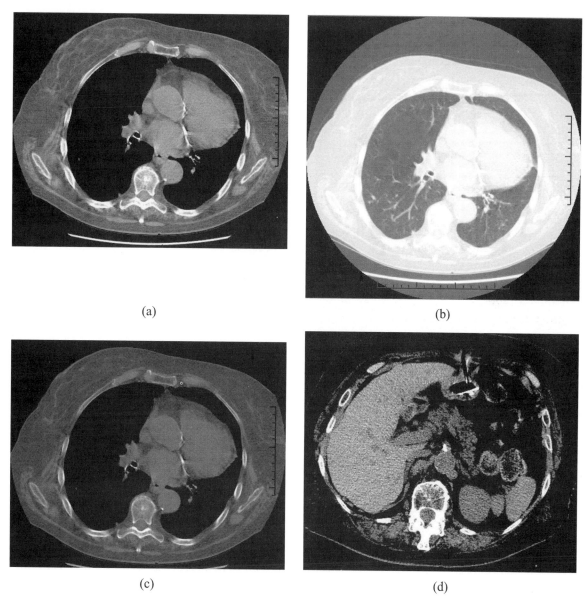

(a) (b)

(c) (d)

Figure 4.2 Viewing CT data: manipulating the viewing window. (a) Tissues from the centre of the range of attenuation values measured by the scanner are displayed in a format in which soft tissues fall in the middle of the range, low attenuation tissues such as fat are seen as dark grey, and high density structures such as bone are seen as light grey or white. (b) Reducing the visible window to very low attenuation values allows detailed analysis of the structure of the lungs. Note that the other soft tissues now fall outside the visible window and are all white. (c) Raising the level of the visible window allows resolution of high attenuation structures. Note the visualisation of the cortex and medulla of the ribs and vertebral bodies. (d) Narrowing the range of the visible window produces a high contrast image, which may be critical to the detection of lesions that do not alter attenuation values very greatly, as in the liver.

Windowing

CT can detect subtle differences in attenuation. However, the attenuations of body tissues and hence their CT numbers cover a wide range. If a CT image is displayed with a grey-scale that varies uniformly with CT number, it will not be possible for the eye to distinguish all the small changes within tissues that CT can detect. Because

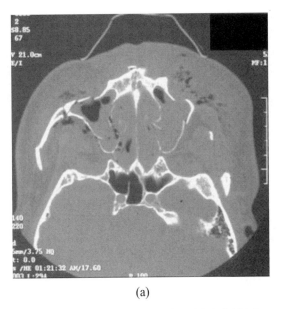
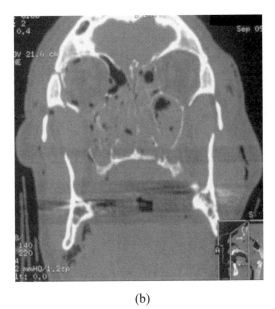

(a)   (b)

Figure 4.3 Multiplanar reformatting. (a) Axial high resolution section through the face at the level of the maxillary antra in a patient who has undergone serious facial injury fracture (see inset at bottom right of second image for position). There are multiple fracture lines involving the walls of the antrum, which are partly filled with blood. Note also that there are bubbles of gas in the soft tissues of the cheek and a fracture of the zygomatic arch on the right. A tiny bubble of air in the left middle cranial fossa is a danger sign, indicating that injury is even more extensive than the axial section shows. (b) Reformatting the data in the coronal plane shows the full extent of the injury. In addition to the maxillary injury there are ethmoid fractures extending to the cribriform plate (almost certainly the source of intracranial air) and two fractures of the lateral wall of the orbit on the right.

of this, viewing consoles display a selective range, or visible "window" (see §3.3.3). This window can be adjusted to concentrate on high or low density structures (for example bone or lung), or widened or narrowed (Figure 4.2). Detection of some diseases requires specific window characteristics, and radiologists usually view images on several different settings when reporting cases.

Image reprocessing

Modern computing methods that permit manipulation of CT image data can be used to bring out different characteristics. Among the simplest are reformatting data from adjacent sections to display different planes (Figure 4.3), or representing the volume of the examination as a 3D image (Figure 4.4). Reprocessing allows the information to be displayed in different ways, which may be more useful for specific applications.

4.3 Use of contrast media and enhancement

In CT, contrast between structures represents differences in attenuation coefficients of tissues. As in other forms of radiography, this natural contrast can be improved by administering external agents, known as contrast media (see §3.4). Iodine-based compounds administered by intravascular injection are retained in the vascular compartment following injection. Perfused structures show an increase in attenuation coefficient to a degree reflecting their capillary circulation and blood pool. This is known as *contrast enhancement*.

Contrast enhancement is frequently used to aid the detection of lesions, as they often have different perfusion to that of surrounding tissue (Figure 4.5). In the brain this effect is increased by breakdown of the blood–brain barrier around lesions (Figure 4.6). Enhancement is also used to distinguish non-perfused lesions (for example cysts, abscesses, haematomas and necrosis) from perfused pathology such as inflammation and neoplasms. Where a contrast medium is used, scans are usually performed before and after its administration.

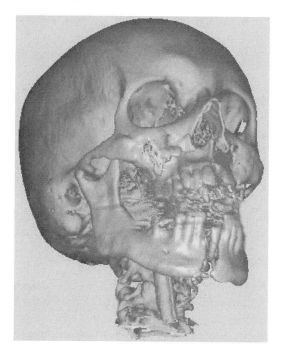

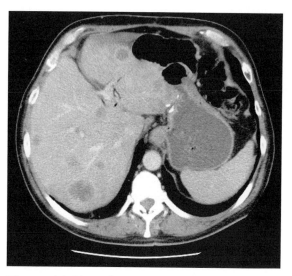

Figure 4.4 Three-dimensional reconstruction from CT data. This patient suffered high impact injury to the anterior face, producing a transverse fracture of the mandible and an impacted transfacial fracture of the maxilla.

Figure 4.5 Use of contrast enhancement, which distinguishes between perfused and non-perfused tissues and also increases contrast between normal and abnormal tissue. Here it is used to aid detection of metastases in the liver, which have lower perfusion than normal tissue and enhance less than the surrounding liver.

With more rapid modern scanners it is possible to synchronise exposure to selective phases of the passage of contrast medium following injection. Timing the exposure to the first circulation after injection provides good demonstration of major arteries (Figure 4.7); later exposure allows veins to be displayed. This is often known as a multiphase study and can be adapted for CT angiography. However, these studies can greatly increase the dose to the patient because of the number of repeat scans.

"*Dynamic CT*" originally meant repeated exposure at one position during passage of a bolus of contrast medium, allowing tissue perfusion to be measured. This technique has been of limited value in clinical practice but the principle of continuous exposure from the X-ray tube was one of the factors leading to the important development of helical CT (see §4.4).

Although contrast enhancement improves the image, it is not used routinely, but is used selectively according to clinical indication. This is because an injection makes the procedure invasive and there are small risks attributable to the contrast medium (see §3.4 and §11.5) and to the increased radiation dose from repeating the exposure.

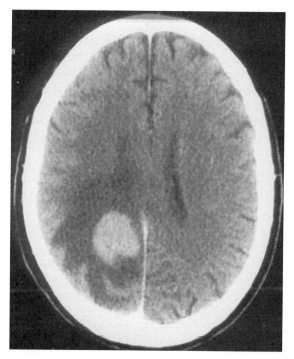

Figure 4.6 Contrast enhancement used in the brain. In this situation the degree of enhancement is increased by leakage of contrast medium across the blood–brain barrier.

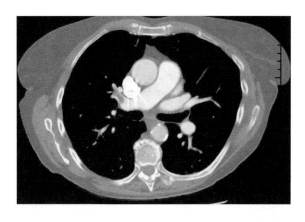

Figure 4.7 CT pulmonary arteriography. Rapid examination with multislice spiral CT and careful synchronisation of the exposure with the bolus of injected contrast medium gives excellent display of major mediastinal vessels, allowing pulmonary emboli to be clearly demonstrated on the right side.

4.4 Helical CT, volume imaging and multislice CT

In conventional CT, table movement between sections and the time necessary to rotate the X-ray tube assembly back to its starting position limit the speed with which the examination can be carried out. These delays are avoided in helical (sometimes called spiral) CT in which continuous exposure is combined with continuous table movement so that the X-ray beam makes a helix along the patient, meaning that much shorter examinations are possible.

Whereas conventional CT collects image data in sequential slices, helical CT acquires data from a volume of the patient, and image reconstruction can be selected retrospectively. Helical CT has meant that anatomical misregistration can usually be avoided, and the shorter examination times reduce movement blurring. Many examinations can be obtained in a single breath-hold, and restless or confused patients, or children, may be examined more easily.

Recently, helical CT has been improved by adding further rows of detectors and by exposing multiple sections simultaneously, allowing table speed to be increased (Figure 4.8). Four, eight and sixteen rows are possible and examination times decrease accordingly. These super-fast "*multislice*" scanners allow large areas to be examined with ease and appear to be the technology platform for the future, making CT a very flexible tool indeed. For example, it is possible in one exposure to image large vessel systems such as the aorta or pulmonary vessels at one phase of enhancement (Figure 4.7). It also becomes possible to reconstruct images with different characteristics (for example different slice thickness or spacing) from a single volume acquisition without further exposure.

Figure 4.8 The principle of multislice spiral CT, with several beams coursing through the examination area simultaneously (reproduced with permission from General Electric Medical Systems, UK).

4.5 CT — a high radiation dose technique

The absorbed radiation dose from some CT examinations is higher than that of most other X-ray techniques. Even a limited examination may involve a radiation dose comparable with that of barium fluoroscopy studies. CT exposures of the abdomen and pelvis are among the highest that a patient may receive from diagnostic radiology and have to be regarded seriously. It has been estimated that CT of the abdomen may give an increased risk of fatal cancer of 1 in 2000 (see Table 11.2). The scan parameters, especially the number of slices in

---

Radiation protection considerations are important in CT because:

- CT usually delivers a high dose.
- CT makes a disproportionate contribution to the exposure of the population compared with conventional radiographic techniques.
- The use of CT is increasing.

---

conventional CT or the scanned length in helical CT, should be optimised for each particular patient to minimise the radiation exposure. The radiologist's training and experience enable him/her to determine the minimum radiation dose required to produce acceptable image quality.

The number of "other examinations" that would deliver a similar dose to one CT examination of the abdomen is shown in the box. It is not, of course, suggested that these examinations have equivalent clinical value, as CT often provides more information. However, it is useful to help remember the order of magnitude of the difference; the clinician who writes a request for CT might think again before requesting 500 chest radiographs!

Comparable doses

Number of studies delivering a radiation dose with comparable risk to that of CT of the abdomen:

- Chest radiograph: 500
- Pelvic radiograph: 15
- Barium meal: 3
- Nuclear medicine bone scan: 2
- Barium enema: 1.5

(Modified from "Making the best use of a department of clinical radiology", Royal College of Radiologists, 2003)

In the early days of CT, its use was largely limited to the brain, as there were no other comparable investigations, and to cancer care, where radiation protection was of secondary importance. Now, however, conditions are radically different. CT has replaced many other techniques on the grounds of providing more information, and many applications of CT are now in young people with benign disease. One department in the USA has estimated that CT is now responsible for two-thirds of the radiation dose delivered in their hospital. These considerations make CT the most important technique over which control of radiation dose needs to be exercised.

Insight: The contribution of CT to collective dose

CT makes a disproportionately large contribution to the collective dose to the population from medical exposures. In the UK, CT comprises only 4% of imaging investigations but represents around 40% of the resulting population dose (compared with chest radiographs, which comprise 30% of examinations but 2% of collective dose). World-wide, it is thought that CT contributes 34% of collective population dose from medical X-rays, but around 90% of all CT procedures are concentrated in the Western World, with around 50 examinations per 1000 population, 6% of which may involve children below the age of 15 years.

What influences radiation dose in CT?

Scanner design is outside the scope of this text, but technological advances in CT have largely been directed at improving image quality rather than reducing dose. However, manufacturers are aware of their responsibilities, particularly in the face of developing international regulation, and developments that allow CT scanners to operate at lower exposures are being investigated. An example of this is modulation of tube output in real-time as the X-ray tube rotates around the patient — a lower intensity of X-rays is used when transmission is through a thinner part of the patient.

> **Three main factors influence the absorbed radiation dose:**
>
> - design of the scanner;
> - size of the patient;
> - the examination technique parameters.

Radiation dose correlates with patient size, as more radiation is absorbed in larger amounts of tissue. However, as many organs have similar attenuation values, a moderate degree of body fat aids distinction of organs by separating them, making interpretation easier than it may be in very thin patients. Beyond this level, increasing stature impedes image quality by increasing noise.

There are ways in which the radiation dose for individual patients can be reduced by modifying technique. However, to do this the radiologist is heavily dependent on receiving accurate information from the clinician. The ideal situation for the radiologist occurs when the clinical question presented is so precise that they can carry out a limited examination, targeted specifically to clinical need, with the minimum image quality that satisfies the clinical requirement.

Insight: Reduction of CT dose

For the individual patient, the main means of reducing radiation dose is by modifying examination technique. The key parameters are:

◊ *the volume of the patient examined;*
◊ *the thickness of the exposed slices;*
◊ *the pitch for helical scanning;*
◊ *the output of radiation from the X-ray tube;*
◊ *the number of repeat exposures (for example after enhancement).*

The relationship between these parameters is complex and choices are usually determined by the clinical indication, which dictates the appropriate slice thickness, the required image quality and the volume of the patient to be irradiated. It must be remembered that tissue outside the main beam, but adjacent to the slice being imaged, will receive a radiation dose from scattered radiation. Thus, when contiguous slices are obtained, each slice receives additional scattered radiation from the adjacent exposures. However, wide separation of sections incurs the risk of disease being overlooked if it falls between sections.

In helical CT, the exposure is continuous and separation of the exposed slice is not possible. However, a similar approach can be applied. The pitch of the helix relates to the distance the patient couch moves during one X-ray tube rotation, and whether this distance is equal to or larger than the thickness of the slices being imaged affects the radiation dose. If the exposure describes a wide spiral through the patient (large pitch), the overall radiation dose to the imaging volume will be lower than if a tight spiral (small pitch) exposure is used.

One of the most important means of reducing radiation dose is to reduce the intensity of the X-ray beam. As already mentioned, this has implications for image quality, as images obtained at low radiation dose have a higher noise level and a lower contrast resolution, which may impede diagnosis. However, in areas of high natural contrast, such as the lung or bone, it may be possible to operate at lower dose levels and still obtain acceptable images.

Some tissues are more radiosensitive than others and protection needs to be more stringent in examinations that include these areas. This applies particularly to examinations covering the lens of the eye, the thyroid gland, gonads and fetus. CT is only carried out in pregnancy for overriding clinical reasons, usually life-threatening conditions. Radiation protection in children must also be more stringent than in adults.

4.6 How to use CT

The golden rule of investigational medicine is that no patient is examined unless the results influence clinical management and therefore outcome (Cochrane's Law, see §13.2). The most important radiation protection step a clinician can make is to decide that an X-ray examination is not required. Quite apart from radiation considerations, unwarranted investigation often raises anxiety in patients, investigations may be invasive and carry additional risks, and valuable resources are wasted. All investigations, including CT, should ideally be used to answer a specific question that has been generated by clinical enquiry and examination.

Another major protection step is to choose a non-radiation test in preference to CT. This usually means ultrasound or MRI (see Chapters 6 and 7). This is particularly important in children and young patients with benign disease. Two possibilities exist:

- The alternative is as accurate or more accurate than CT: CT is contraindicated.
- The alternative is less accurate than CT: alternative investigations may still provide sufficient information for management in some patients, avoiding CT in these patients. The rest may then undergo CT with greater justification.

National guidelines, such as those drawn up in Britain by the Royal College of Radiologists (see §13.4), are valuable in indicating whether CT or its alternatives should be considered. When in doubt, the clinician should always discuss the clinical problem with a radiologist.

Current radiation protection legislation is covered in detail in Chapter 12. Over the last two decades, concern over dose in radiology, and in CT in particular, has risen, culminating in new European law that demands:

- Justification for performing the procedure by clinical benefit.
- Optimisation of examination technique by the X-ray department.

The clinician has to supply sufficient accurate information to allow the radiologist to judge whether the technique is merited. Advice on requesting radiological examinations, including CT, is given in Chapter 13.

Factors relating to a patient's experience in CT are given in the box.

4.7 CT in clinical practice

4.7.1 Current clinical uses

Initially, the main clinical users of CT were neurosciences, oncology, orthopaedics and acute medicine and surgery. Technological advance has been steady and there are now few clinical specialties that do not use CT to some extent.

Insight: The patient experience in CT

Possible starvation beforehand
May be required to undress
May require: contrast medium intravenously
contrast medium orally (GI tract, abdomen)
full bladder (abdomen)
vaginal tampon (female pelvis)
Need to keep still
May need to hold their breath during the exposure
Possible interventional procedure

Information, often in the form of a leaflet, will be given to the patient by the hospital for any examination undertaken.

Table 4.1 gives a summary of the common uses of CT and also indicates where alternative techniques should or might be preferred. It is difficult to give dogmatic recommendations on use, because:

- all techniques may not be equally available locally;
- expertise in techniques may differ and may affect local practice;
- new applications continually develop, while existing ones may gather additional clinical significance;
- benefits of techniques have to be weighed against local costs.

Table 4.1 Common indications for CT and related techniques (only clinical applications where CT is implicated are included)

Indication	Technique of choice	Alternative technique(s)
Acute medicine and surgery		
Abdominal mass	US	CT, MRI
Abdominal sepsis	CT	US, MRI
Abdominal trauma	CT	US
Detecting site and cause of obstructive jaundice	US	CT, MRI
Diagnosis/evaluation of aortic aneurysm/dissection	CT	MRI
Detection of pulmonary embolism	CT	Ventilation/perfusion radionuclide imaging
Endocrinology		
Diagnosis of pituitary disease	MRI	CT
Diagnosis of adrenal disease	US	MRI, CT
Diagnosis of parathyroid disease	US	MRI, CT
Gastroenterology		
Diagnosis of pancreatic disease	US	CT, MRI
Diagnosis of space-occupying lesions of liver	US	MRI, CT
Evaluation of obstructive jaundice	US	MRI, CT
Diagnosis of colonic neoplasms	Endoscopy, barium enema	CT colonoscopy
Gynaecology		
Staging carcinoma of cervix/uterus	MRI	US, CT
Staging and monitoring carcinoma of ovary	US	CT, MRI
Pelvimetry	MRI	CT
Neurosciences		
Diagnosis, staging and monitoring of structural disease of brain	MRI	CT
Cerebral inflammation	MRI	CT
Cerebral haemorrhage	CT	MRI
Evaluation of head injury	CT	MRI
Demyelinating disease	MRI	CT
Diagnosis/evaluation of spinal cord lesions and compression	MRI	CT
Oncology		
Staging of most solid neoplasms	MRI	CT
Treatment monitoring	CT	MRI, US
Computer-assisted treatment planning	CT	MRI

4.7.2 Advanced uses of CT

The cross-sectional display of CT has proved valuable for placing instruments accurately within patients. CT-guided needle biopsy and abscess drainage (Figure 4.9) are now common procedures and in many departments it is standard practice to proceed immediately to guided biopsy or abscess drainage after diagnostic study. These techniques have been shown to be quick and accurate, with a low complication rate.

Vascular uses of CT represent a new development resulting from the combination of contrast medium enhancement, rapid scanning and advanced image processing. CT angiography possesses all the advantages of conventional angiography with the additional benefit of cross-sectional display. Manipulation of exposure factors may result in radiation doses comparable with those from conventional angiography and the technique appears preferable but it is not yet clear whether comparable doses are attained in practice. However, this aspect of CT is likely to increase in the future.

Table 4.1 *Continued.*

Staging systemic neoplasm, *e.g.* lymphoma	CT	MRI
Detecting pulmonary metastases	CT	—
Detecting hepatic metastases	US	CT, MRI
Detecting cerebral metastases	MRI	CT
Orthopaedics and traumatology		
Vertebral trauma	CT	—
Pelvic trauma	CT	—
Discovertebral degenerative disease	MRI	CT
Musculoskeletal neoplasms	MRI	CT
Instability of shoulder/rotator cuff lesions	MRI	CT arthrography
Ischaemic necrosis of joints	MRI	CT
Internal derangement of knee	MRI	CT arthrography
Otolaryngology, ophthalmology and maxillofacial surgery		
Diagnosis/staging of facial neoplasms	MRI	CT
Sensorineural hearing loss	MRI	CT
Maxillofacial trauma	CT	—
Evaluation of sinus disease before endoscopy	CT	—
Planning reconstructive surgery	CT	MRI
Diagnosis of orbital masses/proptosis	MRI	CT
Thoracic medicine and surgery		
Disease of pulmonary parenchyma	CT	—
Diagnosis/staging of pulmonary neoplasms	CT	MRI
Mediastinal trauma	CT	—
Diagnosis/evaluation of thoracic aneurysm	CT	MRI
Evaluation of chest wall disease	CT	MRI
Urology		
Differential diagnosis of renal mass	US	MRI, CT
Staging carcinoma of kidney/bladder	CT	MRI
Evaluation of renal tumour	CT	US
Diagnosis of site and cause of ureteric obstruction	US	CT urography

MRI, magnetic resonance imaging; US, ultrasound.

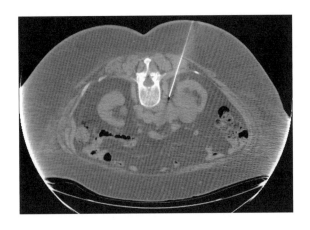

Figure 4.9 Interventional use of CT. The cross-sectional "map" provided by CT images allows accurate placing of biopsy and drainage instruments. Here CT is used to place a biopsy needle deep in the abdomen to obtain a diagnosis in a patient with retroperitoneal lymphadenopathy.

Modern processing of CT image data provides 3D techniques that are valuable in planning surgery and radiotherapy, and in providing a template for the production of prostheses. A more advanced application is "virtual endoscopy", which allows the lumen of some organs to be studied non-invasively, for example CT colonoscopy or laryngoscopy. Their clinical value is currently being evaluated but it seems likely that these applications will increase in the future. An exciting new development is the production of computer programs that allow surgical training under simulation.

4.7.3 Artefacts and impediments

Artefacts from several sources may degrade CT images.

Metal objects
Dense metal objects such as dental fillings and internal or external fixation devices transmit few X-rays and, as a result, they produce serious artefacts. Potential problems are given by:

- metal hip prostheses in examinations of the pelvis;
- aneurysm clips in brain scans;
- barium sulphate in the bowel from barium enema examinations;
- metal items in clothing, and patients may need to undress and remove these before CT.

Movement
Movement during any exposure causes blurring of images. Patients need to lie flat and keep still; often they have to hold their breath for periods ranging from a few seconds to around 20 s. Movement or breathing may also move organs to different locations during exposure, so that lesions may be missed, an effect known as anatomical misregistration.

Partial volume effect (PVE)
CT is a sectional technique and details at the edge of sections may not be clearly seen because the attenuation coefficients will be averaged with those for the normal tissue within the pixels. The radiologist overcomes PVE by adapting section thickness and spacing to the clinical circumstances.

4.7.4 Conclusion

Such has been the increasing utilisation of CT that it has been claimed that the technique is at risk of replacing clinical examination as the most important means of assessing the patient. Many departments have noticed a trend to this practice but it cannot be justified, either medically or legally. New legislation makes it timely to redress the balance. Used appropriately, CT is a powerful aid to clinical management but its use must not be indiscriminate. The clinician who wishes to be conscientious in the protection of their patient should, in addition to knowing when CT should be used, be capable of asking themselves, "when should CT not be used?"

4.8 Summary

- CT produces images of sections through the body that portray X-ray attenuation of the tissues.
- Contrast in the images is primarily due to differences in tissue density.
- CT is a clinically powerful tool that, thanks to technological development, is now applicable to a wide range of clinical conditions.
- Contrast media can be used to produce enhancement related to tissue perfusion.
- In a helical scan the X-ray beam follows a helical path along the patient. This is achieved by moving the couch continuously as the X-ray tube rotates around the patient.
- Modern techniques for processing image data can provide 3D reconstructions, which are valuable in planning surgery and in other applications.
- CT delivers a relatively high radiation dose and special attention must therefore be paid to justification by clinical benefit.
- The clinical referrer and the practitioner share a responsibility for ensuring that the patient is not irradiated unjustifiably.
- The radiologist has the opportunity to reduce radiation exposure significantly by manipulating exposure factors. However, the choice of these is dictated by clinical considerations.
- The clinical referral needs to be as informative as possible to allow the radiologist to adapt examinations to the clinical purpose and to avoid unjustified radiation exposure.

Further reading

Armstrong P, Wastie ML, editors. *Diagnostic imaging* (4th edn). Oxford, London, Edinburgh, UK: Blackwell Science, 1998.

Golding SJ, Shrimpton PC. Radiation dose in CT: are we meeting the challenge? Br J Radiol 2002;75:1–4.

International Commission on Radiological Protection. Managing patient dose in computed tomography, Publication 87. Ann ICRP 2001;30(4).

Royal College of Radiologists. *Making the best use of a department of clinical radiology* (5th edn). London, UK: RCR, 2003.

Chapter 5

Nuclear medicine (radionuclide imaging)

RF Bury

> Nuclear medicine is the umbrella term for diagnostic imaging that relies on the radiation emitted from radioactive materials rather than on X-rays. Although image quality is much inferior to that of X-rays, the techniques are often complementary as the radionuclide image can provide physiological rather than anatomical data.
>
> This chapter focuses on the type of information radionuclide imaging can give, the situations in which it is most useful clinically and some special radiation protection problems arising from using unsealed radioactive materials.

5.1 **Introduction**
5.2 **Underlying principles of radionuclide imaging (RNI)**
5.3 **Capturing and using the image**
5.4 **Positron emission tomography (PET)**
5.5 **Radiation dose and risk**
5.6 **What information does RNI give us?**
5.7 **When to use RNI**
5.8 **RNI in clinical use**
5.9 **Summary**

5.1 Introduction

Nuclear medicine describes the use of radioactive materials not only to produce images, but also to act as tracers in various *in vitro* tests of patient physiology and, in much larger doses, to treat a number of malignant conditions and a few benign ones. Nuclear medicine is a specialty in its own right, and nuclear medicine physicians are, as the name suggests, physicians who have trained in all aspects of the subject and practise the full range of diagnostic and therapeutic techniques. However, a high proportion of the purely imaging nuclear medicine work in the UK is carried out by diagnostic radiologists with a special

> **What's in a name?**
>
> - **Nuclear medicine**: describes the use of radionuclides for diagnostic (imaging and *in vitro* assay) and therapeutic purposes.
> - **Radionuclide imaging (RNI)**: this is the new term that includes the purely imaging component of nuclear medicine, and for which a defined training programme now exists in the UK.
>
> Other names used somewhat loosely to describe imaging with radioactive materials are: *isotope scanning* and *scintigraphy*.

interest in the subject. Until recently, the training required by radiologists taking responsibility for diagnostic nuclear medicine departments was rather nebulous. However, the Royal Colleges of Physicians and Radiologists have now produced joint guidelines for a year of specialist instruction towards the end of the 5 year training in clinical radiology. The training includes all the imaging components of nuclear medicine, but excludes the therapeutic and *in vitro* measurement applications, and will qualify radiologists to hold the appropriate licence governing the medical use of radioactive substances (see §12.7).

A number of different terms are in use to describe imaging with radionuclides (see box), but as this book is principally concerned with diagnostic imaging, we shall stick (more or less) to radionuclide imaging (RNI), with only brief reference to therapeutic applications.

5.2 Underlying principles of radionuclide imaging (RNI)

5.2.1 How is RNI different?

Most of the other imaging techniques in this book rely on the use of an externally generated beam of radiation. This is directed at the patient, and the radiation that is transmitted through them (or reflected from them, in the case of ultrasound) is captured either directly on film or by some other form of detector.

RNI is different. In RNI the patient is injected with radioactive material. This either accumulates in the organ or tissue of interest, or is taken up into a physiological process. The γ-radiation emitted from the patient is detected by a *gamma camera* (see §5.3) and the resulting image is displayed for reporting.

Key points

- The actual radioactive element used is known as the **radionuclide**.
- The combination of radionuclide with its carrier chemical is the **radiopharmaceutical**.

There are a few investigations where a radionuclide alone is used, for example perfusion imaging of the heart using thallium ions.

5.2.2 The RNI process

Whatever the organ or physiological process being imaged, the basic steps involved are the same and they are illustrated in Figure 5.1. Sometimes images will be acquired during and for a variable period after the injection, for example in renography. For other applications images will be obtained after a variable delay, depending on the type of scan being performed. Sometimes a combined approach is needed, requiring both immediate and delayed views.

Following data processing, images are produced for reporting. These may be presented on transparent film, like radiographs, or as colour images on various paper media. Increasingly, though, "soft copy" reporting is used, with the images being viewed on a monitor at a workstation (see §5.3).

5.2.3 Choosing a radionuclide

The radionuclides most commonly used for imaging are listed in the box. Technetium-99m (^{99m}Tc) is deliberately placed at the top because well over 90% of the diagnostic investigations performed in nuclear medicine departments utilise it.

---

choose a pharmaceutical that will attach to the relevant organ/tissue

choose an appropriate radionuclide with which to label the pharmaceutical

administer the radiopharmaceutical (usually intravenously, occasionally by other routes)

acquire images — may be immediately after injection or delayed, depending on the application

---

Insight: Commonly used radionuclides

Technetium	(^{99m}Tc)
Iodine	(^{123}I and ^{131}I)
Indium	(^{111}In and ^{113}In)
Thallium	(^{201}Tl)
Gallium	(^{67}Ga)

Figure 5.1 The steps involved in a radionuclide scan.

The ideal radionuclide

The properties required in a radionuclide are:

- **the right emissions**: γ-rays are required for imaging — α- and β-particle emissions are absorbed almost immediately within the patient's tissues, and therefore increase the radiation dose without contributing to the image.
- **the right γ-ray energy**: the energy of the radiation needs to be high enough for the photons to escape from the patient and hit the gamma camera, but not so high that there are technical difficulties in capturing them.
- **the right half-life** (see box): there are some potentially useful radionuclides whose half-lives are only a few seconds (especially in PET scanning, see §5.4), so unless they are produced on-site and piped direct to the scanning room, they are useless. Equally, if the half-life is too long, the patient will go on accumulating dose, and exposing other members of his or her family, long after the scan is completed.
- **availability**: some radionuclides, such as radioiodine and thallium, may only be available on certain days of the week. They therefore need to be ordered in advance and also tend to be relatively expensive.
- **chemical reactivity**: if it is to be used to scan a range of different organs and tissues, the ideal radionuclide needs to bind to a correspondingly large range of carriers to form the appropriate radiopharmaceuticals.

The reason that ^{99m}Tc is so useful is that it measures up well against all the above criteria.

- It is an almost pure γ-ray emitter.
- The γ-ray energy is close to ideal — 140 keV (keV = thousand electron volts, see §1.7).
- The physical half life is 6 h — long enough that it is still possible to obtain useful information up to 24 h post injection, but not so long that dose becomes excessive.
- It is readily available: ^{99m}Tc is supplied in the form of a "generator", which consists of a column of ion-exchange resin impregnated with radioactive molybdenum-99 (^{99}Mo) (Figure 5.2). This decays into ^{99m}Tc, which can be extracted by drawing sterile saline through the column from a reservoir and into an evacuated vial (a process known as "milking" the generator). ^{99}Mo decays with a half-life of 2.7 days, giving the

---

Insight: Half-life

When using radionuclides for diagnosis or therapy, it is important to remember that there are two half-lives to consider.

The physical half-life: this is the one you (dimly) remember from school physics and it is a constant for the radionuclide concerned. The physical half-life of ^{99m}Tc is approximately 6 h (see §1.2). This means that after 12 h there will be 25% of the original activity remaining, and after 24 h just over 6%.

The biological half-life: if the radiopharmaceutical is excreted by the body, the biological half-life may be less than the physical value, and this fact has important radiation protection implications. For example, in renography the radiopharmaceutical is rapidly cleared from the bloodstream by the kidneys, giving a biological half-life of considerably less than 6 h. Unlike the physical half-life, the biological half-life is not a constant; it will vary with the physiological status of the individual patient. If our renogram patient is dehydrated, ADH levels will rise, water will be retained by the kidney and the biological half-life of the radiopharmaceutical will increase. In practice, patients are given a fluid load prior to the examination to standardise as far as possible the conditions under which the test takes place.

To take another example, the radiopharmaceutical used for bone scanning is bound to bone crystal, but any unbound material is cleared from the blood by the kidneys. Consequently, the critical tissue from the dose point of view is the bladder mucosa, and patients are advised to drink plenty of fluids and empty their bladder at frequent intervals post injection to reduce the biological half-life of the unbound component, and consequently the dose to the patient.

---

generator a useful life of a week. This arrangement ensures that there is a steady supply of ^{99m}Tc available in the department.

- It is chemically reactive: technetium has a number of valency states and is highly reactive, making it a versatile partner for carrier chemicals.

5.3 Capturing and using the image

The patient is positioned with the gamma camera as close as possible to the area under investigation, as shown in Figure 5.3. For static imaging this can be done at leisure after the appropriate delay to allow the radiopharmaceutical to localise in the relevant organ or tissue; for dynamic studies the injection is performed with the camera already in place.

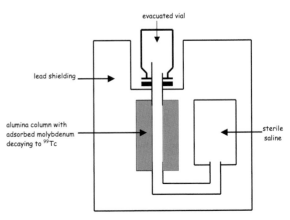

Figure 5.2 Diagram of a technetium-99m generator.

5.3.1 The hardware

The radiation detection system is contained in the "head" of the gamma camera (Figures 5.3 and 5.4), and this is mounted on a circular gantry that allows it to be positioned at any point around the patient and angled to provide the best view of the organ concerned. This arrangement also allows the head to rotate around the patient for *tomographic imaging* (see box on page 51). The detector itself is a large single crystal of sodium iodide, approximately 1 cm thick. When γ-rays are absorbed by the crystal, scintillations (flashes of visible light) are produced. These flashes are detected by an array of photomultiplier tubes, optically coupled to the back of the crystal. Although each scintillation will be "seen" by more than one tube, the relative intensity of the light in neighbouring tubes allows its position in the crystal to be defined. The pattern of radiation hitting the crystal will correspond to the distribution of activity in the patient's body, provided that only γ-rays travelling perpendicular to the patient's body are allowed to impinge on the detector. γ-rays emitted at angles other than 90° to the body surface will give false positional information and are removed by the *collimator* (Figure 5.4). This is a plate of lead with multiple holes perpendicular to its surface, which is bolted to the front face of the camera head.

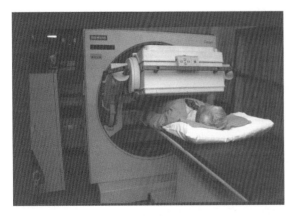

Figure 5.3 Gamma camera in position over a patient.

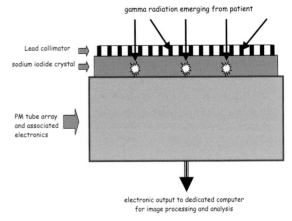

Figure 5.4 Diagram of a gamma camera head (see text for explanation).

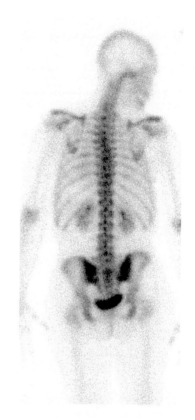

Figure 5.5 A normal bone scan (posterior view).

5.3.2 Static and dynamic imaging

The bone scan is an example of *static imaging*. The radiopharmaceutical is incorporated into actively metabolising bone. At 3 h post injection the gamma camera is positioned close to the patient and several overlapping images each of several minutes duration are acquired, to give full coverage of the skeleton (Figure 5.5).

However, because the image from the gamma camera is recorded electronically and then processed by a dedicated computer system, it is possible to record sequential images very rapidly. This *dynamic imaging* can capture the movement of an organ such as the heart (gated cardiac imaging, see below) or follow the movement of the radiopharmaceutical with time as it is processed by the body. The number of images acquired, and their timing, is controlled by computer, and the exact protocol will depend on the investigation being carried out. For a renogram for example, the camera is triggered as the injection is given, and 200 or more sequential images each of 15–20 s duration are obtained.

5.3.3 Processing and presenting the image

For the bone scan, the images may simply be printed on to film for reporting on a viewing box, like an X-ray. However, as stated above, there is now a general move to soft copy reporting, where the images are viewed on a monitor at a workstation. Even for bone images, where little processing is required, this can be useful, as it allows manipulation of brightness, contrast and window levels. However, for many investigations more specialised processing will be required. This may take the form of drawing regions of interest and plotting changes in activity with time. In the kidney, for example, such simple processing will produce time–activity curves that can diagnose or exclude obstruction to renal drainage, and allow the calculation of relative renal function. For more complex investigations, images can be presented as a cine display. This is particularly useful in cardiac imaging where the acquisition can be gated to the ECG signal, and a moving image can be presented that allows evaluation of ventricular wall movement, ejection fraction and other parameters of cardiac function.

A workstation is also required to process tomographic data (see box on page 51), which is then presented as a series of sections through the organ or region of interest, in any plane selected by the technician or doctor. This type of data can also be presented as a three-dimensional (3D) display, with rotation of the 3D image in real-time.

5.4 Positron emission tomography (PET)

PET is one of the most exciting growth areas in nuclear medicine. It relies on the use of positron-emitting radionuclides. As soon as a positron (positively charged electron, see §1.2) is released in the tissues, it meets an electron and the two particles are annihilated, with the production of two high energy photons travelling away from each other at 180°. The patient lies at the centre of a ring of detectors, which build up an image of a transverse section through the body. As the patient moves through the gantry, successive slices are acquired, allowing reconstruction of images in any plane. The beauty of PET is that it uses radionuclides that can be readily incorporated into organic molecules, allowing imaging of tissue physiology. Some of these are so short-lived that an on-site cyclotron is required. However, one of the most useful PET radiopharmaceuticals is the glucose analogue fluorodeoxyglucose (FDG), which has a sufficiently long half-life to be used by centres within a couple of hours of a production facility. PET already has established roles in oncology (see clinical examples, below), cardiology and, to a lesser extent, neurology. There is likely to be a major investment in PET centres in the next 10 years.

5.5 Radiation dose and risk

Exposure to ionising radiation is potentially hazardous, and patients are becoming increasingly aware of this. This topic is covered in greater depth in Chapters 8, 10 and 11. Typical doses are shown in Table 11.2. Doses in PET tend to be slightly higher than those with ^{99m}Tc because the positron deposits a dose locally before it annihilates. Doses in PET examinations are, however, still generally low. Although sufficiently high doses of radiation can cause tissue damage ranging from skin erythema to full-blown radiation sickness and death, at the relatively low doses used in diagnostic imaging it is only the risk of inducing malignancy in the patient or any fetus which might be present that needs to concern us.

It is important to note that although the doses used in RNI are of the same order of magnitude as those encountered in radiography and fluoroscopy, there are several radiation protection issues that are specific to the use of radionuclides. These all stem from the fact that, in RNI, the radiation source is inside the patient and may be present for some time after they leave the nuclear medicine department. The implications of this are as follows:

- Unlike radiography, where the exposure is limited to the area of interest, the whole body receives a dose of radiation following injection of radiopharmaceutical, even when only performing a bone scan of the wrist.
- The patient continues to be irradiated after the scan is completed.
- Other persons may be irradiated by the patient after they leave the hospital. For most diagnostic RNI procedures the dose to others is minimal, but parents of young children may be advised to avoid prolonged cuddling for a period after the scan.
- Many radiopharmaceuticals are secreted in breast milk, so nursing mothers may need to discontinue breast-feeding temporarily after a radionuclide scan.

5.6 What information does RNI give us?

5.6.1 Structural vs functional information

Most other imaging modalities (with the exception of some of the more recent applications of MRI) produce images of anatomy, that is of structure. Some techniques can produce really exquisite high resolution anatomical images, revealing details a fraction of a millimetre in size. But it's still "just" anatomy. One of the great strengths of RNI lies in its ability to probe the *function* of organs and tissues, and we will see examples of this later in the chapter.

However, in imaging as in life, everything comes at a price, and although RNI techniques have this invaluable ability to reveal function, their spatial resolution tends to be poor. For proof of this, mentally compare the grainy low resolution image of the skeleton in Figure 5.5 with the detailed depiction of bone structure seen in a plain radiograph (Figure 3.2), or compare images obtained by RNI and other techniques in Chapter 2. But of course the type of information required will depend on the clinical problem. Let's take an example involving renal disease.

Staging a renal cell cancer prior to surgery

Here we will want the best anatomical information available, to see whether the tumour has extended through the renal capsule, invaded the renal vein or spread to involve the local lymph nodes. For that we need CT or MRI, with their high resolution images depicting detailed cross-sectional anatomy that can be used by the surgeon to plan the operation.

? urinary outflow obstruction

If, on the other hand, we are dealing with a patient who has undergone surgery to relieve long-standing obstruction at the pelvi-ureteric junction, we do not really mind what the kidney looks like, in fact we would expect it still to be dilated due to the previous disease. What the surgeon needs here is functional information — has normal drainage of urine been restored? For that, radionuclide renography gives us the information we need.

5.6.2 Sensitivity vs specificity

RNI techniques, based as they are on the use of radioactive tracers, tend to be very sensitive. In other words, they will detect small changes in behaviour of the tissue under investigation. The usual example quoted in this context is that of the bone scan in the detection of metastatic disease. Bone metastases will eventually be seen on an X-ray owing to destruction of normal bone by the tumour tissue. However, it has been calculated that for a metastasis to be detectable in this way, it has to have destroyed approximately 50% of the normal bone tissue. Bone scanning, on the other hand, detects the increase in uptake of radiopharmaceutical owing to the bone's attempt to repair the damage done by the tumour cells. This results in a "hot spot" on the scan very early on in the process, sometimes up to a year or more before an X-ray will show any abnormality.

However, here again we come up against that immutable principle of life, the universe and everything; namely that you never get something for nothing, and the price of this high sensitivity is a relatively low specificity. To continue with the bone scanning example, although the scan will detect a problem at a very early stage in its evolution, it will often not tell us what the nature of that problem is, and a hot spot in a bone can be due to any one of a number of disease processes (see box). Sometimes this can be a problem. For example, if a patient with previous breast cancer has a solitary hot spot on her bone scan, it can be difficult or impossible to decide whether it is due to a metastasis or to some other cause. However, the clinical context will often be sufficient to remove any uncertainty arising from the lack of specificity of the technique. Take the case of a fit young long distance runner with shin pain. If the bone scan reveals increased uptake at the typical site on the posteromedial cortex of the tibia, we are not going to start worrying that they might have a metastasis from an unknown primary tumour — we have confirmed the clinical suspicion of stress fracture, and if we wait for a week or two the X-ray will probably show typical findings. Again, if a patient with prostatic cancer and bone pain has a scan that reveals multiple widespread abnormalities, the diagnosis is metastatic disease, regardless of the fact that any of the individual lesions could be due to any of the causes listed in the box.

> ***Insight: Some common causes of increased uptake on bone scan ("hot spot")***
>
> *Tumour (primary or metastatic)*
> *Trauma*
> *Infection*
> *Arthritis*
> *Recent surgery*
> *Paget's disease*

5.7 When to use RNI

The rational use of expensive clinical investigations is a vital skill for all clinicians to acquire and it is something that we tend not to teach very well in medical schools. There is only room for a few general points here.

What is the question? The first step in referring patients for RNI (or any other investigation) is to define the clinical question you wish to answer. Going through this mental process before filling in the request card is useful for two reasons. First, as we saw in our renal example above, the answer will often determine which is the most appropriate investigation to go for. Perhaps even more important, if you are unable to think of a question you are probably wasting everyone's time (not least the patient's) by filling in the card.

What sort of information do we need? As we saw earlier in this section, if only functional information is required, RNI may give the complete answer, but often a combined approach will be required. For example, in a patient with chest pain of presumed cardiac origin, a coronary angiogram may show a 60% narrowing in one of the coronary arteries that is thought to be insufficient to explain the patient's symptoms. A nuclear cardiology procedure (see below) may then be required to show whether this relatively mild stenosis is causing functional ischaemia at tissue level when the patient exercises.

Can we answer the clinical question without using ionising radiation? With the universal availability of ultrasound and with increasing access to MRI, it will often be possible to avoid the use of ionising radiation altogether (see Chapters 6 and 7).

5.8 RNI in clinical use

This chapter does not set out to provide exhaustive coverage of all the clinical applications of RNI, but having already talked about bone scanning and mentioned the role of renography, this final section will present a few clinical situations where scintigraphy is particularly useful, hopefully highlighting some of the modality's specific strengths and illustrating the principles outlined above.

5.8.1 Nuclear cardiology

Although often spoken of as a separate subspecialty, nuclear cardiology is simply the application of RNI techniques to the investigation of cardiac disease. Questions that can be answered in this way include:

Chest pain — ? cardiac: most patients presenting with chest pain will be diagnosed without recourse to nuclear cardiology, but there remains a significant minority who continue to complain of symptoms and where all the initial investigations produce equivocal results. By stressing the patient and then injecting a radiopharmaceutical that gets into the myocardial cells and stays there, it is possible to produce tomographic images through the left ventricle that map the myocardial blood flow (Figure 5.6). Ischaemic areas will show as cold spots since the radiopharmaceutical is not reaching them. This is a very sensitive technique for identifying patients with cardiac ischaemia requiring treatment. Perhaps more importantly, patients with a normal perfusion scan can be reassured that the probability of a future adverse cardiac event is very low.

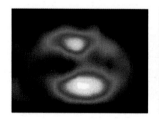 

Figure 5.6 Myocardial perfusion scan showing vertical tomographic slices through the left ventricle at stress (left) and at rest (right). There is a large perfusion defect in the apex and anterior (upper) wall of the ventricle at maximal exercise, which shows good reversibility at rest. This indicates the presence of viable myocardial tissue in the ischaemic area, and so intervention to restore blood flow will be a worthwhile procedure. If the myocardium was dead (infarcted), the defect would have persisted at rest and revascularisation would have achieved nothing.

Abnormal angiogram — ? significant: a coronary angiogram (where radio-opaque contrast medium is injected into the coronary artery via a catheter inserted into the femoral artery and up the aorta) is often regarded as the gold standard for the diagnosis of coronary artery disease, but it only demonstrates the anatomy. As mentioned in the previous section, there may be doubt as to whether a stenosis (narrowing) of a coronary vessel is tight enough to be causing the patient's symptoms. A perfusion scan will demonstrate whether or not there is tissue ischaemia in the muscle supplied by the abnormal vessel.

Recurrent symptoms following treatment: it is not unusual for patients to develop recurrent symptoms some time after surgical treatment to bypass a blocked coronary artery. Perfusion scanning can then show whether there is significant reversible ischaemia (ischaemia occurring on exercise, but normalising at rest; Figure 5.6) that would benefit from further intervention.

5.8.2 Tumour imaging

Following treatment for malignancy, imaging may reveal anatomical abnormalities that are not necessarily the result of residual or recurrent tumour. For example, it is not unusual, following radiotherapy and chemotherapy for lymphoma, for follow-up CT or MRI to reveal a residual mass in the mediastinum at the site of the treated lymph nodes. There is no way of determining whether this represents scar tissue or active tumour. However, PET imaging using FDG will demonstrate high uptake in viable tumour relative to scar tissue, and can reliably differentiate between the two.

There are also more specific markers for some tumours. MIBG is an amine precursor that is taken up by tumours of neural crest origin such as neuroblastoma and phaeochromocytoma. Scanning with ^{123}I-labelled MIBG can be used in the diagnosis of these tumours (Figure 5.7). What's more, if the tumour shows high levels of uptake on the diagnostic scan, a large dose of ^{131}I-labelled radiopharmaceutical can be used to treat disseminated metastatic disease (making use of the short-range β emissions of ^{131}I to kill the tumour cells from within).

Even more specific are *monoclonal antibodies*. These are antibodies raised to specific tumour cell types and then labelled with an appropriate radionuclide. Injected into a patient who has been treated for the tumour in question, these tracers should localise in residual or recurrent tumour tissue, which will be revealed on scanning. In practice, these "magic bullets" have not proved as helpful as had been hoped, but they are used for colonic and ovarian cancer with varying degrees of success. This remains a promising field for development.

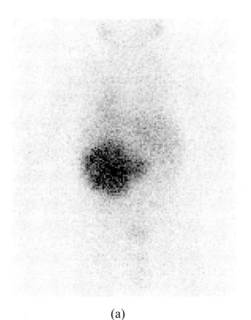 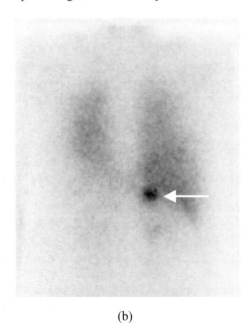

(a) (b)

Figure 5.7 MIBG scans showing (a) an infant with a large neuroblastoma occupying the upper abdomen, but with no evidence of metastasis, and (b) an adult with a phaeochromocytoma in the adrenal gland (arrow).

5.8.3 Gastrointestinal (GI) imaging

There are a number of situations where RNI techniques are of particular value in disease of the GI tract, including:

Gastrointestinal bleeding: intermittent GI bleeding can be a diagnostic problem. The obvious investigation to use is angiography of the vessels supplying the gut. However, a full study of the GI tract requires selective catheterisation of three separate vessels (coeliac, superior and inferior mesenteric arteries), and unless there is active bleeding at the moment the contrast medium is injected, the study will be negative. Scintigraphy can help here by employing a simple *in vivo* technique to label the patient's red blood cells with ^{99m}Tc and then imaging intermittently for up to 24 h. Activity will accumulate in the gut where bleeding is occurring. Although not localising the source of bleeding quite as accurately as a positive angiogram, it can pick up intermittent blood loss and at least tell the angiographer which vessel to target.

Abdominal pain — ? biliary dyskinesia: most patients with biliary symptoms have gallstones, and these are best diagnosed using ultrasound. However, a minority suffer continuing symptoms in the absence of stones, and this can be due to non-coordination of gall bladder and/or sphincter of Oddi contraction. Dynamic imaging using a ^{99m}Tc-labelled pharmaceutical that is rapidly excreted via the biliary tract allows functional abnormalities of biliary excretion to be detected, even though there are no structural defects in the biliary tree.

5.8.4 Imaging infection

In the previous section we saw how labelled red cells could be used to detect haemorrhage. It is also possible to label the patient's leucocytes with ^{99m}Tc, although it is a slightly more complex procedure involving cell separation and labelling *in vitro*. The cells can then be re-injected, and septic foci in the abdomen and elsewhere will be revealed as hot spots on scanning as the white cells accumulate at the site of infection.

5.9 Summary

- Radionuclide techniques generally involve the use of γ-ray-emitting radiopharmaceuticals targeted at specific tissues or physiological processes.
- Nuclear medicine includes the use of radionuclides for imaging (RNI), as tracers in *in vitro* tests and in larger doses to treat various benign and malignant conditions.
- Unlike all other imaging methods, the radiation source is introduced into the patient, usually by intravenous injection. This has important radiation protection implications, not only for the patient but also for those coming into contact with them.
- ^{99m}Tc is an ideal radionuclide for imaging because it emits γ-rays of suitable energy, has a 6 h half-life, is chemically reactive and is readily available.
- Radionuclides inside the body are imaged using a gamma camera.
- RNI studies produce images that reflect physiology and function, data that are often not obtainable in any other way. For this reason they are frequently used to complement investigations that provide better anatomical detail.
- Sequential images can be recorded for dynamic imaging to show movement of an organ or to follow movement of a radiopharmaceutical through the body.
- PET scanning images the γ-ray annihilation photons produced by positron-emitting radionuclides. It enables a number of radionuclides that can be incorporated into organic molecules to be used for imaging.
- Nuclear medicine patients contain radionuclides, so the radiation risk continues after they leave the hospital and may affect members of their family.
- A baby could receive a radiation dose from taking breast milk when its mother has a nuclear medicine investigation.

Further reading

Murray IPC, Ell PJ, editors. *Nuclear medicine in clinical diagnosis and treatment* (2nd edn). Edinburgh, UK: Churchill Livingstone, 1998.

Sandler MP, Coleman ER, Patton JA, Wackers FJTh, Gottschalk A, editors. *Diagnostic nuclear medicine* (4th edn). Philadelphia, PA: Lippincott, Williams and Wilkins, 2003.

Chapter 6

Ultrasound

F Gleeson

<table>
<tr><td>

This is the first of two chapters looking at powerful diagnostic imaging techniques that do not use ionising radiation. This chapter explains how reflection of ultrasound from tissue boundaries can generate anatomical images, and how measurement of frequency changes (the Doppler effect) gives information on flow patterns.
Details of clinical uses of ultrasound, especially in the abdomen, are given.

</td><td>

6.1   **Introduction**
6.2   **Ultrasound**
6.3   **The underlying principles of medical ultrasound**
6.4   **Flow imaging using Doppler ultrasound**
6.5   **Is ultrasound completely safe?**
6.6   **How to use ultrasound clinically**
6.7   **Summary**

</td></tr>
</table>

6.1 Introduction

When a clinician requests an imaging investigation, their aim should be to obtain the information required for management of the patient with the lowest risk to that patient. Every technique using ionising radiation has an associated risk to health. Thus, one aspect of achieving this aim is to consider whether a technique is available that will provide the information without using ionising radiation. Sometimes techniques using non-ionising radiations may be more informative. In other clinical circumstances the non-ionising technique may not give as much information but may still be carried out first because the associated risk is lower. The ionising radiation-based tests are then reserved for patients in whom the initial investigation fails to provide the information required. This represents an aggressive approach to radiation protection and is dependent upon the level of risk from the ionising radiation techniques and the availability of the alternatives. For this reason, replacement of ionising radiation techniques with alternatives, which may not give as much information, tends to concentrate more on investigations that involve a large radiation dose, such as angiography or CT. In clinical practice, ultrasound and magnetic resonance imaging offer the main alternatives to ionising radiation-based tests, and the next two chapters aim to provide background information on these.

6.2 Ultrasound

Ultrasound consists of mechanical vibrations above the frequency that the human ear can detect. Diagnostic ultrasound and its use in medicine developed from SONAR technology used by the Navy in the second world war to detect submarines and by fishing vessels in tracking shoals, and also from industrial techniques to detect flaws within metal. Although developed in the 1940s, medical diagnostic ultrasound did not gain widespread acceptance and use until the 1970s.

<table>
<tr><td colspan="2" align="center">

Insight: Frequencies of sound and ultrasound

</td></tr>
<tr><td>*Human voice*</td><td>*80–1100 Hz*</td></tr>
<tr><td>*Sound audible to the human ear*</td><td>*20 Hz–20 kHz*</td></tr>
<tr><td>*Ultrasound*</td><td>*>20 kHz*</td></tr>
<tr><td>*Bat echo location system*</td><td>*1–120 kHz*</td></tr>
<tr><td>*Medical therapeutic ultrasound*</td><td>*1–3 MHz*</td></tr>
<tr><td>*Medical diagnostic ultrasound*</td><td>*2–20 MHz*</td></tr>
</table>

1 hertz (Hz) = 1 cycle per second; 1 kHz and 1 MHz are one thousand and one million hertz, respectively.

6.3 The underlying principles of medical ultrasound

6.3.1 The pulse–echo technique

The technique involves sending pulses of ultrasound into the body and detecting the *echoes* reflected back from the tissues. Echoes are produced from boundaries between tissues with different mechanical properties. The amount of ultrasound reflected from an interface between two tissues depends on the difference in a quantity called the *acoustic impedance* (*Z*), which is determined by the elasticity and density of the tissue. The acoustic impedances of most soft tissues are fairly similar (see box), so the proportion of a sound pulse that is reflected at each interface is relatively small and most of the ultrasound energy is transmitted further into the body.

Insight: Acoustic impedances of tissues (T) relative to water (W) (Z_T/Z_W)	
Air	*0.0002*
Fat	*0.88*
Water	*1.00*
Muscle	*1.11*
Liver	*1.12*
Bone	*3.8*

6.3.2 Formation of the image

The depth of any structure giving rise to an echo can be determined from the time taken for the sound pulse to reach it and the time for the echo to return to the surface, because the velocity of sound is similar in all soft tissues. After the echoes from one ultrasound pulse have been detected, another pulse is generated and the echoes from each pulse are displayed as the brightness on a screen. If each successive ultrasound pulse is transmitted in a slightly different direction, it is possible to build up a two-dimensional image of a slice within the body. This is the type of ultrasound image that you may be familiar with, known as a B-mode scan or grey-scale image (Figures 6.1–6.3). Further images are produced by repeating the whole process, so images of tissues and structures within the body are generated in real-time showing their natural movement. Ultrasound can also provide information on blood flow from the Doppler effect (see §6.4).

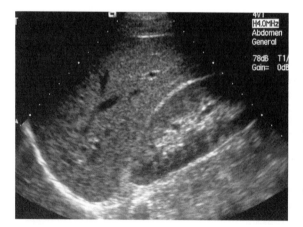

Figure 6.1 Sagittal ultrasound image of the liver and right kidney. There are strong echoes from the abdominal wall behind the liver, from boundaries between the liver and kidney, and from the calyces. Bile ducts and blood vessels in the liver show as echo-free spaces, with stronger echoes from blood vessel walls.

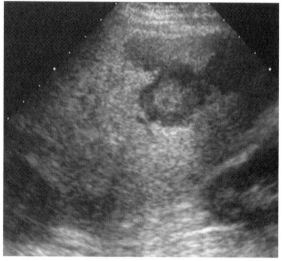

Figure 6.2 B-mode images of a liver with metastases. The structure of the metastatic tissue is different from normal tissue and this shows up in the different pattern of echoes.

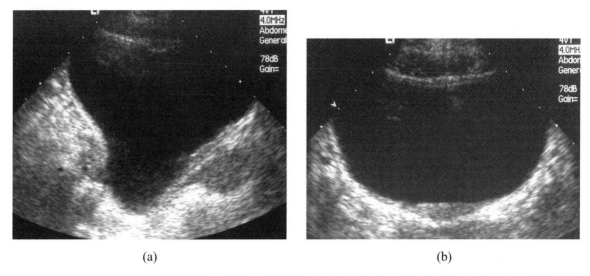

(a)   (b)

Figure 6.3 Ultrasound B-mode scans showing images of the bladder in (a) sagittal and (b) axial planes. Fluid-filled organs contain few echoes and ultrasound is reflected strongly from the rear wall.

6.3.3 Ultrasound scanner components and facilities

Some of the key elements and components of medical ultrasound scanners are described here.

The ultrasound transducer

Ultrasound pulses are generated and echoes are detected by a single device called a transducer, which converts one form of energy into another. Ultrasound transducers are made from piezoelectric crystals, which have the property that an applied electric voltage changes the thickness of the crystal. If an alternating voltage is applied, the crystal vibrates and generates a sound wave. Conversely, if a sound wave causes the crystal to vibrate, this generates an alternating electric voltage. Thus medical ultrasound transducers convert electrical energy into mechanical energy to produce ultrasound waves, and then convert the received echoes back into electrical signals that are used to produce an image.

Ultrasound techniques and display methods

- **A-mode** (A for amplitude): display in one dimension, which shows the depth of the echo-producing interface, with the height of the signal indicating the strength of the echo.
- **B-mode** (B for brightness): two-dimensional images of slices in which echoes of different magnitudes are displayed as different shades of grey. The directions or positions of successive ultrasound pulses are changed to build up an image.
- **M-mode** (M for movement): if the ultrasound beam is pointing in one direction, then movement of structures such as the heart valves can be displayed as a trace of depth against time.

Transducer arrays

The series of ultrasound pulses required for an image can be produced by a probe with an array of transducer elements. These transducer probes can be moved over the patient's skin and allow the operator to see real-time images of the part of the body being examined.

Attenuation and time gain compensation (TGC)

Ultrasound is attenuated as it passes through tissue owing to absorption and scattering. Since the intensities of the ultrasound pulses are quite rapidly reduced as they pass deeper into tissue, echoes returning from greater depths must be amplified to compensate for the attenuation.

Ultrasound frequency

Higher frequency ultrasound gives better image resolution than lower frequency, but it is more heavily absorbed. For this reason, higher frequency transducers (>10 MHz) can be used to image objects near to the skin surface, such as the thyroid, testes or eye, while lower frequencies (3–5 MHz) are used for tissues deeper within the body.

Insight: Ultrasound echoes and what they can show

Specular reflection*: Specular echoes are reflections from tissue boundaries, such as walls or capsules of organs or vessel walls. These give strong echoes predominantly towards one direction and appear as bright signals.*

Tissue echo patterns*: Diffuse echoes are scattered from small structures within a tissue. Each tissue contains a framework of collagen fibres that forms a structural skeleton. These fibres have different elastic properties from the parenchyma and produce multiple echoes of low intensity. Each tissue has a different collagen framework that gives an echo pattern characteristic of that organ, for instance making liver appear brighter than kidney (Figure 6.1). A tumour or other abnormal tissue growth will have a different structural framework, often with less connective tissue, so the echo pattern will be different from that of normal tissue, allowing ultrasound to detect different pathologies (Figure 6.2).*

Cystic structures and echo enhancement*: Fluid transmits sound with little scatter and less attenuation than tissue. As a result, fluid-filled viscera usually contain few echoes and the echoes from the rear wall appear brighter. This is because the echo signal has been amplified by time gain compensation (TGC) to compensate for the greater attenuation that would have occurred in tissue (Figure 6.3).*

Shadowing behind stones*: Because rigid objects such as bone or stones have a very different acoustic impedance from tissues, almost all the ultrasound will be reflected from the surface and little will penetrate. The* **shadowing** *produced can itself be useful in detection of gallstones.*

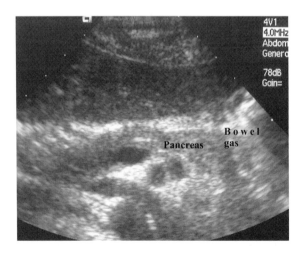

Figure 6.4 Ultrasound scan showing transverse image of the pancreas with bowel gas preventing a view of the tail of the pancreas.

6.4 Flow imaging using Doppler ultrasound

Doppler techniques

- **Continuous wave (CW) Doppler**: Velocity can be portrayed as a function of time for showing blood flow patterns in the arteries by a simple CW Doppler device with two transducers, one for transmitting and one for receiving.
- **Pulsed Doppler**: The spatial distribution of blood flow can be obtained from Doppler analysis of ultrasound pulses. Different velocities are portrayed in a range of colours in a two-dimensional image. By convention, red represents flow towards and blue away from the transducer. Different intensities of colour represent velocity and turbulence.
- **Duplex scanning**: B-mode images with superimposed Doppler information in colour.

The Doppler principle is used to portray more rapid movements, in particular blood flow. The Doppler principle relates to the shift in frequency of a sound wave as the source of the sound (or the echo) moves relative to the observer. It is responsible for the drop in pitch of a siren as an ambulance drives past. There is also a frequency shift if sound is reflected back off a moving boundary. The change in frequency is related to the velocity of movement and so enables the velocity of flow to be measured. The flow may be represented as:

- a trace showing change in flow velocity with time;
- sounds emitted at frequencies equal to the difference between the transmitted and returning signals, which lie in the range audible to the human ear;
- the spatial distribution of flow portrayed by superimposing flow information in colour on a grey-scale B-mode image.

Ultrasound contrast media and enhancement

Use of contrast media enables flow in smaller vessels and patterns of vascular enhancement to be seen. Gas bubbles are used as contrast agents as they have very different acoustic impedances from soft tissue, and these bubbles may be stabilised by a shell of albumin or lipid. The ultrasound contrast medium is injected into a vein and as it passes through the tissues the microbubbles are broken up by the ultrasound waves. The large number of small bubbles increases scatter and produces more echoes and this enables areas that are well perfused to be identified. The microbubbles enable abnormalities within the liver to be characterised, allowing, for instance, differentiation of a haemangioma from a metastasis.

6.5 Is ultrasound completely safe?

One of the great strengths of ultrasound is its safety. This is apparent from its use throughout medicine and the confirmation by many studies of its safety in examination of the fetus. Follow-up studies of the growth and development of children subjected to ultrasound *in utero* have not shown evidence of any harm, even in organs that may be vulnerable, such as the eye.

Particle vibration induced by ultrasound leads to energy dissipation by heat. In fact this is the desired effect when ultrasound is used at the higher power levels in physiotherapy treatment. Very high intensity ultrasound is able to damage tissue, and this is used deliberately in lithotripsy to break up kidney stones and in hyperthermia to heat tissues and ablate tumours such as hepatic metastases. The very high powers used can vaporise water in tissues, producing minute gas bubbles that can vibrate violently or collapse, contributing to tissue damage. These bubble-related phenomena are termed cavitation. However, although these effects are known to occur at high intensity, current opinion remains that the ultrasound intensity levels used in medical diagnosis are safe.

> **Insight: General guidelines to maintain ultrasound safety**
>
> ◊ *Default output settings should be chosen to give low output power and high receiver gain.*
> ◊ *The acoustic output settings should be at the minimum levels consistent with good diagnostic accuracy.*
> ◊ *The transducer should be in contact with the skin for the minimum time, that is only when the image is being studied or recorded for diagnostic purposes.*

6.6 How to use ultrasound clinically

As explained above, ultrasound produces images related to the structure and mechanical properties of tissues. Thus, it is complementary to the ionising radiation techniques described in earlier chapters. It is able to visualise changes in organ shape, but not function. Ultrasound has had an enormous impact on medicine. Ultrasound is now ubiquitous in medicine throughout the world, and is one of the cheapest and most efficient means of imaging. Scanners have improved immeasurably over the years and this, along with their low cost, portability and new techniques such as the use of microbubble contrast agents, is responsible for the continued expansion of the use of ultrasound.

Ultrasound is able to show movement and flow, and this has established echocardiography as a primary technique in cardiac investigation. It is able to image the fetus safely and so has an important role in assessment of pregnancy and fetal development. It is also a valuable technique for investigating a wide range of abdominal organs. A range of applications practised in most departments today is given here. It is likely that, in the near future, an ultrasound scan will become part of a routine clinical examination. Indeed this is already the case in many areas of medicine. It is clearly not possible to review in any depth the clinical role of ultrasound here and for more information the reader is directed to textbooks listed under "Further reading".

Neurosciences
Ultrasound has a place in paediatric neurology to assess ventricles and other intracranial aspects until the fontanelles close. It is often used in eye disease, *e.g.* assessment of the retina.

Musculoskeletal disease
Ultrasound is used for the assessment of joints, effusions, muscles and tendons for atrophy/tears and tumours. It can also be used to look at periosteal reaction from non-radiologically apparent fractures.

Neck disease
Lumps in the thyroid and salivary glands are well delineated by ultrasound.

Chest disease
Ultrasound has a role in the assessment of pleural fluid and chest wall tumour invasion.

Abdominal and gastroenterological disease

The large abdominal organs are generally assessable by ultrasound, especially the liver, gall bladder, pancreas, kidneys, bladder and spleen. Fluid collections and abscesses may be amenable to ultrasound detection.

Pelvic disease/assessment

Obstetric assessment is the most common use of ultrasound. It is the prime medium for gynaecological disease, and may include both transbladder and transvaginal approaches. The prostate is also approached by the transrectal route.

Superficial organ assessment

Ultrasound is well suited to assessment of the breast and the scrotum, and it is often used as part of screening.

Interventional radiology

Despite the name, ultrasound is often used to guide a radiologist during interventional procedures.

Vascular disease

The aorta is easily assessed for aneurysm development and progress. The deep veins of the limbs are generally amenable to assessment for thrombosis.

Other clinical applications of ultrasound are shown in Table 4.1.

6.7 Summary

- One of the most effective radiation protection moves in clinical imaging is to replace an ionising radiation-based technique with one that uses non-ionising radiation.
- Ultrasound imaging detects echoes from ultrasound pulses to locate structures within tissue.
- Ultrasound images the elastic and density properties of tissues.
- Ultrasound is impeded by gas and bone and performs better in thin patients.
- Doppler ultrasound provides information on blood flow.
- Current evidence indicates that ultrasound is the safest imaging technique.

Further reading

Armstrong P, Wastie ML, editors. *Diagnostic imaging* (4th edn). Oxford, London, Edinburgh, UK: Blackwell Science, 1998.

Kurtz AB, Middleton WD, editors. *Ultrasound: the requisites*. St Louis, MO: Hanley & Belfus, 1996.

Chapter 7
Magnetic resonance imaging

S Golding

This chapter looks at the second powerful diagnostic imaging technique that does not involve ionising radiation, namely magnetic resonance imaging (MRI).

Applications of MRI are increasing and diversifying so rapidly that a comprehensive treatment is well beyond the scope of this book. This chapter explains the type of information available in an MR image and provides an overview of current clinical uses.

7.1 Introduction

The nuclear magnetic resonance (MR) effect — in essence an electromagnetic phenomenon that can be used to characterise chemicals by an induced electromagnetic effect — was first discovered in the 1930s by Bloch and Purcell working at the Universities of Harvard and Stanford, respectively. In 1973 Paul Lauterbur showed that the signal could be coded to display chemical information as a two-dimensional image, and the Universities of Nottingham and Aberdeen played a major role in the practical development of the technique. Finally, the addition of modern computer array processing produced practical clinical imaging by magnetic resonance imaging (MRI).

MRI is now a powerful clinical tool. It provides high quality cross-sectional images of tissues within the body and is therefore an obvious alternative to CT. Like other imaging techniques, its major use is in structural imaging, but it has the advantage that images are based on chemical information. MRI therefore almost always offers better discrimination between normal and abnormal tissues than CT. In many situations an MRI scan would be requested in preference to a radiological investigation. For example, lumbar spine radiographs can be replaced by MRI for investigation of the majority of patients with non-traumatic problems. As well as using non-ionising radiation, MRI is more sensitive to pathology involving discs, ligaments, bone marrow and spinal roots, and thus is the technique of choice. MR spectroscopy can be used to evaluate patterns of chemical activity in tissues, and functional MRI uses advanced techniques to map metabolic changes in tissues during function or to observe the effect of pharmacological agents. This account is concerned solely with clinical imaging by MRI.

7.2 The basics of MRI

MRI is the most complex imaging technology currently available and a complete account is beyond the scope of this book. The key elements of an MRI device are a high power magnet and coils to generate and receive radiofrequency signals.

Static magnetic field

The technique is based on the fact that nuclei that contain unpaired protons or neutrons behave like magnets. Since the hydrogen nucleus contains a single, unpaired proton and is the most commonly occurring element in biological tissues, hydrogen nuclei can be used to generate a strong signal. When a large static magnetic field is applied, the nuclear magnets either align with the field (parallel) or against the field (anti-parallel). There is a small excess of magnets parallel to the field, enough to give a measurable resultant magnetisation. The main element of an MRI scanner gantry is a large magnet, usually superconducting in nature.

Radiofrequency signal

When the proton magnets have been aligned by the static field, the direction of their resultant magnetisation can be rotated by application of an external radiofrequency signal. This signal must be at a resonant frequency that is characteristic of the strength of the static field. This requires an additional set of magnet coils, controlled by a computer to allow the rapid switching needed to generate the radiofrequency signal.

MR signal

When the resultant magnetisation is no longer aligned with the static field, it rotates (precesses) around the static field. This rotation generates a radio signal that can be detected by a coil acting as an aerial placed around the patient. The strength of this signal is proportional to the number of hydrogen atoms in the sample, so one of the quantities that influences the MR signal is *proton density*. This signal is maximum initially and then decays, with the pattern of decay, or *relaxation*, being a function of the chemical charges surrounding the protons, *i.e.* their biochemical environment. This is how MRI conveys chemical information about the tissues.

The important characteristics of MRI

- It is ionising radiation free.
- It is multiplanar.
- It usually provides the best tissue discrimination of any imaging technique.

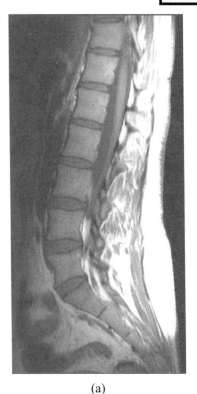

(a)

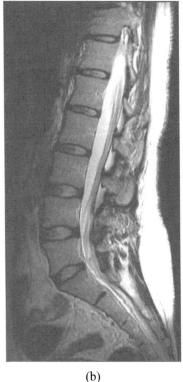

(b)

Figure 7.1 Magnetic resonance images recorded at the same position through the lumbar spine in the mid-sagittal plane showing the contrast between (a) a spin echo T_1 weighted image and (b) a T_2 weighted image at the same position. Note the difference in tone of the spinal cord between the two images.

Insight: The significance of relaxation time, field gradient and scan sequences

T_1 and T_2: *The time constants of the relaxation processes with which signals decay (T_1 and T_2) represent specific characteristics of the tissue. T_1 relaxation refers to the return of the protons to their equilibrium positions; T_2 relaxation refers to dephasing of the resonating protons after withdrawal of the radiofrequency pulse. MR images contain signals reflecting both forms of relaxation, but the images can be weighted to either one or the other by adjusting the amplitude, timing and phase of the radiofrequency stimulation pulse.*

Field gradients and position: *Three-dimensional array processing in MRI is achieved by superimposing a phase and frequency shift on the MR signal by applying gradients to the main magnetic field. This means that the magnetic field varies with position in the body. When the shifts are decoded, they allow the signal from individual points in the patient to be localised in space and make image construction possible. The gantry therefore contains a further set of coils to create field gradients. The image data are set out in a matrix of voxels in exactly the same way as information is displayed in CT (Chapter 4), but in MRI the brightness of the voxel as displayed in the image reflects the amplitude of signal coming from that point.*

Scan sequences: *There is a wide range of different types of "scan sequences" available in MRI, involving the application of radiofrequency signal pulses in different time sequences that are designed to bring out different forms of information from the tissue. In practice the reader is most likely to encounter the spin echo sequence, with gradient echo imaging the second most common. Most examinations consist of some T_1 weighted images and some T_2 weighted images (Figure 7.1). T_1 weighted images usually offer the best definition of anatomy, whereas T_2 weighted images in general bring out differences in cellular water. T_2 weighted images are valuable for showing differences between normal and abnormal tissues as there are frequently differences in cellular water in these states (Figure 7.2).*

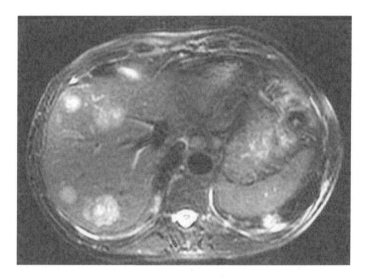

Figure 7.2 Axial T_2 weighted spin echo image of the liver, showing several well defined foci of high signal intensity within the right lobe of the liver, consistent with metastases. The image has been obtained with a fat suppression technique, which reduces the signal from fat surrounding the organs.

An electrically stimulated phenomenon

Because the scanning operations in MRI are controlled electrically rather than requiring mechanical movement such as rotation of the X-ray tube as in CT, it is relatively easy to adjust sequence parameters and direction. This allows images to be obtained in different planes without the need to move or manipulate the patient. In practice this is one of the most valuable imaging characteristics of MRI (Figure 7.3).

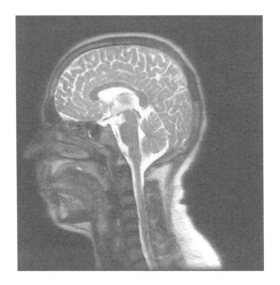

Figure 7.3 T_2 weighted spin echo images showing the multiplanar capacity of MRI in displaying the face. (a) Image in the mid-sagittal plane. (b) Coronal image through the maxillary antra, showing a large inhomogeneous tumour expanding the antrum on the right. The effect on the orbit above can be clearly appreciated. (c) Axial image through the lesion showing the tumour expanding into the subcutaneous tissues of the right cheek.

(a)

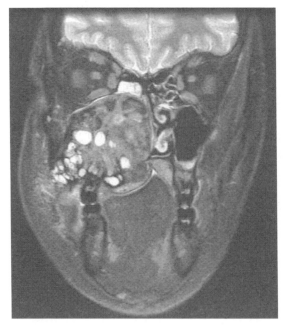

(b)

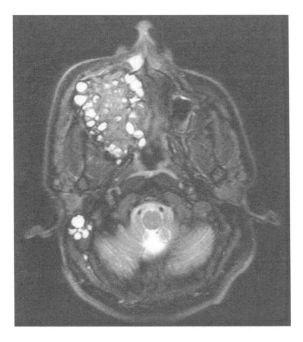

(c)

7.3 MRI contrast media and enhancement

As in CT and ultrasound, the information from MR images can be enhanced by administration of an external agent. In CT, enhancement depends on the presence of contrast medium in the tissues and its effect on X-ray absorption, whereas in MRI contrast media affect the magnetic environment of the protons from which signal is being generated and alter their relaxation characteristics. They are therefore effective in much smaller amounts than are required to produce radiographic enhancement.

The most common agents are paramagnetic in nature, meaning that they have a positive effect on the local magnetic field. The commonest agent is gadolinium, administered in the form of a chelate, which is mostly excreted by the kidney within a few hours. At diagnostic doses, gadolinium produces enhancement of T_1 weighting (Figure 7.4), although T_2 effects can also be influenced at larger doses. Gadolinium-based contrast media have a good safety record and adverse reactions are rare.

Other agents that may be used include compounds containing ferrous oxide, which have a powerful effect on images. MR contrast media represent a rapidly developing field, with new agents appearing regularly.

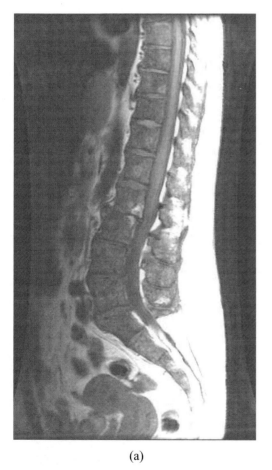
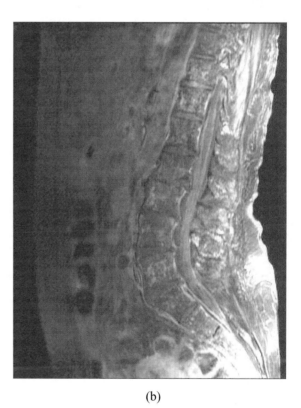

(a)   (b)

Figure 7.4 The use of enhancement in MRI. (a) Mid-sagittal T_1 weighted spin echo image of the lumbar spine in a patient with carcinoma of the breast, metastatic to the vertebral marrow; note the difference in appearance of the marrow from Figure 7.1. The image shows a relatively normal spinal cord and conus, although there is the impression of increased density of tissues in the cauda equina (compare with Figure 7.1). (b) An enhanced image shows extensive enhancement in the roots of the cauda equina, characteristic of metastatic infiltration of the nerve roots. The patient had severe sciatica and was thought clinically to have spinal cord compression due to vertebral metastases. Note the variable enhancement of the disease within the vertebral bodies.

As in CT, dynamic examination to assess tissue perfusion is possible, but the examination of perfusion by MRI is much more sensitive than with CT. To date this technique has been most commonly used in characterising breast lesions. This aspect of MRI is also used in functional MRI to evaluate blood flow changes representing metabolic activity. More recently, enhancement has been combined with three-dimensional display techniques to develop vascular imaging by MRI, a great advantage in radiation protection as conventional angiography and CT angiography both involve significant absorbed doses.

7.4 MRI — a risk-free procedure?

Within the context of this book, the key point about MRI is that it does not use ionising radiation. However, there are a number of risks associated with the technique that may limit its use. Some of these are important safety restrictions that require careful control of the magnetic environment.

The missile effect
Ferromagnetic items are powerfully attracted to magnets of the field strength used for MRI. Departments therefore have to exercise careful control over entry to the magnetic environment to ensure that accidents do not occur to patients or staff. If a missile enters the magnet, removal may be very difficult and may mean putting the system out of action.

Effect on metal implants
Any ferromagnetic items in the body represent a serious risk in MRI. Large pieces of metal such as shrapnel residue undergo severe heating due to electromagnetic induction and this may result in serious burns. Moreover, if these items are not firmly fixed in the tissue they may experience a torque, which causes significant movement and damage to tissue. Even the risk from tiny pieces of metal can be significant, depending on their location. For example, patients working with metal who have had previous penetrating injuries to the eye are precluded from examination owing to serious risk of ocular damage. Elsewhere, tiny ferromagnetic objects anchored in scar tissue may not represent serious risk, but ferromagnetic material causes considerable disturbance of the image by susceptibility artefact (see box on page 73).

Large non-ferromagnetic materials such as joint replacements or prostheses also undergo heating, although to a lesser extent than ferromagnetic material, and the energy gain is usually dissipated by normal blood flow. However, even small objects made from these materials experience a torque in response to the radiofrequency pulse. The significance of this depends on their situation. Small items such as arterial clips become anchored by fibrosis 6–8 weeks after insertion and examination is usually safe after this time. However, in the brain fibrosis does not occur and intracerebral clips may preclude examination, depending on the type. Similarly, metallic implants to the middle ear may be at risk of serious movement, so patients with these are precluded from examination.

A wide range of implants are used in modern medicine, some of which are safe for MR examination and others that are not. A register of implants tested for MRI has been produced by national testing agencies and this register needs to be consulted before patients are cleared for examination. Imaging departments can advise on the risk status of patients before referrals are made.

Radiofrequency power and interaction with tissues
In the same way that metals are heated by electromagnetic induction, body tissues experience a similar but weaker effect. Sometimes patients undergoing intensive examination feel heating in dense areas of tissue such as around the hip. The risks from overheating are greatest in tissues where the blood supply is poor, such as in the eyes, or in tissues susceptible to thermal damage, such as the testes. There is currently no evidence that this effect or the general effects of magnetism at the levels used in diagnostic imaging have any long-lasting effect on tissues. However, empirical limits are in operation for power deposition in patients. When beginning an examination, the patient's weight is entered in the identification data and the scanner automatically prevents the operator from conducting a sequence that would exceed recognised safety limits.

Insight: Artefacts and impediments

Like other imaging techniques, MRI is subject to a range of specific artefacts. Some of these arise from the nature of the imaging sequence and are beyond the scope of this book; those of clinical importance are described here. Some of the effects of magnetism are also responsible for safety restrictions on MRI, and are described below.

Magnetic susceptibility: The basis of MRI is a powerful magnetic field and the presence of metal in the scanning volume disturbs the lines of field strength. This results in altered excitation at the point of interference, and also affects spatial decoding, so that the image at this point may be lost. This applies around prostheses and is a highly sensitive effect — even the traces left by previous orthopaedic drilling may degrade images. Patients therefore need to be screened for metal objects before examination and all items removed where possible. Ferromagnetic items represent significant risks and are dealt with as safety issues on page 72.

Movement: The data for reconstructing the MR images are collected from a volume during the scanning period, which may last several minutes, and any movement may cast an effect over all the images in the sequence. Patient immobilisation and restraint are important. There are a number of technical methods for removing artefact due to predictable patterns of movement such as blood flow and respiration.

Flow-related artefact: Flow-related artefact, for example from large blood vessels, can produce troublesome artefacts in MRI but this can usually be alleviated by technical programmes designed to counter it. Conversely, the effect can be used to produce images of flow in MR angiography.

Apart from the above considerations and questions of safety for the patient (see §7.4), the main impediment to examination by MRI is claustrophobia. Patients with this problem may not be able to tolerate lying in the gantry tunnel. Sometimes these patients respond to simple manoeuvres such as reassurance, company in the examination room or a blindfold. Occasionally sedation or even general anaesthesia is required to achieve a successful examination. Anaesthetic equipment has to be specially designed to operate in the magnetic environment, and patients who require continuous monitoring equipment or support systems may not be suitable for examination. Occasionally patients are too large to enter the gantry, or exceed table loading restrictions.

Electronic interference

The static magnetic field or radiofrequency pulse may interfere with patient support devices that rely on electromagnetic induction. The most important example is the in-dwelling cardiac pacemaker, some models of which may be deactivated by MRI pulses. Hearing aids associated with electronic implants are also affected. These patients have to be excluded from the magnetic environment by the department's safety controls on entry.

Pregnancy

Although there is no proven pathological effect of magnetism on tissues, MRI follows the recognised principle that no external agent should be applied to the patient during the first trimester of pregnancy, unless there is an overriding clinical need for this. It is also conventional to avoid MRI throughout the remainder of pregnancy whenever possible, although in the late stages of pregnancy the technique has some valuable applications in problems affecting the uterus and fetus.

Control and prevention are the secrets to running a safe MRI service. Departments exercise a safety screen of anyone undergoing examination, as well as anyone else who may enter the area of the magnet. The questions usually asked in this are given in the box.

Insight: Questions asked in screening for MRI safety

◊ *Do you have a pacemaker or artificial heart valve?*
◊ *Have you ever had an operation on your head? If so what have you had?*
◊ *Do you have a programmable hydrocephalus shunt?*
◊ *Do you have any metal implants (joint replacement etc.)?*
◊ *Do you have an artificial limb?*
◊ *Do you wear a calliper or surgical corset?*
◊ *Do you have any shrapnel from a war injury?*
◊ *Have you ever sustained any injuries involving metal to the eyes or any other part of the body?*
◊ *Are you wearing:*
    dentures with metal?
    a metal plate?
    a hearing aid?
    body piercing/jewellery?
◊ *Have you ever had a fit or blackout, or suffered from epilepsy or diabetes?*

To be answered by women of childbearing age.
◊ *Do you have an intrauterine contraceptive device (i.e. coil)?*
◊ *Could you be pregnant?*

7.5 How to use MRI clinically

Although MRI is free of the risks associated with ionising radiation, it is still important that it is used only when justified by clinical benefit. Unwarranted investigation remains an intrusion on the patient, even when free of risk, and each investigative event may increase the patient's anxiety about their health. Moreover, inappropriate use of scarce resources must be considered.

The introduction of MRI has had a major impact on practice in CT, for which it has replaced a number of applications, often with increased diagnostic capability. Only in evaluation of fine detail of bone and acute haemorrhage and in speed of operation does CT now exceed the diagnostic capability of MRI. The relationship between the two techniques is summarised in Table 4.1. However, although MRI has undergone considerable technological development, it remains less readily available than CT, and examinations are generally slower because of the number of scan sequences recorded. For this reason, complete replacement of CT with MRI is unlikely because of the implications of limited resources. None the less, MRI has made a powerful impact on investigative medicine, most especially in neurological, musculoskeletal and oncological investigation.

The summary included here gives a general guide to the clinical value of MRI; for more detail the reader is referred to "Further reading".

Neurosciences
MRI has become the leading technique in the demonstration and assessment of all structural disease of the brain, orbit, cranial nerves and spinal cord. CT is now largely limited to the evaluation of head injury and cerebral haemorrhage, as the latter is frequently difficult to characterise on MRI.

Musculoskeletal disease
MRI has become the technique of choice for the investigation of structural disease of the vertebral column and all major joints. It is also the investigation of choice for diagnosing and staging musculoskeletal neoplasms. CT remains indispensable for the investigation of major trauma. Although simple fractures can be readily demonstrated by MRI, the ease of obtaining radiographs and the low radiation dose associated with these make it unlikely that conventional radiography will be replaced in assessing common fractures of the limbs.

Oncology

MRI has made a major impact in the practice of oncology. Whilst it is not frequently the main form of diagnosis for most solid tumours, it would be indispensable in the staging of all these neoplasms prior to treatment if it were more widely available. It is at least as reliable as CT and ultrasound in detecting metastases to lymph nodes and equally valuable in demonstrating distant metastases to the brain and liver. It is the sole technique that can supply structural assessment of metastases to bone marrow.

Gynaecology

Here ultrasound remains the major technique. However, MRI offers considerable advantage as a complementary technique, especially in staging gynaecological tumours and in the characterisation of some benign disease, notably ovarian masses and endometriosis. It is also complimentary to ultrasound in the assessment of the pregnant uterus and fetus.

Abdominal and gastroenterological disease

MRI has proved a valuable adjunct in the characterisation of lesions in the liver and the detection of small pancreatic masses. Cholangiography by MRI has been introduced and is rapidly overtaking endoscopic cholangiography.

Face and neck

The multiplanar capacity of MRI has been particularly important in investigation of the face and neck. It is the technique of choice for detecting and staging cervicofacial neoplasms and in the investigation of orbital masses and sensorineural hearing loss. As in other areas, CT remains important in trauma and in assessment of the sinuses before endoscopy, but otherwise MRI is applicable to most cervicofacial disease.

Vascular disease

MRI is making a contribution to the investigation of vascular disease in several ways. First, lesions of major vessels are conveniently examined by conventional sectional MRI, which has the advantage over CT of not requiring contrast enhancement in order to evaluate aneurysms, dissection or thrombosis. Second, imaging sequences that highlight flow have been used to create three-dimensional demonstration of vessels, producing an equivalent to conventional angiography of major arteries, including those in the periphery. Finally, bolus injection of contrast medium has been shown to give very accurate demonstration of blood vessels well into the peripheral branches. Conventional angiography techniques are often only used for therapeutic purposes such as stent insertion and angioplasty.

Possibly the most interesting aspect of MRI is its potential for further development. The technique has expanded dramatically over the last decade and this process is clearly not yet complete. It seems certain that MRI will play an increasing role among the techniques available for clinical investigation for the foreseeable future.

7.6 Conclusions

From the point of view of radiation protection, it would be reasonable to ask whether, wherever possible, we should carry out non-ionising radiation techniques on patients using ultrasound or MRI, reserving the ionising radiation-based approaches for those clinical applications not solved by this approach. This would clearly be of greatest priority for those radiographic techniques that involve the largest radiation doses. However, this approach is not currently within reach, largely because the resource implications would be serious. Currently, many ultrasound services are heavily subscribed owing to the large number of applications, and MRI is of limited availability owing to the high cost of the equipment. However, it is clear that ultrasound and MRI have considerable potential in minimising radiation doses to patients. Table 4.1 shows how they can be considered in preference to one technique, namely CT. More general guidelines are available, such as those published by the Royal College of Radiologists, "Making the best use of a department of clinical radiology", but it is difficult to make hard and fast rules about substituting techniques because this approach is subject to variations in local resources and local expertise, and departments will have their own individual approaches. However, both techniques are still undergoing technological development. For these reasons, a progressive rise in the use of ionising radiation-free investigations in common practice is likely and the reader may well find that the "non-ionising radiation first" approach becomes viable in the course of their career.

7.7 Summary

- MRI is one of the main non-ionising radiation alternatives to ionising radiation imaging in clinical practice.
- MRI utilises the hydrogen nuclei within tissue.
- MRI gives information on the biochemical environment.
- Paramagnetic contrast agents are used to assess perfusion as well as for vascular imaging.
- Implanted metal objects and electrical devices within tissue give rise to hazard for MRI.
- MRI is currently limited by availability.
- Safety restrictions prevent examination in a small number of patients.

Further reading

Armstrong P, Wastie ML, editors. *Diagnostic imaging* (4th edn). Oxford, London, Edinburgh, UK: Blackwell Science, 1998.

Royal College of Radiologists. *Making the best use of a department of clinical radiology* (5th edn). London, UK: RCR, 2003.

Westbrook C. *MRI at a glance.* Oxford, UK: Blackwell Science, 2002.

Chapter 8
The effects of radiation on cells

B Dixon and PP Dendy

An understanding of biological damage by radiation must begin at the molecular level. This chapter summarises our knowledge on the ways in which ionising radiation can damage DNA and chromosomes, and kill cells. It provides an insight into radiation-induced transformations of cells and cancer induction, and the influence of cellular repair. Operational quantities for use in radiation protection are introduced.

8.1 Introduction

This chapter presents some basic ideas on the physical, chemical and biological interactions of ionising radiation with human cells. These apply to X-rays and γ-rays and also to particulate radiations such as electrons, neutrons and α-particles. The potential damage to tissue from these interactions is assessed in terms of radiation dose, which relates to the amount of radiation energy that is absorbed in the body.

Radiobiology has contributed substantially to our understanding of the potentially harmful effects of ionising radiation. This chapter outlines the mechanisms for understanding the exceptional sensitivity of mammalian cells to ionising radiation. Important aspects include effects on DNA, disturbances in cell biochemistry and division, information on the genetic transformation of cells, and the earliest stages of cancer induction. The various stages in the complex sequence of events that may be initiated by ionising radiation are summarised in Figure 8.1.

The evidence that irradiated cells have powerful repair mechanisms is presented. These mechanisms, together with tissue regeneration, have an important role in limiting the overall response of the body to high doses of radiation, for example in radiotherapy.

Finally, another important principle of radiobiology will show that not all forms of ionising radiation are equally harmful. Since, for radiation protection purposes, the risks for different types of radiation exposure must be compared (for example between diagnostic X-rays in radiology, γ-rays in nuclear medicine and natural background radiation), this chapter concludes by introducing a unit of radiation dose that allows for different types of exposure and variation in their potential to cause harm.

8.2 Ionisation

X-rays have wave-like properties, illustrated, for example, in X-ray diffraction. However, when considering their physical and subsequent biological effects in cells and tissue, it is easier to think of X-rays (or γ-rays) as a stream of small particles or "photons".

When photons "collide" with orbital electrons of an atom, the interaction may be so violent that the electron is ejected from the atom and, once free, often travels away with significant energy (see Figure 1.1), leaving behind

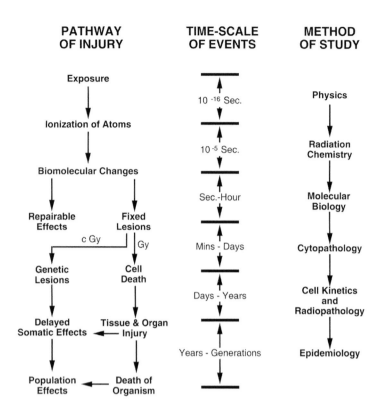

Figure 8.1 Pathways of injury, time-scale of events and methods of study following exposure of the body to ionising radiation.

a positively charged atom that is missing an electron. This formation of a positive–negative ion pair within the exposed cell is known as *ionisation*.

X-rays and γ-rays form part of the very large spectrum of electromagnetic radiation that includes, for example, visible, ultraviolet and infra-red. Only X-ray and γ-ray photons have enough energy to ionise atoms. In addition to X-rays and γ-rays, several charged and uncharged particles, for example β-particles (electrons), neutrons and α-particles (the nuclei of helium atoms), will also cause ionisation.

8.3 Absorbed dose

The ways in which X-ray photons may interact with the body were discussed in §1.3 and §3.2. They are summarised here for convenience.

The last three processes (see box) all result in *attenuation*, that is removal of photons from the initial incident direction of travel through the body. The total or partial loss of photon energy in the third and fourth processes results in tissue *absorption* of energy.

Only absorbed energy can cause biological damage. Therefore, the starting point for understanding such damage is to quantify

> **Ways in which X-ray photons may interact with the body**
>
> - Pass through unaffected.
> - Change direction but lose no energy (*elastic scattering*).
> - Be stopped completely and lose all energy (*photoelectric effect*) — total absorption.
> - Change direction and lose some energy (*inelastic scattering* or *Compton scattering*) — partial absorption.

the *absorbed dose*, a measure of energy deposited in joules per kilogram (J kg^{-1}). However, when measuring absorbed doses from ionising radiation a special unit is used, the *gray* (Gy), where 1 Gy = 1 J kg^{-1}.

For radiation protection purposes, a gray is often too large a unit of absorbed dose, so subunits — milligray, mGy (10^{-3} Gy), and microgray, μGy (10^{-6} Gy) — are frequently used. The relatively large doses used in radiotherapy are usually prescribed in gray or sometimes centigray, cGy (10^{-2} Gy).

8.4 The molecular basis of biological sensitivity

In terms of absorbed energy, ionising radiation is much more harmful than chemical or other physical agents. An acute dose of X- or γ-radiation that would be lethal to 50% of the population through bone marrow failure within 60 days ($LD_{50/60}$), if distributed uniformly throughout the body, would only result in a temperature rise of about one thousandth of a degree. This would be virtually undetectable and far less than the natural daily variations in body temperature.

The key point is that energy absorption associated with ion pairs is **not** distributed uniformly. Each ionisation results in a small cluster of ion pairs. However, each of these clusters represents only a very small amount of energy (~100 eV per cluster) and therefore even the small radiation exposure required in, for example, a dental X-ray, will create millions of ion pairs in the exposed tissues.

At the biomolecular level, the energy deposition is highly localised and non-uniform. Relatively large volumes of each cell, and the macromolecules in it, receive no energy at all. But where ionisation occurs, the energy deposited is very high compared with that usually associated with cellular biochemical events — for example, an ionising radiation event produces approximately 70 times more energy than that required to break a hydrogen bond in DNA.

Thus, even very small but detectable doses (μGy) of ionising radiation will produce a large number of random submolecular events in cells, any one of which may damage a sensitive macromolecule without raising the temperature of the cell outside its normal physiological range. This unique form of radiosensitivity only occurs with ionising radiations. Other forms of radiation may of course also cause biological damage, but the amount of energy involved is much greater and there is usually measurable, biologically significant thermal heating of the whole cell.

8.5 Initial effects in cells

Because energy absorption events rarely occur close to important cellular macromolecules, only about 1% of the events that produce ionisations are potentially harmful. The most abundant cellular molecule is water (~80% of the cell) and therefore radiation energy-absorbing events, although clustered, will mostly ionise H_2O molecules throughout the cell. This occurs within nanoseconds during exposure and for X-rays, γ-rays and β-particles this is the most important energy event.

Insight: What are the important cellular targets for radiation damage?

Since ionisation occurs randomly throughout an irradiated cell, there are many potential cellular targets that may be damaged by free radical attack. Intracellular membranes undergo transient changes that temporarily suppress the activity of, for example, lachrymal and salivary glands as well as other tissues that have secretory functions. Free radical attack on the external cell membrane may also temporarily reduce cell-to-cell adhesion, or increase cell wall permeability and motility. After high doses, these changes contribute within hours to a transient tissue oedema, inflammation, skin erythema and other effects.

However, there is significant evidence, e.g. from experiments with intracellular α- or β-particle irradiation and also from external microbeam irradiation of cells, that the most important sites of free radical interactions in the cell are mostly within the nucleus. Free radical damage to DNA forms a common "starting point" for clinically significant acute tissue injury after moderate and high dose (Gy) exposure, and genomic damage and increased risk of cancer development after low dose (mGy) exposure.

When radiolysis of water molecules occurs, transient free radicals OH˙ and H˙, together with hydrated electrons (e^-_{aq}), are formed. They are highly reactive and within milliseconds usually recombine to re-form water molecules. However, if these radicals are formed within a few nanometers of large biological macromolecules or cell membranes, they may interact with these cellular components and by this *indirect action* may initiate a chain of subcellular events that will produce temporary or permanent microscopic, detectable changes in cells.

Even after low doses, free radical effects may therefore lead to delayed but increased risks of cancer in the exposed individual or genetic changes in future generations. Following high doses, microscopic damage due to free radical attack is more severe and is more likely to kill cells and lead to clinical signs of temporary or permanent changes in normal tissue function. The OH˙ radical is the most damaging of the free radicals and is believed to initiate about two-thirds of all the effects of external exposure of the body to X- or γ-rays.

8.6 Attack on DNA

When free radicals are formed from water molecules immediately surrounding cellular DNA, even with their very short millisecond lifetimes they can diffuse, reach and chemically attack this most important biological macromolecule. It is this indirect attack on DNA that produces most of the known high or low dose effects of ionising radiation.

The relatively smaller negatively charged free electrons produced by the initial ionisation of water molecules can also cause damage by direct interaction with DNA; but heavier, more densely ionising charged particles, *e.g.* α-particles from internally absorbed radionuclides, are much more likely to cause direct damage through this mechanism.

Insight: Effects of radiation exposure on nuclear DNA

Base modification/deletion: *causing genetic defects and increased mutation rate in reproductive cells; or, if not repaired or eliminated, increased risk of malignant cell transformation in somatic cells.*

Bond breakage: *between complementary DNA strands of the double helix, facilitating the loss of a base and changes in molecular shape and structure.*

Cross linkage: *the additional covalent binding of two adjacent strands of DNA; this potentially inhibits semi-conservative replication of DNA.*

Single-strand breaks: *occur at random in either strand along the DNA double helix.*

Double-strand breaks: *may be formed either by a single event, e.g. when the track of a densely ionising particle passes through or close to the DNA helix, or, more likely with X- or γ-rays, by random coincidence of two single events occurring at the same time on complementary DNA strands. This process becomes more probable the higher the X-ray dose and dose rate.*

8.7 Cellular response and DNA repair

The initial response of a cell, even to low dose irradiation, is activation of early and late response genes, *e.g.* the tumour suppressor gene p53. These genes:

- regulate the control of gene expression and transcription;
- arrest the progress of cells through the cell cycle;
- promote DNA repair;
- induce differentiation;
- initiate apoptosis.

Modified and deleted bases, *i.e.* point mutations and single-strand breaks, are mostly repaired within a few hours following up-regulation of early and late response "housekeeping" genes and their products. They rejoin breaks using "cut and patch" enzymes, *e.g.* endonucleases and ligases, that semi-conservatively replicate and replace the damaged part of the single strand. These changes in irradiated DNA may not therefore contribute significantly to acute radiation effects. There is, however, about a one in a thousand chance of mutations occurring through misrepair of single-strand breaks.

"Checkpoint" genes also act to arrest cells in the cell cycle to facilitate repair and to prevent single-strand breaks becoming double-strand breaks during DNA synthesis. High dose radiation exposure produces about a 10% lengthening of the cell cycle per gray of radiation exposure. A similar but less well understood repair mechanism also exists for the more difficult rejoining of double-strand breaks. With these repairs the correct chromosomal sequence of bases and of the cell's genome may not be re-established, resulting in sister chromatid exchanges and the formation of hybrid chromosomes.

If double-strand breaks cannot be repaired, a cell may become permanently prevented from progressing to mitosis by checkpoint genes, or induced to differentiate or be removed by apoptosis. The clustering of double-strand breaks has been clearly linked to radiation lethality in cells. The enhanced clinical radiosensitivity of some patients, *e.g.* those with *Xeroderma pigmentosum* or *Ataxia telangiectasia*, may be linked to their severely reduced capacity for DNA repair. Even in apparently normal individuals, the accuracy of the DNA repair mechanisms may relate to an increased radiation susceptibility to oncogenic and genetic risks.

8.8 Chromosomal aberrations

Cells in the cell cycle, or cells entering the mitotic cycle in a tissue after high dose radiation exposure, may have higher or lower than normal DNA content. Failure to repair single-strand and, more importantly, double-strand breaks after irradiation results in the formation of imperfect chromosomes when preparing for mitosis. Individual chromosomes may show what appear to be chromosomal or chromatid breaks, abnormal staining regions and fragmentation. If radiation exposure has occurred before DNA synthesis then, as the cell reaches mitosis, both arms of the chromatid will show aberrations. If exposure occurred after DNA synthesis, only one chromatid will be abnormal.

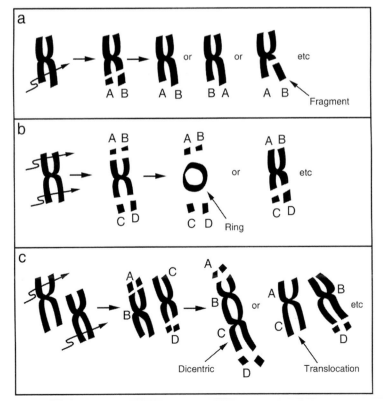

Figure 8.2 Formation of chromosomal aberrations in irradiated cells. (a) Possible consequences of a single-strand break. (b,c) Ring chromosomes and dicentrics caused by faulty rejoining of two breaks can be identified readily in chromosome spreads and examples are shown arising from (b) two breaks in the same chromosome and (c) breaks in two adjacent chromosomes.

Insight: Chromosomes as a biological radiation dosemeter

Chromosomal aberrations scored in mitotic cells prepared from a blood sample may, in exceptional circumstances, be used as a retrospective biological dosemeter in radiological protection. An example would be where an individual had been accidentally exposed and had not been wearing an appropriate dosemeter.

With X- and γ-rays there is a well established relationship between the number of aberrations and the radiation dose.

The system is only useful, however, when the suspected dose is relatively high, i.e. more than approximately 50 mSv (50 mGy for X-rays; see § 8.11).

Lethally irradiated cells typically show failure of chromosome condensation, dicentric chromosomes, ring chromosomes and acentric fragments (Figure 8.2). Dicentric and ring chromosomes are particularly damaging to cells since they may lead to failure of separation of chromatids and death of the cell when it attempts mitosis. Chromatid bridges may also form between daughter nuclei at mitosis leading to the formation of micronuclei with comparable loss of genome to daughter cells, which are no longer able to contribute to cell replacement in the irradiated tissue.

8.9 Transformation of cells and cancer induction

After low doses, a few mGy of X-rays, alteration of some genes increases the risk of malignant transformation of cells in irradiated tissues and organs in the exposed individual. These proto-oncogenes normally control cellular growth, proliferation and differentiation, for example through regulation of:

Insight: The link between radiation and development of cancer

Radiation can mutate, translocate or cause the overexpression of proto-oncogenes, e.g. up-regulation of the mic gene in myeloid leukaemia. More generally, the conversion of proto-oncogenes into oncogenes leads to inappropriate gene expression and malfunction of many cellular regulatory activities, often demonstrated by the transformed cells located in initially benign, but later malignant, areas of irradiated normal tissues. However, clinical cancer develops through a multistage process requiring not only initiation but also progression and promotional events. In this respect, the loss of tumour suppressor genes, e.g. p53 and Rb1, may be particularly important with irradiation. The ability to induce acentric chromosomal fragments can lead to loss of relatively large parts of the cell genome.

However, the exact role of radiation exposure in the multi-step carcinogenic process still remains to be fully established. Currently it seems that an increased risk resulting from radiation exposure:

◊   *is most likely owing to gross genome loss;*
◊   *needs at least two events, e.g. for leukaemogenesis;*
◊   *requires 50 or more cell cycles of the transformed oncogenic cells after their initial exposure;*
◊   *involves no particular genetic locus or chromosome.*

Initiation is a common occurrence but requires many other promotional events, possibly involving other risk factors, e.g. hormonal or viral exposure, before a cancer may develop, usually many years later.

- the production of cytokine molecules;
- cell membrane receptor sites;
- intracellular transduction of signals;
- gene transcription.

Cell transformation increases with initial exposure but then decreases with increasing dose as cells begin to sustain lethal radiation injury. Transformation occurs more readily with densely ionising α-particles than with X- or γ-rays (see §8.11). No specific cancer is associated with radiation exposure and these conclusions, based on experimental data, are consistent with the clinical epidemiology of increased radiation cancer risk (see §11.2).

8.10 Cell survival after irradiation

Induction of gross chromosomal aberrations and the formation of micronuclei following high dose therapeutic or accidental radiation exposure usually leads to unacceptable loss of genome and hence to clinically significant loss in the mitotic ability of, for example, clonogenic stem cells in normal tissues. If such cells are removed from a tissue immediately after radiation exposure, or they are first cultured and then irradiated, the fraction of clonogenic cells that retain this ability — the surviving fraction — can be assayed to obtain their survival curve. Such curves give a quantitative measure of radiosensitivity. Cells may also be assayed in this way to determine how their sensitivity or overall survival will be influenced by different dose patterns, dose rates and exposure to different types of radiation (Figure 8.3). (See box on page 84 for explanation.)

Why radiotherapy works

- The radiobiological properties of cancer cells are not different from normal cells.
- High dose radiation therapy is possible if the dose is localised.
- Cancer tissue usually contains many more actively proliferating cells.
- This usually makes the tumour more radiosensitive than the surrounding normal tissues necessarily included in the treatment volume.
- Normal tissue repair and regeneration functions may also give a therapeutic advantage.
- If the tumour is localised but is growing close to or in a critical tissue containing many rapidly dividing normal cells, *e.g.* in the small intestine, then surgery may be preferred to radiotherapy.
- If the tumour has seeded distant metastases or is diffuse, *e.g.* leukaemia, chemotherapy is likely to be the treatment of choice.

8.11 Radiation weighting factors

A smaller dose of radiation is required for neutrons than for X-rays to cause the same killing effect (Figure 8.3d). This is related to the difference in ionisation density of the two radiations relative to the twin strands of DNA (see Figure 8.4). Moreover, the survival response curve is more linear than for X-rays, indicating that the cells have reduced capacity to repair injury after neutron irradiation. These are very important factors both in radiotherapy and in radiation protection.

Different types of radiation are compared with X-rays by using the term *relative biological effectiveness* (RBE). RBE is defined as:

$$\frac{\text{dose of X-rays}}{\text{dose of other radiation}}$$

required to produce a defined biological or clinical effect.

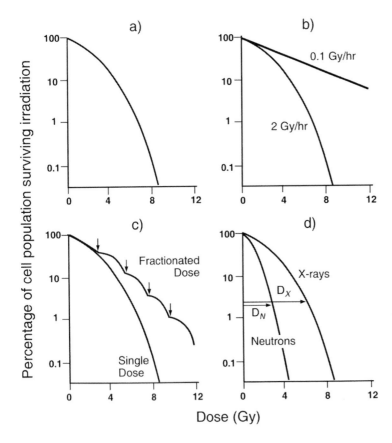

Figure 8.3 Examples of cell survival responses. (a) Single exposure to X-rays at high dose rate. (b) Exposure to X-rays at high and low dose rate. (c) Increased survival (recovery) when cells are exposed to five fractions of X-rays. (d) Survival curves drawn on the same axes comparing responses to X-rays and neutrons. Relative biological effectiveness (RBE) (shown at about 2% survival) = D_X/D_N.

Insight: Explanation of different cell survival curves

The non-linear "shoulder" on a simple survival curve (Figure 8.3a) shows that for X- or γ-rays, fewer cells are killed per gray at low doses that at higher doses. Fewer cells are also killed per gray if exposure is at low dose rate rather than at high dose rate (Figure 8.3b). Put simply, this is because at low doses and dose rates the natural DNA repair capacity of the cell is, to some extent, still effective. Recovery can occur, even during exposure, and this may repair less serious forms of DNA damage, e.g. single-strand breaks. With large acute doses (Figure 8.3a) and at higher dose rates (Figure 8.3b), the DNA repair capacity of the cells is overwhelmed and more cells are then sterilised per gray dose.

Similarly, even with high dose rate exposure, if the total dose is divided into two or more fractions (Figure 8.3c), each separated by more than a few hours (e.g. 24 h as used in conventional radiotherapy of cancer patients), the maximum possible repair of sublethal and even of some potentially lethal DNA damage, e.g. double-strand breaks, occurs between exposures. The net effect is an increase in the overall radiation tolerance, i.e. survival, of clonogenic cells. In radiotherapy this is a very significant clinical factor in protecting the normal tissues of patients and in minimising the acute effects of necessary but localised high dose ionising radiation exposure.

The survival of cells after exposure to different forms of radiation, for example X-rays or neutrons, is also clearly different (Figure 8.3d).

Table 8.1 Radiation weighting factors w_R according to the International Commission on Radiation Protection (1990)

Radiation type	w_R
X- and γ-rays	1
Electrons	1
Slow (thermal) neutrons	5
Fast neutrons	20
α-particles	20

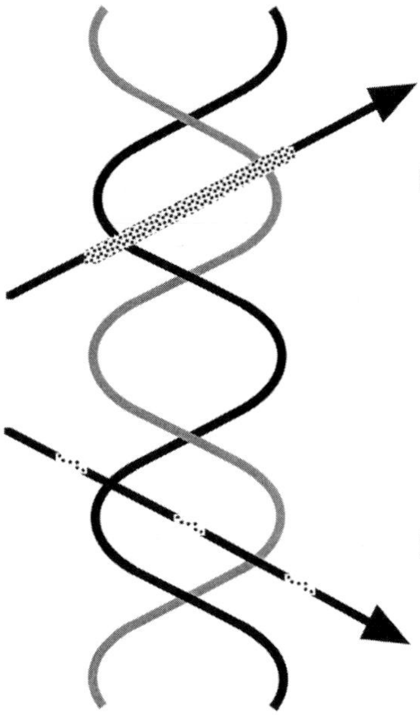

Comparison of the curves in Figure 8.3d shows clearly that the purely physical concept of absorbed dose, as measured by the gray, is inadequate when attempting to predict the possible harmful effects of radiation.

However, RBE is a difficult concept to quantify, since it varies not only with the type of radiation but also with dose, dose rate and fractionation, physiochemical conditions, the biological effect being measured and the time after irradiation at which the measurement is made. This is especially true for the low doses used in diagnostic radiology and nuclear medicine, or considered more likely to occur accidentally when working with radiation.

To incorporate these complex radiobiological factors into radiation protection, simpler *radiation weighting factors* (w_R), based on established RBE values, have been internationally agreed (Table 8.1).

Figure 8.4 Schematic illustration of the different patterns of energy deposition for radiations producing high and low density radiation tracks relative to the double strands of the DNA helix. X- and γ-rays produce low density tracks; neutrons and α-particles produce higher density tracks.

To provide a more practical radiation protection unit for each type of radiation, the appropriate weighting factor is then used to convert the absorbed dose measured in grays for a particular exposure to an *equivalent dose* now expressed in *sieverts* (Sv). For example, for fast neutrons:

$$1 \text{ mGy} \times 20 \ (w_R) = 20 \text{ mSv}$$

The use of mSv or μSv denotes that the type of radiation has been taken into account for the purpose of estimating risk. For most medical applications $w_R = 1$, so 1 mSv equals 1 mGy.

It is important to note that the concepts of radiation weighting factor and equivalent dose should only be used for low doses (a few mSv) usually encountered when dealing with radiation-related cancer, genetic and fetal risks and other radiation protection matters. In cancer therapy, appropriate clinical RBE values are used.

8.12 Summary

- Absorbed dose from ionising radiation is measured in terms of the energy deposited in tissue. The unit is the gray (Gy), equal to a J kg^{-1}.
- Ionising radiation is more damaging than other forms of radiation exposure because, at the molecular level, energy deposition is highly localised and non-uniform.
- The effect is mediated via the formation of highly reactive, short-lived free radicals. The most damaging sites of free radical interactions in the cell are mostly within the nucleus, with DNA particularly at risk.
- Chromosomal aberrations provide evidence that ionising radiation can damage genetic material.
- Significant repair of DNA can occur after irradiation, but failure to repair or misrepair is common.

- Clinical cancer develops through a multistage process requiring not only cellular initiation but also progression and promotional events. The exact role of radiation exposure is still not clear.
- Cellular changes in response to different types of radiation, dose rates and radiation energies require the use of radiation weighting factors, equivalent dose and millisieverts for radiation protection purposes.
- The advent of molecular radiobiology is providing valuable information on the mechanisms involving oncogenesis, and the part played by low dose radiation exposure.

References and further reading

Denekamp P, Hirst DG, editors. Radiation science — of molecules, mice and men. *Br J Radiol* 1992;Suppl. 24.

Dixon B. Therapeutic radiobiology. In: Joslin CFA, editor. *Cancer topics in radiotherapy.* London, UK: Pitman, 1982:17–30.

Hall EJ. *Radiobiology for the radiologist* (5th edn). Philadelphia, PA: Lippincott, Williams & Wilkins, 2000.

International Commission on Radiological Protection. 1990 Recommendations of the International Commission on Radiological Protection, ICRP 60. *Ann ICRP* 1991;21(1-3):91–161.

Jones RR, Southwood R. *Radiation and health: the biological effects of low level exposure to ionising radiation.* Chichester, UK: John Wiley and Sons Ltd., 1987.

National Radiological Protection Board. Mechanisms of radiation tumourigenesis. *Docs NRPB* 1993;4:19–31.

National Radiological Protection Board. *Living with radiation* (5th edn). Chilton, Didcot, UK: NRPB, 1998.

Travis EL. *Primer of medical radiobiology* (2nd edn). Chicago, IL: Year Book Medical Publishers, 1989.

Chapter 9

Radiotherapy

EGA Aird and P Diez

Cell killing by radiation is put to beneficial effect in radiotherapy. Here the primary objective is to kill as many tumour cells as possible, whilst sparing normal tissue. This chapter explains how this may be achieved with careful treatment planning and radiation beam delivery from modern equipment. Treatments with both external radiation beams and radioactive sources (either sealed or unsealed) are used in appropriate circumstances.

9.1 What is radiotherapy?

Some definitions

- **Dose (absorbed dose)** is the energy deposited in a medium (*e.g.* tissue) per unit mass. It is measured in *gray* (Gy).
- **Fractionation** is the delivery of a treatment dose in several, usually daily, fractions in order to allow normal tissues to recover.

Radiotherapy is the treatment of lesions by radiation. Generally these lesions are cancerous tumours, but some benign diseases are also treated. Radiotherapy is mainly used as a curative technique (radical radiotherapy), although approximately 10–15% of all treatments are palliative, where the purpose is to reduce symptoms (*e.g.* pain) arising from the malignant disease for patients who do not have a positive prognosis. The aim of (radical) radiotherapy is to deliver an accurate dose of radiation to the target volume, *i.e.* cancerous cells, whilst avoiding healthy tissue and, particularly, critical structures.

The ultimate goal of any radiotherapy treatment is to deliver the highest possible *dose* to the tumour without exceeding the tolerances of the surrounding healthy tissues. However, the maximum dose that can be given in a single treatment without causing any acute or long-term side effects in healthy tissue is usually not sufficient to sterilise all the tumour stem cells. For this reason, treatments are usually delivered in several fractions. The time between fractions must be long enough that the damage inflicted on the healthy tissue can be repaired, but not so long that the tumour also begins to recover.

It is usual to give doses of radiation on a daily basis for several weeks. Total doses of 60–70 Gy are usually given in a *fractionated* treatment of 2 Gy per fraction to sterilise most tumours, depending on their type and size.

9.2 Forms of radiotherapy

There are three main types of radiation therapy:

- **External beam radiotherapy** is the most common type and can be used to treat tumours at depth in different parts of the body and of varying morphology. The beam is usually provided by a linear accelerator, although cobalt-60 units and kilovoltage X-ray tubes are still in common clinical use. The beam can consist of high energy photons (*e.g.* 1–20 MV), electrons of varying energies, or kilovoltage photons. The latter is used exclusively for superficial tumours since kilovoltage photons deposit most of their energy at the skin surface. Megavoltage photons are used to treat deep-seated tumours, and electron beams are used to treat superficial tumours as well as those located near to particularly radiosensitive organs.

- **Brachytherapy** (or "short distance" radiotherapy) is a form of radiotherapy that makes use of sealed radioactive sources placed directly into or immediately adjacent to the tissue to be treated. This gives a high radiation dose to the tumour, but only a low radiation dose to surrounding healthy tissue. Unfortunately brachytherapy can only be applied to small, localised tumours that are situated in accessible locations. Examples of this are iodine-125 seed implants for the treatment of prostate cancer, use of iridium-192 (^{192}Ir) for treatment of cervix tumours or strontium-90 keloid treatment.

- **Unsealed source radiotherapy** involves the introduction of unsealed radioactive material into the body in a chemical form that is taken up by tumour tissue. The material may be in the form of either a liquid that can be injected or a capsule that can be taken orally. Examples of this are iodine-131 (^{131}I) to treat carcinoma of the thyroid or strontium-89 (^{89}Sr) to treat bony metastases. This form of radiotherapy is usually conducted in the nuclear medicine department, where radionuclides are in common use as tracers for diagnostic investigations.

9.3 External beam radiotherapy

9.3.1 Treatment planning

Treatment planning determines the best way to direct the incoming radiation beam(s) relative to the patient in order to achieve a uniform dose distribution across the tumour volume, whilst avoiding critical organs where feasible, and minimising the dose to healthy tissue. The methods used to achieve this dose at depth whilst avoiding critical structures include the following:

- The tumour must always be in each beam.
- The position of the tumour is normally at the centre of rotation (isocentre) of the machine.
- Irradiate the tumour from a number of different angles.
- Avoid hitting critical structures and normal tissue (in any one position) with all beams.

Treatment plans

- A **treatment plan** is (in two dimensions) a single transverse section (CT slice) of the patient onto which the target volume and critical structures have been marked.
- The **dose distribution** resulting from a number of radiation beams entering the patient at different angles, but centred on the target, is superimposed onto this.

Insight: How treatments are planned

Treatment planning systems (TPSs) incorporating sophisticated computer systems are used to design treatment plans for individual patients. To produce an accurate plan it is usual to use CT scans of the patient over the region of interest. These are loaded into the TPS in the radiotherapy department. To take prostate as an example, a typical abdominal set of CT scans may be 50–70 CT slices at 5 mm apart. A modern TPS can automatically outline the surface of the body on all these slices. The clinical oncologist will then mark on each relevant slice the clinical target volume (CTV). This volume will include the gross tumour, affected lymph nodes, metastases and an extra margin for any subclinical spread. Critical organs will also be outlined. In the particular case of the prostate, most clinicians now define the CTV as the whole of the prostate gland unless the cancer is more advanced and will then include the seminal vesicles. A margin is then drawn around the CTV to expand this volume in three dimensions to produce the planning target volume (PTV). This volume allows for organ movement and any patient set-up errors during treatment.

The treatment planner will then plan this individual treatment to direct a number of radiation fields at the PTV to ensure a high and uniform dose throughout, whilst keeping the doses to critical structures, particularly the rectum, as low as possible.

Insight: What do the dose distributions look like?

In the plain field isodose chart (Figure 9.1a) the most important feature to note is the change in dose with depth. The higher the energy of the X-rays, the greater the penetration of the beam and the more spread out the percentile lines. Figure 9.1b shows the same X-ray beam as Figure 9.1a but with a beam modifier — a wedge — to tilt the isodoses to allow a degree of optimisation of the dose distribution when planning a multifield treatment, particularly, for example, when opposed beams cannot be used. Figure 9.1c shows an isodose chart for an electron beam. Electrons have much less penetration into tissue than X-rays, so electron beam radiotherapy is used for superficial treatment, especially to avoid irradiating underlying critical structures such as the spinal cord.

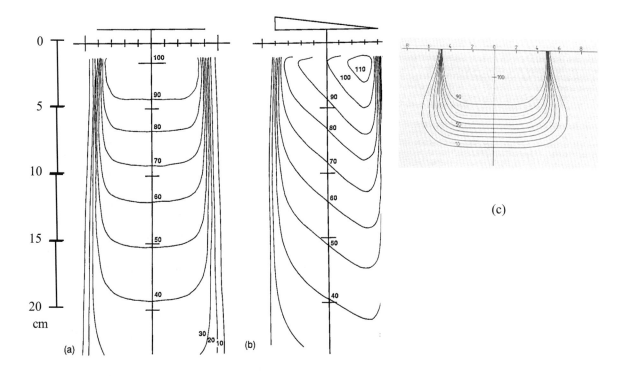

Figure 9.1 (a) Plain field isodose chart (8 cm × 8 cm field size) for 6 MV X-rays. (b) Wedged field isodose chart (8 cm × 8 cm field. 45° wedge) for 6 MV X-rays. (c) Electron beam isodose chart for a 17 MeV beam.

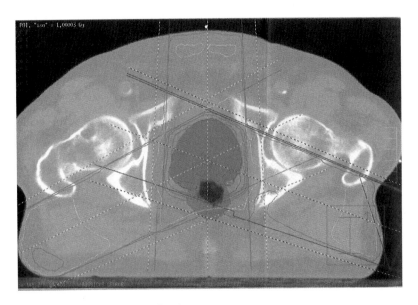

Figure 9.2 Treatment plan for the prostate.

Two-dimensional planning

Beams used for conventional planning have rectangular or square cross-sections. The dose distribution from a single beam can be shown as an isodose chart, which is a set of isodose curves at the 10 percentile levels, *i.e.* 100% dose, 90% dose etc.

The most basic plans use only a single cross-section of the patient. Simple rectangular radiation beams are used from three or four directions (see Figure 9.2) to achieve a uniform dose across the target volume. The same distribution is produced throughout the extent of the radiation field so an unnecessary amount of normal tissue is irradiated.

Three-dimensional (3D) planning

3D treatment planning systems allow the possibility of more accurate planning of the radiation distribution using conformal blocks or multileaf collimators (MLCs) (see box on conformal radiotherapy on page 92). These adjust the shapes of the radiation beam to fit that of the target. This is called conformal radiotherapy and is now widely available.

9.3.2 The delivery system

There is only space here to describe the most commonly used piece of equipment to deliver beam-directed radiotherapy to deep-seated cancers: the linear accelerator (linac). This first came into clinical use in the 1950s and has been developed and refined in various ways during every decade since then.

The modern linac (see Figure 9.3) produces high energy X-rays by accelerating electrons to very high energies, typically 5–25 MeV. The electrons come from a tungsten filament (called an electron gun) and are produced in the same way as in a conventional X-ray tube (§3.2). However, the potential difference in the electron gun is only approximately 50 kV, sufficient to get the electrons started. Electrons are then accelerated to very high energy before reaching the X-ray target. The anode target is thin, typically about 2 mm of tungsten, or its equivalent, and the X-rays are produced by "transmission" through the target, *i.e.* in the same direction as the "stimulating" electron beam. (In electron ream radiotherapy the target is moved out of the way.) The X-rays then pass through various parts of the treatment head (see Figure 9.4 and box).

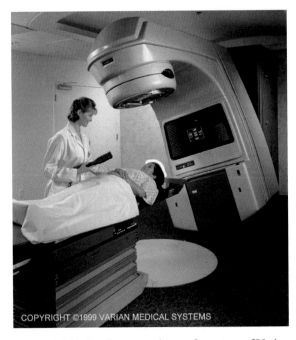

Figure 9.3 Varian linear accelerator [courtesy of Varian Medical Systems].

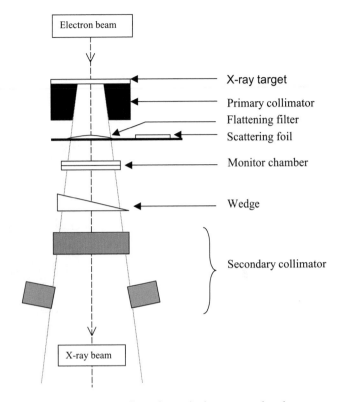

Insight: Components of a linear accelerator treatment head

The primary collimator, which determines the maximum field size at the patient plane and reduces the "leakage radiation" in all other directions.

The flattening filter, which ensures a uniform intensity of X-rays across the beam.

The scattering foil, which replaces the flattening filter in electron beam radiotherapy to provide a flat uniform treatment field.

The monitor chamber, which is an ionisation chamber that measures the amount of radiation given by each beam.

The wedge, which is used to modulate the intensity across the beam.

The secondary collimator and/or multileaf collimator, which shapes the beam to the chosen field size and shape.

Figure 9.4 Cross-section of a typical treatment head.

9.3.3 The treatment process

The treatment machine is always in a specially designed concrete room (sometimes known as a *bunker*), which contains sufficient concrete in the walls to absorb the high energy X-rays. This reduces the radiation outside the room to a negligible level. The entrance to this room is along a corridor, referred to as the *maze* (see Figure 9.5 on page 94), to scatter the radiation many times to reduce its intensity to a very low level at the door. The patient is taken by the radiographer along the maze into the treatment room and prepared for treatment.

For the most accurate treatment, immobilisation devices are used. Examples of these are headshells, leg and ankle supports, and bags of polystyrene pellets. The patient is placed on the treatment table and fitted with their immobilisation device as necessary. Various optical devices are used to set up the patient as accurately as possible. These include room lasers, optical front and back pointers, distance indicators and tattoos on the patient's skin. The most modern design for patient positioning includes reflectors on the skin that are viewed with a special television camera. The daily set-up is adjusted until the set of reflectors registers with the planned set-up.

The radiographers then leave the room and operate the X-ray beams from outside the room whilst observing the patient with closed circuit television. The dose accuracy is determined by the monitor units (MU) set on the linac control for each beam. The geometric accuracy is checked using the treatment X-ray field, which passes through the patient and then forms an image on film or a digital detector system. This image contains less contrast than a conventional radiograph because of the high energy of the radiation beam, but can still be compared with the planned image for positional accuracy. Digital systems give a real-time image of the treatment beam through the patient and can also be used to observe the movement of the MLC leaves while the beam is on to check correct operation during intensity modulated radiotherapy (IMRT) (see Insight boxes on page 92).

Insight: How does conformal radiotherapy shape the beam to the tumour?

Conformal block

A manufactured customised block that is placed in the path of the beam to shield a part of the patient or to define the beam shape. This is used in conformal radiotherapy to reduce the dose to surrounding normal tissue, especially when the tumour is near a critical organ.

Multileaf collimator

A secondary collimator consisting of a number of opposite leaves that move independently. This allows beam shaping to conform to the treated volume in a similar way to a conformal block.

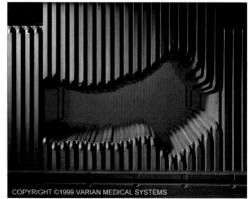

COPYRIGHT ©1999 VARIAN MEDICAL SYSTEMS

Varian multileaf collimator [courtesy of Varian Medical Systems]

Insight: Intensity modulated radiotherapy (IMRT)

A special case of conformal radiotherapy is the most recently developed IMRT. Here, not only are the radiation fields shaped to fit around the projection of the target volume in the direction of fire, but the intensity of the beam can be modified in a series of segments across its 2D area, using multileaf collimators. This makes it possible to create dose distributions that are uniform across an irregularly shaped 3D target (more recent thinking suggests that it is possible to produce hot or cold small volumes within the target to give more dose to the active tumour volume and lower dose where necessary, such as the path of the urethra through the prostate).

9.3.4 Fractionation

The total radiation dose and dose distribution given to the treatment volume in the patient is critical to tumour control and morbidity. However, the way the total dose is subdivided into dose per day and the overall time in which the dose is given also have an effect on these outcomes.

In *conventional fractionation*, a typical curative dose in, say, head and neck cancer is 60–66 Gy in 2 Gy fractions of 1 fraction per day, with an overall time of 6–7 weeks (no treatment at weekends).

Recent radiobiological evidence now suggests several alternative possibilities that may improve tumour control and reduce, or at least make no worse, the morbidity.

9.3.5 Clinical aspects

The most common sites to be treated by radiotherapy are the breast, prostate, lung, head and neck, gynaecological sites and bladder. The role of radiotherapy is different for different cancers and their staging, and is also dependent on the overall management of the disease in terms of surgery and chemotherapy.

Insight: New treatment regimens

Two new treatment concepts are:
1. *that a lower dose per fraction will reduce late morbidity;*
2. *that a shorter overall time, especially in a rapidly growing tumour, will prevent proliferation during treatment and will improve overall survival by improving tumour control.*

*Both these concepts have been used in a multicentre trial of CHART (**C**ontinuous **H**yperfractionated **A**ccelerated **R**adio**T**herapy) (Saunders et al, 1997). When low doses per fraction are given it is necessary to give more than 1 fraction per day in order to reach the same total dose in a reasonable time. This is called **hyperfractionation**. CHART uses 3 fractions per day of 1.5 Gy per fraction with no gaps for weekends (continuous) to a total dose of 54 Gy in only 12 days. An interval of 6 h is maintained between fractions to allow sufficient normal tissue recovery to take place.*

Role of radiotherapy in various treatments

- **Breast**: to reduce the risk of locoregional recurrence following surgery.
- **Prostate**: as an alternative curative treatment to surgery.
- **Lung**: mainly palliative, but some radical treatment for certain patients.
- **Head and neck**: mainly post-operative radiotherapy of primary tumour together with lymph nodes.
- **Cervix uteri**: a mixture of surgery, surgery with radiotherapy, or radiotherapy alone, is used to control this disease depending on staging.
- **Bladder**: a mixture of surgery, surgery with radiotherapy, or radiotherapy alone is used to control this disease depending on staging.

9.3.6 Quality control

Ever since linacs were first used in radiotherapy, it has been recognised by physicists that quality control (QC) is essential. Although at first the main concern was to maintain accurate output of radiation by linacs, it was soon recognised that, if overall accuracy of treatment was to be within the tolerances expected by radiotherapists, other parameters needed continual checking.

In very approximate terms, these tolerances are:

Accuracy of delivered dose to ±5%
Accuracy of beam edges ±2 mm

Thus, routine QC sessions became standard. As well as providing assurance of continuing accuracy of dose delivery, QC also provides the radiotherapy department with an invaluable record of the safety of treatment given by the centre so that, in case of litigation, machine error can be eliminated.

9.3.7 Radiation protection

Staff and members of the public are protected from the very powerful beams used in treatment by a series of safety measures. These include the thick-walled concrete bunkers and the general design of the treatment room, as specified earlier (see Figure 9.5); manufacturer's features in the treatment head; provision of safety interlock systems for machine operation to prevent accidental radiation exposure; and warning lights and notices. Staff are also monitored using film badges, thermoluminescent dosimeters (TLDs) or optical dosimeters, and records of their exposures are kept in accordance with regulations. There is also a system of local rules to ensure safe working practice.

The patient is the only person allowed in the treatment room when radiation is on. Procedures are in place to ensure that the patient receives an accurate dose as prescribed and these cover all areas of the treatment process including planning, QC, calibration of equipment and staff training.

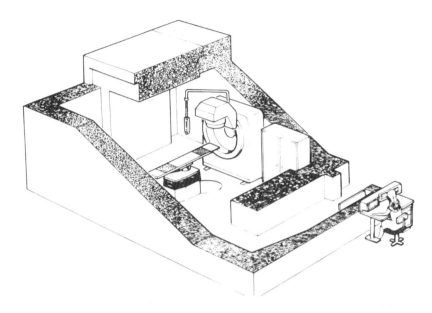

Figure 9.5 A radiotherapy linear accelerator concrete bunker [courtesy of CGR Medical Ltd, taken from Mould, 1985].

9.4 Brachytherapy

The first radiotherapy treatments were performed with radioactive sources (radium at the time) early in the 20th century. Some of the techniques using small, sealed sources have changed little over the intervening century, but the sources now give less potential hazards, *e.g.* ^{192}Ir and caesium-137 (^{137}Cs).

Standard brachytherapy treatments throughout the middle of the 20th century used small, low activity sources for interstitial head and neck (*e.g.* tongue, neck nodes) and intracavity gynaecological sites (*e.g.* cervix, vagina). *Afterloading* systems were introduced in two stages. Manual systems, particularly for gynaecological treatments, were first introduced mainly to reduce the dose to theatre staff. The applicator was placed in the patient in theatre and the patient returned to the ward where the active sources could be quickly inserted. *Remote afterloading systems* were developed to reduce the dose to all staff to a minimum. The patient is treated in a room with sufficient radiation protection for the given radioactive source type and strength (activity). Low dose rate systems are still used in some centres for gynaecological treatments, where the patient is connected to the machine for up to several days. Staff or visitors can enter the room without any risk of radiation exposure by automatically removing the sources from the patient into a lead safe at the press of a button. The advent of high dose rate (HDR) afterloading brachytherapy has allowed new types of treatments to be attempted, whilst keeping some of the old. This is possible because the source (a very small source on a long motor-driven thin cable) can be

> *Insight: Commonly used sources for brachytherapy*
>
> | | |
> |---|---|
> | Caesium | (^{137}Cs) |
> | Iridium | (^{192}Ir) |
> | Iodine | (^{125}I) |
> | Strontium | (^{90}Sr) |
> | Yttrium | (^{90}Y) |

> *Insight: Source types*
>
> **Needles**: interstitial implantation, e.g. ^{192}Ir wire for tongue or breast.
>
> **Seeds**: interstitial implantation, e.g. ^{125}I low dose rate (LDR) for prostate.
>
> **Tubes**: intracavitary brachytherapy, e.g. ^{137}Cs for manual afterloading.
>
> **Pellets**: in remote afterloading machines, e.g. ^{192}Ir high dose rate (HDR) for cervix.

computer driven to any position in the catheter in the patient and left there for any length of time (dwell time) so that a particular distribution of dose can be achieved. Treatment times for this type of brachytherapy are similar to those for external beam radiotherapy.

9.4.1 Radiation protection in brachytherapy

Radiation dose to staff has reduced markedly with the introduction of afterloading techniques for both interstitial and intracavitary treatments, such as ^{137}Cs or ^{192}Ir gynaecological work. The use of afterloading equipment allows the implementation of similar safety features to those applied in external beam radiotherapy. The treatment room is designed like a high energy external beam room to absorb most of the radiation incident on the walls and ceiling. Thus, members of staff are not exposed to radiation.

> **Insight: Types of brachytherapy**
>
> **Interstitial**: *sources surgically inserted into tissue, e.g. ^{192}Ir pellet for high dose rate (HDR) treatment of vaginal wall or ^{125}I seeds for low dose rate (LDR) treatment of prostate.*
> **Intracavitary**: *sources inserted into a body cavity, e.g. ^{192}Ir for gynaecological malignancies or palliative bronchus treatment.*
> **Surface applicators**: *for superficial lesions, e.g. ^{90}Sr for keloid scars (although their usefulness has diminished with the increased availability of electron beams).*
> **Intralumen**: *sources inserted in blood vessels to treat or avoid re-stenosis, e.g. ^{90}Y, ^{32}P, ^{192}Ir.*

However, some interstitial treatments do not use remote afterloading but use manual loading techniques, such as in ^{125}I seed prostate implants and the use of iridium wire (or hairpins) for implants. Special care must be taken in preparing and loading these sealed sources and during treatment on the wards to reduce the doses to staff. Written instructions must be followed carefully.

Procedures will be available that will ensure that doses to visitors are kept *as low as reasonably practicable* (ALARP) (see also Chapter 14). ^{125}I seed implants of the prostate are permanent; the seeds are left in the patient for all time. This has implications for sending the patient home where they may be in close contact with other members of the family. Guidance is given regarding the amount of contact, particularly close contact with children or spouse, that can be allowed. The recommended dose constraint per procedure is 5 mSv for "comforters and carers" who are (a) knowingly and willingly exposed and (b) not pregnant; and 1 mSv for other members of the household. For a reminder on the sievert (Sv) see §10.4 and for a reminder on the risk associated with a dose of 1 mSv see Table 11.1.

Some of the issues that must be considered for manual loading techniques and surface mould treatments are the time spent near the radioactive source and the distance from the source and shielding. Consequently, all radioactive sources used in brachytherapy are stored in a Sealed Source Room behind appropriate shielding or, as is the case with the ^{192}Ir HDR source, in the treatment room in a lead-shielded container, which is part of the afterloading system itself. All sources should be transported in adequately shielded containers.

9.5 Unsealed source radiotherapy

Unsealed radioactive sources are introduced into the body either orally (by means of a capsule or a liquid) or intravenously, to be taken up by malignant tissue and destroy it. The most common treatment is the use of radioactive iodine (^{131}I) to treat thyroid cancer or thyrotoxicosis. Another form of unsealed source radiotherapy is the use of radioactive strontium to treat bony metastases, and for palliative care (to reduce the pain induced by these metastases).

9.5.1 Radiation protection in unsealed source radiotherapy

Nuclear medicine or radiotherapy departments, depending on the institution, must take responsibility for the execution of an extensive QC programme in order to support these clinical applications safely. Most radiation protection issues are very similar to those that apply to manual loading techniques in brachytherapy. An added problem with ^{131}I radiotherapy is that the source also emits γ-rays, which will escape the patient's body. This can be a problem as the patient cannot be shielded by a container and is mobile. Also, all body fluids, particularly urine, excreta and saliva, contain radioiodine that could be ingested or absorbed by other persons. To ensure safety of staff and members of the public, a set of protection measures are in place, which are detailed below.

Restrictions on discharge

Patients cannot be discharged from the hospital unless the amount of radioactivity is below set limits, the patient is willing to follow instructions and restrictions, and he/she is not incontinent or dependent on others for physical care.

Thyroid carcinoma patients

Doses given to thyroid carcinoma patients are very high. They must therefore be treated as inpatients and are confined to a shielded room. Written procedures, which must be read by all persons coming into contact with these patients, will determine the amount of contact with visitors or other patients and will also restrict contact with members of staff for a period of 3–4 days.

Insight: Examples of treatments

Thyrotoxicosis: The thyroid does not distinguish between stable and radioactive iodine, so ^{131}I can be used very effectively for the treatment of thyrotoxicosis (hyperthyroidism). Most of the dose is delivered through β particles (from ^{131}I decay), so a very high dose can be delivered to the thyroid whilst keeping the dose to the rest of the body relatively low.

Thyroid carcinoma: Differentiated cancer of the thyroid may be treated using ^{131}I after the bulk of the tumour has been surgically removed. The same principle may apply as for thyrotoxicosis, but the size of the dose administered can be up to ten times higher in some cases.

Strontium therapy: A secondary effect of prostate cancer is the formation of bony metastases, where bone absorbs extra calcium and can be very painful. If hormone therapy is unsuccessful, strontium therapy might be used for palliative care. Strontium behaves in a similar way to calcium in the body so it will collect in these metastases.

In hospital

To minimise the spread of contamination outside the patient's room, treatment rooms have their own washing and toilet facilities. In addition, disposable crockery and cutlery and other items are used by the patient. Protective clothing is worn when handling the patient and all waste generated is treated as radioactive.

At home

One of the restrictions imposed on patients returning home immediately after radio-iodine treatment, or discharged later from hospital wards, is staying away from pregnant women and children for particular periods of time, depending on the amount of radioactivity they have been given.

9.6 Summary

- Most radiotherapy is given with beams of high energy X-rays. Several beams are normally used to concentrate the dose around the tumour whilst sparing normal tissues and critical structures.
- Some radiotherapy is given with small sealed sources (brachytherapy) or unsealed sources.
- The efficacy of radiotherapy is very dependent on the total dose of radiation, the total treatment time and the dose per fraction.
- To ensure accuracy of treatment as well as safety for the patient in a radiotherapy department, there is a quality system in place as well as ionising radiation legislation.

Further reading

Dobbs J, Barrett A, Ash D. *Practical radiotherapy planning* (3rd edn). London, UK: Arnold, 1999.
Joslin CA, Flynn A, Hall EJ, editors. *Principles and practice of brachytherapy using afterloading systems.* London, UK: Arnold, 2001.

Mould RF. *Radiation protection in hospitals*. Medical Science Series. Bristol, UK and Boston, MA: Adam Hilger Ltd, 1985.

Saunders M, et al. Continuous hyperfractionated accelerated radiotherapy (CHART) versus conventional radiotherapy in non-small cell lung cancer: a randomised multicentre trial. *Lancet* 1997;350:161–5.

Chapter 10

Effects of human exposure to ionising radiation and risk estimates

PP Dendy and B Dixon

This chapter focuses on the harmful effects of ionising radiation on the whole body, with much of the data derived from epidemiological studies. The important distinction between stochastic and deterministic effects is introduced, and a model is developed to allow estimation of the risk to individual patients from low doses of radiation.

10.1 Introduction

Our concern when using ionising radiation is the potential hazard to us as human beings. In Chapter 8 we looked at how radiation can injure cells. In this chapter we develop these ideas to provide an understanding of effects on tissues and the whole body. The effects of large radiation doses become apparent within a few days of the exposure, but the doses that a patient might receive from a diagnostic medical test are far below the threshold to produce any of these early effects. However, there may be a small increase in the long-term risk of developing an illness such as cancer, even for these small exposures. A great deal of epidemiological evidence has been accumulated from various population groups exposed to large doses of radiation. This has been used to develop a simple model giving an *effective dose* from which the long-term risks can be estimated for exposure of any part of the body. This chapter attempts to explain more about these effects and the factors that influence them. It also includes an explanation of how exposures are quantified in terms of radiation dose.

Table 10.1 Threshold doses for the most sensitive deterministic effects

Tissue and effect	Absorbed dose for a brief exposure (Gy)
Skin	
Early transient erythema	2
Temporary epilation	3
Lens of eye	
Detectable opacities	>0.5
Cataract	>2.0
Bone marrow	
Depression of haematopoiesis	>0.5
Gonads	
Temporary sterility in males	0.15
Permanent sterility	>2.5

10.2 Deterministic effects of radiation

Large doses of radiation will produce effects on the body within a few days. There are definable threshold doses for these effects below which no damage, in terms of measurable clinical response, can be detected (Table 10.1). Examples of effects that fall into this category include skin erythema, hair loss, cataract and death.

Above the threshold, the severity of effect increases with dose in a way that can be predicted. Such effects are referred to as "deterministic effects". A typical dose–response curve for a

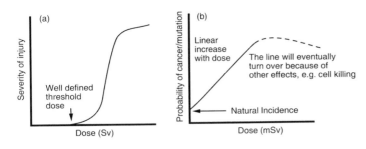

Figure 10.1 Typical dose–response curves for (a) deterministic effects and (b) stochastic effects.

deterministic effect is shown in Figure 10.1a.

Deterministic effects are initiated in cells, but clinically they affect tissues and have the following features.

- An absorbed dose to the tissue of 150 mGy or more is required to observe an effect.
- The dose threshold varies from one tissue to another.
- The exposed individual is affected (*i.e.* a somatic effect).
- Repair and recovery can occur.
- The severity of the effect depends on dose/dose rate/number of exposures.
- The effect usually occurs shortly after exposure, *i.e.* days or weeks.
- An initial mild response may repair quickly, but a higher exposure may cause progressive damage, *e.g.* secondary ulceration of the skin perhaps 80 weeks after exposure.

Protection of normal tissues from high doses of radiation is a major feature of radiotherapy, discussed briefly in Chapter 9.

Threshold doses for even the most sensitive of deterministic effects, summarised in Table 10.1, are well above the doses received by patients in conventional radiology (see §11.2).

However, some prolonged interventional procedures in which dose rates to the skin during fluoroscopy exceeded 0.1 Gy min^{-1} have caused skin damage (see for example Figure 10.2) or epilation (hair loss). This cannot now be discounted as a possible side effect of some lengthy radiological procedures but should be avoidable with an optimised technique.

Note that it is relatively straightforward to establish dose limits well below the relevant threshold for persons working with radiation in order to avoid deterministic effects.

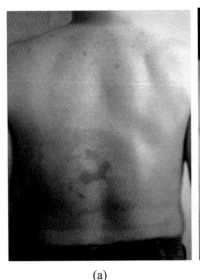
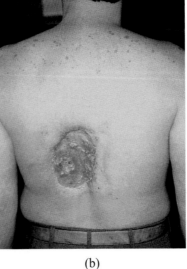

Figure 10.2 Skin injury attributable to X-rays from fluoroscopy following multiple coronary angiography and angioplasty procedures: (a) 6–8 weeks and (b) 18–21 months; tissue necrosis is evident. [Acknowledgment to T Shope from ICRP Publication 85 (2000).]

(a) (b)

10.3 Stochastic effects of radiation

A stochastic effect is one that is governed by the laws of chance. Since a single ionising event may cause radiation damage to the DNA and even diagnostic examinations result in millions of ionisations, it is usual to assume that there is no threshold dose for stochastic effects of ionising radiation. Thus the curve relating probability of stochastic effect to dose has the form shown in Figure 10.1b. A further feature of a truly stochastic process is that the effect of multiple doses is additive, with no ability to repair or recover from injury.

The most important stochastic hazards of radiation are carcinogenesis and heritable effects. We shall use the term carcinogenesis to include leukaemias, sarcomas and other rare tumour types as well as carcinomas. Steps leading to malignant transformation were discussed in Chapter 8. Heritable effects may result from DNA damage in a germ cell.

Another feature of stochastic effects is that their frequency increases with dose, but their severity does not. Thus, the degree of malignancy of a radiation-linked cancer is not related to the dose.

> **Insight: The probability of stochastic effects**
>
> *The model of stochastic damage has many features in common with the National Lottery (LOTTO).*
>
> *(a) If you buy a ticket, you have a chance of winning the jackpot (there is no threshold).*
>
> *(b) Although the probability of winning the jackpot (a chance effect) increases with the number of tickets bought, the size of the jackpot (severity of effect) does not.*
>
> *(c) The concept of* **collective dose** *(see §10.6) is analogous to a syndicate pooling their resources to increase their chances of winning.*

10.3.1 Carcinogenesis

There is extensive evidence that ionising radiation increases the risk of malignant disease in humans (Table 10.2). Some of the evidence comes from occupational exposures, for example in the period 1929–1949 American radiologists exhibited nine times as many leukaemias as other medical specialists, some from approved medical procedures. Some of the cited sources are stronger than others, and in many situations there are confounding factors. For example, it is often difficult to distinguish a second or third radiation-related tumour in a patient receiving radiotherapy for cancer from possible secondaries arising from the original primary or other "spontaneous" tumours.

The most carefully followed-up group are the Japanese nuclear weapons survivors. Five key points can be made from data collected over a period of 50 years (see box). All these points have an important influence on current radiation protection practice.

> **Key points derived from epidemiological studies**
>
> - The risk of cancer is not the same for all parts of the body. Many organs are affected, but not all to the same degree.
> - There is a long latent period before cancer develops — excess leukaemia occurred between 5–14 years but the risk of solid tumours was still increasing 40 years after the bombs.
> - There is no evidence of a threshold dose for most tumour types.
> - In terms of relative risk, cancer was highest in those under 10 years of age at the time of exposure.
> - The data agree with that from other sources and permit a risk estimate.

Table 10.2 Sources of evidence that ionising radiation increases the risk of cancer in humans

Generic source	Examples
Occupational	Uranium miners, especially resulting from inhalation
	Radium ingestion by dial painters who licked their brushes
	American radiologists carrying out screening procedures without image intensifiers
Medical diagnosis	Prenatal X-rays
	Thorotrast (α-particle emitting ^{232}Th) injected as a contrast agent
	Multiple lung fluoroscopies (screening for tuberculosis), increasing breast cancer
Medical therapy	Cervical and breast radiotherapy
	Treatment for ankylosing spondylitis
	Many reports of radiotherapy causing new tumours
Atomic bombs	Hiroshima and Nagasaki survivors
	Marshall Islanders near nuclear test sites

10.3.2 Heritable effects

The situation is less clear for radiation-induced germ line mutation in humans, although the circumstantial evidence is very strong. Mutations have been observed in a wide variety of other species, including plants, bacteria, fruit flies and mice. In Chapter 8, the ease with which ionising radiation can damage DNA was discussed.

For the purposes of risk estimation, the dose of radiation that would double the natural incidence of germ line mutation is estimated from animal work to be approximately 1 Sv.

Insight: Heritable effects in humans — the statistical uncertainty

Notwithstanding the circumstantial evidence, researchers have so far failed to demonstrate convincing statistical evidence of hereditary or genetic changes in humans as a result of radiation, even in the offspring of Japanese survivors. This failure relates to the difficulty of showing a significant increase in the overwhelming presence of spontaneous genetic abnormalities. It is a common failing of epidemiological studies designed to estimate directly the genetic (or cancer) risk associated with small doses of ionising radiation that they do not have sufficient statistical power to detect such low level risks.

A reminder on dosimetric quantities

- Absorbed dose: measure of the energy deposited in tissues; unit — gray (Gy)
- Equivalent dose: allows for the effectiveness of different radiations in producing biological damage; unit — sievert (Sv)
- Effective dose: adjusts for different tissue sensitivities to radiation; unit — sievert (Sv)

10.4 Effective dose

Among the conclusions from the study of Japanese survivors was that many tissues are affected but not all to the same degree. In radiological examinations, only part of the body is irradiated, therefore some system is required that will allow risks from different patterns of exposure to be compared.

The International Commission on Radiological Protection (ICRP, 1991) has assigned tissue weighting factors (w_T) to the various body organs, related to their radiosensitivity (see Figure 10.3).

An *effective dose* has then been defined as the weighted *equivalent dose* for all the organs and tissues in the body. It is the whole-body dose that would carry the same risk as the delivered dose distribution. In later chapters, risk estimates for different radiological examinations are based on effective doses.

10.5 Models of radiation cancer risk

Current estimates for the risks of very low doses of ionising radiation should be regarded as uncertain, even though they are based upon data from relatively large epidemiological study groups, *e.g.* survivors of atomic weapons used in Japan.

The smallest dose that has provided clear evidence of an increased cancer risk (data for breast cancer after multiple lung radiographs of patients with tuberculosis and Japanese bomb survivors) is approximately 200 mSv (Figure 10.4).

There are, however, a variety of ways to extrapolate from these data down to the much lower doses, typically 1–2 mSv, used for many radiological procedures. Currently the ICRP recommends a linear no-threshold (LNT) extrapolation model. This assumes that the incidence is directly proportional to the dose (curve A; Figure 10.4), but other models (B, C, D) may be equally valid in the absence of adequate low dose data.

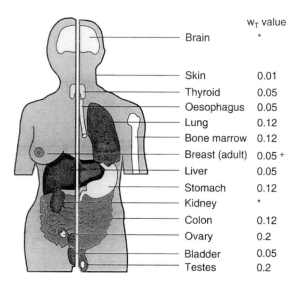

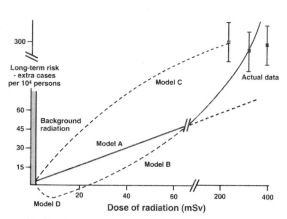

Figure 10.3 Schematic diagram showing that the radiation risk to different organs is not the same. The higher the tissue weighting factor (w_T), the greater the risk. *Brain and kidney are part of the "remainder" organs with lower risk; also including adrenals, upper and small intestine, muscle, pancreas, spleen and uterus. They have an aggregated weighting factor of 0.05. +The weighting factor for the breast is, at first sight, rather low since it is known that the risk of cancer in the female breast following radiation exposure is quite high. It is primarily the consequence of quoting a value of w_T for a mixed population, half of whom will be males.

Figure 10.4 Curves showing the possible variation in human long-term risk with radiation dose. The solid line (model A) represents current convention — a linear increase at low doses with no threshold. At higher doses (well above protection and diagnostic levels), the curve turns upwards. The dotted curves represent other possibilities: a non-linear increase, possibly with a threshold (model B); a supralinear model in which low dose effects would be higher than predicted (model C); radiation hormesis (model D as an extension of model B). Doses from background radiation (typically 2 mSv per annum) and many radiological examinations (up to 2 mSv) are shown shaded.

A variety of reasons are put forward for using model A.

- It is similar to the model for all stochastic effects (Figure 10.1(b)).
- Biophysical considerations of radiation events resulting in non-repairable DNA damage suggest a LNT model at very low dose.
- The LNT model errs on the side of safety.
- It is historically accepted and is the basis of extensive Europe-wide legislation.

Model A is therefore currently used by the ICRP, and accepted internationally, to quote cancer risks factors applied to very low doses (Table 10.3). These numerical values of cancer risk as well as other radiation protection concepts, *e.g.* collective dose (see §10.6 below) and the ALARP principle (as low as reasonably practicable — see §12.3.3), depend on the LNT model being correct.

Table 10.3 A summary of the main risk factors (% risk per Sv)[a]

	Radiology work force	Whole population
Fatal cancer	4.0	5.0
Non-fatal cancer	1.0	0.8
Hereditary effects	0.8	1.3
Total (rounded)	5.6	7.3

[a]Note that a 5% risk per Sv means, literally, that if 100 persons representing a broad cross-section of the population were each exposed to 1 Sv of radiation there would be 5 additional fatal cancers.

Insight: Questions about the validity of the LNT model

Model A does have significant disadvantages. It implies that "No radiation dose is safe" (as does model C) and the public takes this to mean "All radiation doses are dangerous". Such fears can have considerable social consequences, for example it is estimated that over 10,000 women in Europe may have chosen to have unnecessary abortions after Chernobyl on groundless fears of deformed births.

The alternative models B and D (Figure 10.4), for which some supporting evidence is now emerging, do not have such severe practical and social implications resulting from very low dose radiation exposure. Some radiation scientists have made very detailed analyses of existing low dose epidemiological data and suggest there may be a threshold for cancer induction (model B). Others, mostly involved in studies of DNA repair genes, believe that natural radiation defence mechanisms in cells may be switched on by very low doses (less than 20 mSv), thereby reducing the cancer risk below normal levels (radiation hormesis — model D). At higher doses these defence mechanisms are overcome. Either model B or D, if adopted for radiation protection, would lead to dramatic changes in risk evaluation for all forms of low dose radiation exposure.

10.6 Collective doses and the man-sievert

One direct consequence of adopting the stochastic LNT model is that, for the somatic radiation effects of carcinogenesis and germ line mutation, all radiation doses are additive. This applies not only for an individual but also for groups of individuals, so we can compute the *collective dose* for an exposed population and estimate the "collective" risk. The collective dose is calculated by summing the doses for all the exposed individuals and is quoted in *man-sieverts*.

Thus, a more flexible way to interpret the risk factors shown in Table 10.3 would be to say that if a group of persons/patients received a collective dose of 100 man Sv, 5 additional fatal cancers would ensue. To retain a sense of proportion, it should be noted that if this collective dose had arisen from diagnostic radiology, it would have resulted from about 100,000 persons each receiving on average 1 mSv. The 5 additional fatal cancers then have to be set against about 30,000 naturally occurring cancers in a population of this size.

10.7 Risks to individual patients

Medical exposures deliver radiation doses to individuals. There are situations where average risk factors based on the total population will be misleading. Some of these will be considered briefly.

Age distribution

The use of diagnostic X-rays as a function of the age of the population is substantially skewed. More than 50% of examinations are on patients over 45 years and more than 25% are on patients over 64 years of age. This has an effect on detriment, which includes a contribution from years of life lost as well as compromised quality of life. Consideration of the age factor, which is rarely done, could reduce the effective collective dose from diagnostic radiology by as much as 37%.

Sex

For some organs, the risks to males and females are different (see footnote to Figure 10.3). It would not be appropriate, for example, to use a general population risk factor when estimating the risk from asymptomatic breast screening.

Irradiation of children, neonates or the fetus

Exposure during childhood or *in utero* carries an enhanced radiation risk. This may in part be due to an inherently greater sensitivity, in part due to a greater opportunity for damage expression.

For irradiation of children, neonates or the fetus, most of the available data come from Hiroshima and Nagasaki and relate primarily to leukaemia. Note that the "bone" marrow stem cell distribution is different in children, being more widespread in the body than in adults. When children are exposed it is likely that:

- the probability of cancer induction is about twice as high as in adults;
- the possibility of heritable changes is higher than for adults.

For exposures of the fetus, likely risks are as follows.

- The increased risk of cancer up to 15 years after irradiation *in utero* is approximately 6% Sv^{-1} (6×10^{-4} for 10 mSv). Half the cancers will be fatal. One reason for stating the risk to 15 years is that direct comparison can be made with the natural incidence in the UK of childhood cancers up to that age (1 in 1300 or 7.7×10^{-4}). Again, about half will be fatal.
- Mental retardation due to exposure *in utero* can result from irradiation of the nervous system if the exposure is during the critical period of organogenesis from about 8–15 weeks. Fortunately, the reduced intelligence quotient (IQ) that might be caused by a diagnostic exposure would not be detectable.

For all these reasons, a higher level of clinical justification is required before deciding to perform an X-ray examination for a child. X-ray examination below the diaphragm of a patient who is pregnant should be postponed unless the condition is life-threatening. Tests that do not involve ionising radiation may be more appropriate.

When a patient is found to be pregnant only after an X-ray examination, expert advice should be sought. A careful estimate of the dose to the fetus should be obtained. Mostly this will be below 2 mGy and will carry a risk that is well below both the natural incidence of malignant disease and the other risks of pregnancy. If the fetal dose estimate is somewhat higher, it can serve as a starting point and guideline for a reasoned decision by parents concerned about a possible abortion.

Heritable effects

The highest tissue weighting factor is assigned to the gonads (see Figure 10.3). However, for individual patients this is a most unreliable figure since it is an average value for the whole population. It is more appropriate to consider the genetically significant dose (GSD). The contribution to the GSD for a patient who has passed the reproductive age, frequently the case in radiology, will be zero. For children and teenagers with a normal life expectancy it will be higher than average.

Genetic predisposition

Since ionising radiation is known to cause extensive DNA damage, especially double-strand breaks (see §8.6), those individuals who, for genetic reasons, carry an elevated risk for "spontaneous" cancer may also be at increased risk for cancer following irradiation.

Evidence for this view comes from only a small number of relatively rare familial cancers where there is a high probability that the mutant gene will be expressed as neoplastic disease (high penetrance genes).

The potential consequences of the very incomplete data currently available are as follows.

- This genetically susceptible group will have minimal impact on the overall population risk factors because it is such a small percentage of the population.
- At diagnostic doses, the impact for an "at-risk" patient would be relatively small. From Table 10.4, an equivalent dose of 100 mSv would increase the lifetime risk for a "high-risk" breast cancer patient from 40% to 40.4% if the suggested elevated risk of 10-fold were confirmed.
- On the other hand, for a radiotherapy patient, the increased risk of a second cancer may be substantial (see Table 10.4). There already appears to be sufficient evidence to consider alternative therapies for known high-risk patients.

Insight: How much is known about genetic predisposition?

The most common familial cancers show an approximate prevalence per live birth of between about 1 in 500 (prostate cancer) and 1 in 800 (breast/ovarian cancer). A range of other rare disorders, including retinoblastoma and nevoid basal cell carcinoma, have a prevalence between 1 in 10,000 and 1 in 50,000. Cancer-prone individuals comprise well below 1% of the population.

For radiation hypersensitive persons, a reasonable aim is to ensure that their exposure to medical sources of radiation should not knowingly result in an unacceptable risk.

Radiation risk estimates are very uncertain for the very small numbers in the genetically "at-risk" group. The tissue-specific cancer risk following exposure to moderate to high doses of radiation is thought to be in the range 5–100 times greater than normal, probably nearer the lower end. For the purpose of assessing implications for radiation protection, a factor of 10 has been suggested (see Table 10.4).

Table 10.4 Calculated risk of fatal radiogenic breast cancer in women with high genetic risk

	Individual risk (%)	
	All individuals	At-risk group
Spontaneous risk	4.0	40
100 mSv[a]	0.04	0.4
2 Sv[b]	0.8	8.0

[a]50 years of background radiation with a risk estimate of 0.4% Sv^{-1}.

[b]Estimated dose to the unaffected contralateral breast during radiotherapy.

There are many uncertainties to be resolved. Some recent work has suggested that a much higher percentage of individuals than the 1% with high penetrance genes carry germ line mutations in low penetrance genes that predispose to common cancers. If this larger radiosensitive group were confirmed, it might have a greater impact on the non-uniformity of population risk than the high penetrance group because of higher prevalence.

10.8 Summary

The effects of human exposure to ionising radiation are summarised in Figure 10.5.

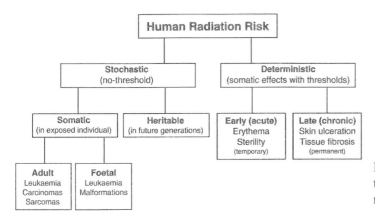

Figure 10.5 A block diagram summarising the main categories of human radiation risks.

- Deterministic effects are somatic effects in the exposed individual, have well defined threshold doses for different tissues and show increasing severity with increasing dose.
- Stochastic effects obey the laws of chance, showing increasing probability with increasing dose but no dose level at which the risk becomes zero. Stochastic effects may be genetic, *i.e.* heritable changes in descendants, or may be somatic. The most important stochastic somatic effect is radiation-induced cancer.
- The risk of cancer is not the same for all parts of the body, so when only part of the body is irradiated, *e.g.* in diagnostic radiology, allowance must be made for this.
- The effective dose is the whole-body dose that would carry the same risk. Effective doses from different patterns of exposure can be compared directly.
- The risk from very low doses has to be extrapolated from the observed risk at much higher doses. This is done using the linear no-threshold model, although alternative models cannot be refuted on the basis of existing evidence.
- The risk of fatal cancer from a medical exposure of 1 mSv is estimated to be approximately 5 in 100,000. Recall that the lifetime risk of cancer from all causes is currently about 1 in 3.
- The collective dose, for example to a group of patients who all have the same diagnostic examination, is calculated by assuming that radiation doses are strictly additive. The (theoretical) number of excess cancers can then be estimated.
- For individual patients there are several factors that distort risk estimates based on a broad cross-section of the population. Age is very important. Elderly patients have a below-average risk, and children, neonates and the fetus have the highest risk. There is also increasing evidence that certain families are genetically more sensitive to radiation than the average population.
- The risk factors quoted in this chapter will be applied to specific situations in Chapter 11.

Acknowledgment

We thank Dr David Scott for helpful comments on genetic predisposition to elevated radiation sensitivity.

References and further reading

Granier R, Gambini DJ. *Applied radiobiology and radioprotection*. London, UK: Ellis Horwood Ltd., 1990.

Hall EJ. *Radiobiology for the radiologist* (5th edn). Philadelphia, PA: J. B. Lippincott & Co., 2000.

Hendee WR, Edwards FM, editors. *Health effects of exposure to low level ionising radiation*. London, UK: IoP Publishing, 1996.

International Commission on Radiological Protection. 1990 Recommendations of the International Commission on Radiological Protection, ICRP Publication 60. *Ann ICRP* 1991;1(3).

International Commission on Radiological Protection. Genetic susceptibility to cancer. *Ann ICRP* 1998;28:1–2.

International Commission on Radiological Protection. Avoidance of radiation injuries from medical interventional procedures, ICRP Publication 85. *Ann ICRP* 2000;30(2).

National Radiological Protection Board. Genetic heterogeneity in the population and its implications for radiation risk. Report of an Advisory Group on Ionising Radiation. *Doc NRPB* 1999;10(3):1–47.

Point/counterpoint. Controversial issues: the linear no-threshold debate. *Med Phys* 1998;25:273–300.

Scott D. Individual differences in chromosomal radiosensitivity: implications for radiogenic cancer. In: Sugahara T, Nikaido O, Niwar O, editors. *Radiation and homeostasis*. Proceedings of the International Symposium of Radiation and Homeostasis; Kyoto, Japan; July 2001. Excerpta Medica International Congress Series 1236. London, UK: Elsevier, 2002:433–7.

Sumner D, Wheldon T, Watson W. *Radiation risks: an evaluation*. Glasgow, UK: Tarragon Press, 1991.

Chapter 11

Risks from radiological examinations

CJ Martin and J Shand

This chapter gets to the heart of the justification process. Guidelines are given on the doses and risks from a wide range of radiological examinations, and the way in which this information should be used to justify medical exposures in a variety of different situations is discussed.

The chapter also discusses ways in which radiation risks can be minimised and suggests ways in which radiation risk can be explained.

11.1 Introduction

Images obtained using ionising radiation provide answers to numerous questions about patient illnesses. The benefits in treatment of disease and improvements in patient management are obvious, and failure to carry out an examination that is indicated may have a significant detrimental effect on a patient's health. However, there are risks associated with radiation exposures that should not be ignored. If a procedure will not influence the management of a patient or give another similar benefit, it should not be carried out. This chapter considers the risks involved and the methods used to reduce them.

11.2 The risk of long-term stochastic effects

The main health effects of radiation to be considered when deciding whether a diagnostic examination should be carried out are the stochastic effects; cancer and hereditary disease (§10.3). For stochastic effects, the chance that any one person will be affected is very small, but the implications for an individual who is affected will be great. This type of risk phenomenon is often difficult for people to grasp and put into the context of everyday life. Everyone faces risks all the time, but they seldom think of the consequences as individuals, because the chance of being affected is very small. This begs the question as to why there is a need to take them into account for medical exposures.

The answer is that, whilst the risks are small for any individual, potentially a large population may be exposed. Although the chance of a significant effect occurring for any given individual is small, there will be serious consequences for a few of the many individuals exposed. It is impossible to identify the individuals affected because of the relatively high baseline incidence of the types of disease involved. Nevertheless, the number of affected individuals will increase as the total population dose rises. The criteria used to decide whether examinations should be undertaken will determine how many persons undergo radiation exposures.

Many studies have been carried out on the effects of radiation. There are a great deal more data available for assessing the risks from radiation than the risks from other environmental carcinogens, although, as has been explained in Chapter 10, there are uncertainties because these data are derived from groups who received much higher doses than those from diagnostic medical exposures. The concept of effective dose has been developed based on the assumption that risk is directly proportional to dose. This allows risks of stochastic effects from radiation exposures to different parts of the body to be evaluated and compared. For any exposure, an effective dose can be derived that is equivalent to the uniform "whole-body" dose that would give rise to a similar health risk (§10.4). The factors used to represent the radiation sensitivity of different organs have been derived from epidemiological studies and represent the "best guess" at this time. Radiation protection physicists using practical measurements of radiation dose quantities can evaluate the effective dose received by a patient.

The risks of potential harm associated with a radiation exposure giving an effective dose of 1 mSv are given in Table 11.1. This dose is similar to that received from a lumbar spine examination. The risks are quoted as 1 in so many thousand, a form often used for presenting this type of data. Average effective doses and approximate lifetime risks of fatal cancer for a variety of diagnostic examinations are given in Table 11.2. The examinations have been divided into groups of similar order of magnitude of risk, and terms are included that might be used in describing the magnitude of the risk.

Table 11.1 Risks of stochastic effects from a dose of 1 mSv to the population[a]

Effect	Risk
Adult exposure (1 mSv)	
Fatal cancer (all types)	1 in 20,000
Fatal leukaemia	1 in 200,000
Non-fatal cancer	1 in 100,000
Heritable effects	1 in 80,000
Childhood exposure (1 mSv)	
Fatal cancer	1 in 10,000
Fetal exposure (1 mSv)	
Fatal cancer to age 15 years	1 in 33,000
All cancers to age 15 years	1 in 17,000
Heritable effects	1 in 42,000

[a]Risks are calculated from ICRP 1990 data given in Table 10.3 for the whole population. Values are rounded to the nearest 10 or 100 thousand because of the large uncertainties in the data. Risks of cancer are over the individual's lifetime, unless otherwise stated.

Insight: Practical patient dose measurement quantities in radiology

Entrance surface dose is the dose to the skin where an X-ray beam enters the body. It can be measured with small thermoluminescent crystal dosimeters placed on the skin or can be calculated from the radiographic factors (kVp and mAs) coupled with measurements of X-ray tube output.

Dose–area product is the product of the dose within the X-ray beam and its area. It quantifies all the radiation that enters a patient and is measured by a meter fitted to the X-ray tube.

Computed tomography dose index (CTDI) is the integral of the dose across the volume irradiated in producing a CT image. It is normally measured with a special radiation detector placed across the slice. A weighted CTDI, derived from measurements made in a Perspex phantom, is used in evaluation of patient doses.

Dose–length product is equal to the weighted CTDI multiplied by the length of the body scanned and is used to assess the dose to the patient for a particular CT examination protocol.

Insight: How can effective dose be estimated for a medical exposure?

Estimates of effective dose can be calculated from any of the practical dose measurement quantities by using coefficients derived from computer simulations of the interactions of radiation as it passes through the body. Anthropomorphic phantoms have been used to assess doses to individual organs in deriving the coefficients, which relate to particular body projections, exposure factors and techniques. A similar model has been used to evaluate effective doses from administration of radiopharmaceuticals that collect in particular organs.

Table 11.2 Effective doses and lifetime risks of cancer from some common diagnostic medical examinations for adults in the UK[a]

Term for risk	Examination	Mean effective dose (mSv)	Risk of fatal cancer
	Incidence of cancer in population		1 in 3
	Radiology		
Negligible	Intraoral dental radiograph	0.002	1 in 10 million
	Panoramic dental radiology	0.007	1 in 3 million
	Limb and joint radiographs	<0.01	<1 in 2 million
Minimal	Chest radiograph (PA)	0.02	1 in 1 million
	Skull radiograph (PA)	0.03	1 in 700,000
	Cervical spine	0.08	1 in 250,000
Very low	Hip	0.3	1 in 60,000
	Abdomen or pelvis radiograph (AP)	0.7	1 in 30,000
	Lumbar spine examination (AP and Lat)	1.0	1 in 20,000
Low	Head CT scan	2	1 in 10,000
	IVU	2.5	1 in 8000
	Barium meal (fluoroscopy and images)	3	1 in 7000
	Barium enema (fluoroscopy and images)	7	1 in 3000
	Chest CT scan	8	1 in 2500
	Abdominal CT scan	10	1 in 2000
	Pelvic CT scan	10	1 in 2000
	Nuclear medicine		
Minimal	[57]Co GI absorption (Schilling test)	0.1	1 in 200,000
Very low	[99m]Tc lung ventilation (aerosol)	0.4	1 in 50,000
	[99m]Tc kidney (MAG3)	0.7	1 in 20,000
	[99m]Tc lung perfusion (MAA)	1.0	1 in 20,000
Low	[99m]Tc bone scan (diphosphonate)	3	1 in 7000
	[99m]Tc dynamic cardiac scan (RBC)	7	1 in 3000
	[18]F tumour (PET)	10	1 in 2000
Moderate	[201]Tl myocardial perfusion	18	1 in 1000

[a]Data taken from various sources, including Hart et al 1996, and Administration of Radioactive Substances Advisory Committee 1998.

PA, posteroanterior; AP, anteroposterior; Lat, lateral; IVU, intravenous urogram; GI, gastrointestinal.

Particular thought should be given to whether those examinations with higher risks are really required and whether alternative ones could be used. For radiological examinations it is organs in the vicinity of the part of the body being X-rayed, particularly lying within the X-ray beam, that will receive higher radiation doses. So X-ray examinations involving exposure of the abdomen and pelvis, where there are several organs that are sensitive to radiation (Figure 10.3), tend to have higher effective doses. However, for nuclear medicine examinations, the radiation dose depends on the organs in which the radiopharmaceutical accumulates and this may include parts

---

Insight: Some notes on lifetime risks for medical examinations

The risks in Table 11.2 have been derived using the linear no-threshold model (§10.5), with the assumption that the additional risk is related to the natural incidence of cancer in the population, as this model gives the best fit to the epidemiological data. According to this model, since the natural incidence of solid cancers in the population increases with age, the risk of developing radiation-induced cancers also increases. The excess risk of cancer from a single radiation exposure will change as the person gets older, as shown in Figure 11.1. In fact, the period when death from solid tumours induced by radiation exposure is most likely to occur will be when a person is between the ages of 60 years and 90 years. Leukaemia follows a different pattern, with the main period of increased risk extending from 2 years to 20 years following an exposure. The probability of someone developing cancer during their lifetime as a result of a radiation exposure also depends on the age at which they were exposed (§10.7). Figure 11.1 also shows how the risk is thought to vary for exposures received by a child, an adult and a senior citizen. The differences are partly owing to changes in the sensitivity of the tissues and partly to changes in the opportunity for expression. The risk of fatal cancer associated with radiation exposure of a child below 15 years of age is about double that for an adult.

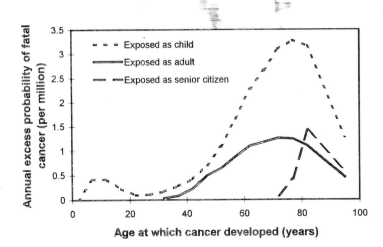

Figure 11.1 Predicted probabilities of the variation in excess risk of fatal cancer throughout life induced by an effective dose of 1 mSv to a female. Data are shown for exposures received by a child (1–4 years), an adult (30–34 years) and a senior citizen (70–74 years).

away from the organ of interest. In particular, as radionuclides are excreted they will accumulate in the bladder and thereby expose sensitive pelvic organs.

The frequency of different X-ray examinations in the UK and the contribution of each to the collective dose is shown in Figure 11.2. It is apparent from this that the examinations giving the highest dose are CT scans of the trunk and certain nuclear medicine examinations. Doses from CT scans make up nearly 40% of the collective patient radiation dose received from X-rays, although they form less than 4% of the examinations carried out, whilst chest X-rays make up 20% of the examinations performed but contribute less than 1% to the collective dose from medical exposures. The flexibility of new CT scanners, the variety of image presentations that can be produced and the speed with which scans can now be performed have led to a proliferation of CT examinations (Chapter 4). Their use for a wider variety of conditions may be justified, but each case should be given careful consideration. The types of examination having the next highest doses are those that involve contributions from fluoroscopy to view parts of the body in real-time, usually using contrast media. Simple radiographic images tend to have lower doses, and digital images recorded as part of fluoroscopic procedures tend to have the lowest doses.

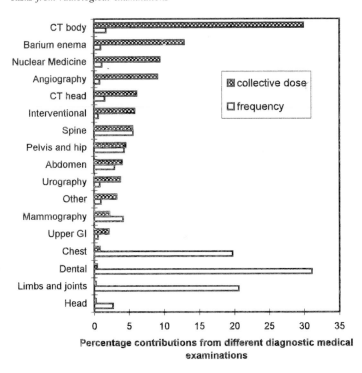

Figure 11.2 Relative frequencies and collective doses for groups of diagnostic medical radiation examinations, expressed as percentages of the total in the UK during the period 1995–2000. X-ray data taken from Hart and Wall (2001); nuclear medicine data taken from UNSCEAR (2000).

11.3 The risk of short-term deterministic effects

Large radiation doses to the skin can cause short-term effects, such as skin erythema and temporary hair loss. Complex and lengthy interventional X-ray procedures do very occasionally lead to short-term effects from high skin doses. The risks are directly related to the radiation dose that the skin receives and every effort will be made to avoid such high doses. If doses are found to have been high enough that injury is likely to occur, the radiology department will pass on the information to the clinician. The patient should be informed of what to expect, since the effects may not be obvious immediately after the exposure and may subsequently cause discomfort and distress. It should be stressed that such effects are extremely rare and it is important not to arouse concern in the patient unnecessarily, since any skin reaction that does occur is more likely to be related to some form of allergic reaction rather than to radiation exposure.

> **Insight: Procedures that could give deterministic effects**
>
> *RF cardiac catheter ablation, transjugular intrahepatic portosystemic stents (TIPS), coronary angioplasty, renal angioplasty, interventional neuroradiology*

In nuclear medicine, deterministic effects such as pruritus and erythema occur occasionally when an injected radiopharmaceutical has extravasated. Radiation doses from diagnostic exposures will not be high enough to produce deterministic effects in organs other than the skin.

The purpose of radiotherapy exposures is to induce deterministic effects to destroy malignant cells. The treatment is planned so that a prescribed dose is delivered to the target and optimisation is performed to minimise the dose to adjacent tissues (Chapter 9). However, deterministic effects will occur in organs surrounding a malignant tumour being treated by radiotherapy and the decision on the radiation dose to be given is a delicate balance between maximising the chance of a successful treatment and minimising the effects on surrounding healthy tissue. There is considerable risk to the patient if the exposure is larger than the prescribed value, while if the dose to the malignant tissue is too small, the treatment is unlikely to be successful.

11.4 Risks to the fetus and the breast-feeding child

11.4.1 The pregnant patient

Risks of inducing harmful effects in a developing embryo or fetus are greater than for adults. The main concern is that the unborn child may develop cancer in the future, and doses of tens of millisieverts more than double the natural risk. The possibility that a child may be more likely to develop cancer before the age of 15 years is of particular concern. Fetal doses from a selection of examinations and associated risks are given in Table 11.3.

The risks during the menstrual cycle and pregnancy are considered to be as follows:

- During the first 10 days of the cycle, there is no increased risk from diagnostic medical exposures.
- In the first 3 weeks post conception, when pregnancy may not have been confirmed, the risk of cancer appears to be much lower than during the remainder of pregnancy. The most likely effect of exposure at this early stage is failure of the pregnancy to develop further. However, because the fetus is so small at this stage, the chance of any effect occurring is extremely low.
- During the remainder of pregnancy, the risks of cancer are those given in Tables 11.1 and 11.3.
- Doses that would be recorded from diagnostic procedures are much less than the threshold for deterministic effects, such as malformation or mental illness.

Table 11.3 Fetal doses and risks of fatal cancer for exposures *in utero* from some diagnostic medical examinations

Term for risk	Examination	Mean fetal dose (mGy)	Risk of cancer to age 15 years for *in utero* exposure
	Incidence in the population		1 in 1300
	Radiology		
Negligible	Chest radiograph (PA)	<0.01	<1 in 3 million
Minimal	Chest CT scan	0.06	1 in 500,000
Very low	Pelvic radiograph (AP)	1.1	1 in 38,000
	Abdominal radiograph (AP)	1.4	1 in 30,000
	Lumbar spine examination (AP and Lat)	1.7	1 in 24,000
	IVU	1.7	1 in 24,000
Low	Barium enema	7	1 in 6000
	Abdomen CT scan	8.0	1 in 4000
	Pelvic CT scan	25	1 in 1300
	Nuclear medicine		
Very low	^{99m}Tc lung perfusion (MAA)	0.2	1 in 160,000
	^{99m}Tc lung ventilation (aerosol)	0.3	1 in 110,000
Low	^{99m}Tc bone scan (phosphate)	3.3	1 in 10,000
	^{99m}Tc dynamic cardiac scan (RBC)	3.4	1 in 10,000
	^{201}Tl myocardial perfusion	3.7	1 in 9000

Data taken from various sources, including National Radiological Protection Board, 1998, and Administration of Radioactive Substances Advisory Committee, 1998.

PA, posteroanterior; AP, anteroposterior; Lat, lateral; IVU, intravenous urogram.

Even the highest fetal doses from diagnostic procedures are unlikely to justify either the risks associated with performance of invasive fetal diagnostic procedures (such as amniocentesis) or the termination of a pregnancy. Following doses in the range tens to hundreds of millisieverts, termination may need to be considered. A dose of 100 mSv during the middle part of pregnancy would be likely to reduce the IQ of the child by 3 points and give an additional risk of 1 in 200 of childhood cancer (§10.7).

Special precautions are taken to minimise the risks when dealing with pregnant patients. The advice about diagnostic radiation exposure of women who may be pregnant is as follows.

- A woman should be treated as though she were pregnant if her period is overdue or clearly missed. This must be taken into account in justification of any exposure.
- No special limitations need apply during the first 3 weeks for most radiation examinations.
- Exposures of tens of millisieverts to the fetus, which could double the natural risk of childhood cancer, should be avoided even in early pregnancy unless there is an overriding clinical need. This risk can be greatly reduced by restricting these procedures to the first 10 days of the menstrual cycle. This will only be necessary for a few procedures, such as CT examinations of the abdomen and pelvis (Table 11.3). High dose procedures for a pregnant patient that are important for management of the patient should only be rearranged if they can be safely postponed until after delivery of the child (Sharp et al 1998).
- Any therapeutic radiation exposure of a woman who may be pregnant must be discussed with the radiotherapy practitioner to decide the appropriate course of action.

11.4.2 The breast-feeding child

In the case of nuclear medicine examinations it is also important that steps are taken to determine whether any female patient is breast-feeding, since some radioactivity will appear in the milk. It may be necessary for breast-feeding to be interrupted following administration of some radiopharmaceuticals (§14.5). The nuclear medicine department will provide the patient with appropriate information if precautions are necessary.

11.4.3 Avoidance of conception following an exposure

In a small number of examinations there may be a need for the patient to avoid conception for a period of time after a medical exposure. This may be because a parent's germ cells have been irradiated or, in nuclear medicine, there is a potential for irradiation of the embryo by a longer half-life radionuclide retained in the mother or appearing in the father's ejaculate and sperm. Precautions for diagnostic examinations would rarely be required and in this case specific instructions would be given by the nuclear medicine department. However, restrictions are more likely to be necessary for therapeutic procedures and these must be discussed with the radiotherapy practitioner.

11.5 Other risks in radiology

While the subject of this book is ionising radiation, the chapter would be incomplete without a mention of other risks that the patient may be exposed to while attending the radiology department. Apart from the obvious ones that are not specific to radiology, such as falling off tables, there are others of more relevance. These can be divided into three categories.

Contrast media

This term is used to describe anything of a differing radiodensity to soft tissue that is administered to a patient to outline a specific organ or organs. They are broadly divided into water soluble and non-water soluble, although gas is used in the GI tract and occasionally in angiography. Water soluble contrast medium is almost always a variation on a tri-iodinated benzene ring, as described more fully in §3.4. As a family of compounds, they have the potential to be allergenic, this being exacerbated in atopic and especially asthmatic patients. The range of reaction types may vary from mild urticaria to anaphylaxis. The latter consists of some or all of a combination of laryngeal oedema, bronchospasm and hypotension and, if not treated promptly with oxygen, adrenaline and intravenous fluids, can be fatal. The incidence of such reactions can be reduced by administration of steroids in the 24 h preceding the examination. It is therefore important that any history of allergies, atopy or asthma should also be sought prior to referring a patient for an examination that involves contrast medium. This must be included with the clinical details. Failure to do this will often lead to the postponement of an examination. Examinations involving intravascular injection of water soluble contrast medium would include intravenous urograms (IVUs), angiography and many CT examinations. Water soluble contrast media can also be used in the GI tract where there is clinical suspicion of a perforation, and they may be either swallowed or administered rectally. Gastrograffin was the original contrast medium for this purpose; it is a high osmolar contrast medium (see §3.4 for a full explanation) but, because of the risk of severe and sometimes fatal pulmonary oedema if aspirated, it has largely been replaced by low osmolar contrast media. The non-water soluble contrast medium is almost exclusively barium sulphate and is used in the GI tract. This is an inert substance that, apart from causing granulomata in the peritoneal cavity if there is a perforation, is relatively safe. Occasionally, patients do suffer allergic reactions but this is in response to the flavourings and other additives rather than the actual barium sulphate.

Anaesthesia

Historically, many patients required a general anaesthetic for pain control during radiology procedures, but with the advent of low osmolar contrast media and modern catheters this is now rare. One procedure where anaesthetic is required, which is currently on the increase, is vertebroplasty involving injection of bone cement into a diseased vertebral body. Many procedures are now performed using local anaesthetics and mild sedation prior to the placement of needles and catheters. General anaesthesia or deep sedation is still used in situations where patients have to be stationary and are unable to co-operate for reasons of age or other medical condition or if already ventilated for intensive care. This is most commonly required in CT and MRI. Both local and general anaesthetics have their attendant risks that should be borne in mind.

Procedure

As alluded to in the previous paragraph, radiology has an ever-increasing number of procedures that are invasive, involving the placement of assorted needles, wires and catheters into virtually any body cavity, whether anatomical or pathological. No invasive procedure is without risk, whether that be damage to the organ that is being treated, to structures that require to be traversed to reach the target organ or structures that are inadvertently hit. Such procedures would include guided biopsy, drainage, angiography and embolisation to mention a few simple ones from a list that continually grows. The risks are specific to the individual procedure and there are books devoted entirely to the subject.

11.6 Justification of medical exposures

11.6.1 Objectives of medical exposures

Because of the risks from ionising radiation, legislation in the UK and other European States requires that every medical exposure is justified (§12.3.1). The broad objectives encompassed within the term medical radiation exposure fall into four categories.

Examinations or treatments directly associated with illness or injury

Almost all the examinations that you will request as a clinician will be within this category. The potential clinical benefit associated with each type of procedure should be sufficient to offset the risk of harm from the radiation exposure. This depends on how the practice will influence the subsequent management of the patient and on what alternative investigations are available.

Exposures forming part of a medical research programme

The subject of research involving medical exposures is dealt with in Chapter 15.

Mass screening of asymptomatic patients and health checks

Mass screening must be justified by weighing the benefit to the individuals who are treated as a result of the screening process against the risk of harm from the radiation exposure to the population being screened. This is dealt with in more depth in Chapter 16.

Medicolegal exposures

The term medicolegal exposures encompasses exposures made for a wide variety of reasons unconnected with clinical management of the person. In some cases there may be a component that relates to a need of the individual, for example:

- assessment of health status for persons seeking insurance;
- occupational health assessment;
- health screening prior to emigration;
- investigation of injury in cases of civil litigation;
- assessment of health status for top class athletes.

These types of request should be treated with caution if the individuals do not have any symptoms, since medically they are not in the direct interest of the individual and so may appear unjustified.

In other cases there is no benefit to the individual and they may prefer not to have the exposure. Here the benefits to society as a whole must be considered in the justification process. Examples of these types of examination are:

- investigation of child abuse;
- search of individuals suspected of concealing drugs within their bodies;
- search of prisoners suspected of concealing objects within their bodies;
- assessment of asylum seekers.

Since these examinations are not linked to the health of the individual, assessment of the need for such exposures and consideration of the risk involved is particularly important.

11.6.2 Justification of individual exposures

Exposures for individual patients must be justified by a trained health care professional with expertise in radiation. This person is called a practitioner and is usually a radiologist, oncologist or radiographer, but may be another individual such as a cardiologist who has had training regarding the appropriateness of relevant radiation examinations and the risks from radiation. Patients may be referred for examinations involving radiation exposure by clinicians from many different specialties. The clinician who refers the patient must supply sufficient, legible, clinical information to enable the practitioner to:

- assess the relevance of the investigation;
- determine how the diagnosis or treatment will affect management of the patient;
- determine whether relevant previous examinations might provide the information required;
- ensure that relevant clinical questions are addressed in the evaluation;
- take account of whether the patient may be pregnant.

Guidance on requesting an examination is given in Chapter 13.

11.6.3 Justification for pregnant patients

Because of the higher risks from radiation exposure of a fetus, a variety of procedures will be in place in an imaging department to identify any female patient who may be pregnant.

- The request form must ask whether the patient may be pregnant and the date of the last menstrual period.
- Signs are displayed prominently in waiting areas, often written in multiple languages, asking patients to inform staff if they are pregnant.
- Female patients of child-bearing age (12–55 years) are questioned directly just before any radiation examination.
- A pregnancy test may be carried out for high dose procedures, such as therapy with radioactive iodine, although it should be remembered that this will miss pregnancies up to 4/5 days post conception.

If the patient may be pregnant, then the justification for the examination will be reviewed (§11.4.1), taking into account questions such as:

- Is the procedure essential at this time or can it be delayed until after childbirth?
- Is there an alternative procedure not involving a radiation exposure?

11.7 Optimisation to minimise risks

11.7.1 Optimisation of technique

In radiology departments, procedures and techniques are optimised to minimise radiation doses from examinations performed without affecting the chance of obtaining the diagnostic information required. Guidance on dose levels is provided by diagnostic reference levels, which can be used in audits of patient dose. The methods use in this optimisation process are discussed in §14.3 for diagnostic radiology and in §14.5 for nuclear medicine.

> **Insight: Examples of optimisation**
>
> **Protection of radiosensitive organs** near to the examination site.
>
> **Taking particular care with high dose procedures** to ensure that skin doses are not large enough to induce deterministic effects.
>
> **Instructions** for stopping medication, food or drink that may interfere with the investigation. These are issued before the procedure and it is important that they are understood by the patient.

11.7.2 Radiation incidents

Imaging departments will have procedures in place to minimise the risk of any incident involving an unintended exposure of a patient to radiation. However, incidents will occur from time to time. Important lessons can be learned from these incidents, as they show how procedures can fail. Hospitals will have systems in place to ensure that any incident is investigated, an assessment made of the radiation dose received and a report prepared.

In the event of an incident involving an unintended exposure, it is advisable for the clinician to inform the patient as soon as possible in order to maintain their confidence, unless there are overwhelming reasons to the contrary. Information on the excess radiation dose that the patient has received and the risk will be provided by the radiation protection service, and the clinician will need to put this in perspective in discussions with the patient.

> **Insight: Action following an incident**
>
> ◊ Recording all necessary data and all actions taken.
> ◊ Notifying the clinician responsible for the patient.
> ◊ Determining whether the incident is notifiable to external statutory agencies (the Department of Health or Health and Safety Executive).
> ◊ Carrying out an investigation to determine how the error occurred and deciding whether procedures need to be revised or equipment replaced.

11.8 The perception of risk

11.8.1 Explanation of risks to patients

There are a variety of circumstances in which a clinician may need to explain the risks from radiation to his/her patient and/or members of the patient's family. The patient may:

- be concerned about the risk from an exposure he/she needs to undergo;
- have received an unintended exposure or an overexposure;
- be involved in a research project using ionising radiation;
- be pregnant and need to have an examination involving a fetal exposure;
- be breast-feeding and need to undergo a nuclear medicine procedure;
- be asked to undergo a medicolegal exposure.

The explanation in these cases is likely to be given by the referring clinician with advice from a medical physics expert, since the risks will depend on the patient's clinical condition and circumstances. The perception of risk by members of the public often relates to the situation or practice that causes the risk rather than the risk itself. Risks from radiation tend to be viewed as being more hazardous because of the nature of the effects. Radiation causes hidden damage that may lead to cancer, itself an illness arousing particular dread. Moreover, there is a greater danger to pregnant women and small children as well as a risk of effects in future generations. The sense of unease and distress is likely to be heightened in the case of an incident where a higher exposure than was intended has imposed an involuntary risk on the patient.

It is important to adopt an open approach when communicating ideas about risk to a patient in order to gain their trust. All the information should be set out clearly, including the benefit from the exposure and the potential risk if it is not carried out. It is best to find out about the patient's view of risk at an early stage. Some patients may be absorbed by the risks inherent in their disease, while others may be more concerned about the side effects of treatment. The explanation should be tailored to the patient's needs, and given in terms that they can readily understand. Particular attention should be paid to any questions raised.

11.8.2 How is risk quantified?

Risk can be described in a variety of ways. An evaluation may be carried out in terms of relative risk, for instance a simple comparison of the effective dose from the medical procedure with that from another, more familiar source of radiation exposure. An example commonly used is natural background radiation; others that may be useful are given in Table 11.4. This technique gives a comparison with the dose from an activity for

Table 11.4 Radiation doses from various sources

Activity	Dose (mSv)
Natural background radiation in UK (1 day)	0.006
Return flight London to Paris (2 h)	0.01
Return flight London to Madrid (4 h)	0.02
Natural background radiation in UK (1 week)	0.04
Return transatlantic flight to New York (14 h)	0.08
Return flight London to Los Angeles (26 h)	0.14
2 weeks in Cornwall (radon)	0.2
2 weeks in a Scandanavian country (radon)	0.4
Average annual dose from radon in UK	1
Annual dose from background radiation in UK	2.3

Table 11.5 Community risk scale

Risk	Comparable population
1 in 10	family
1 in 100	street
1 in 1000	village
1 in 10,000	small town
1 in 100,000	large town
1 in 1 million	city
1 in 10 million	small country
1 in 100 million	large country

which the risk is perceived as being acceptable, and so provides reassurance. However, it does not give a direct indication of absolute risk.

The absolute lifetime risks of stochastic effects (Tables 11.1–11.3) allow risks to be defined in terms of effects on populations. However, small risks such as 1 in 10,000 are difficult to visualise and use of a familiar group with which the patient can relate, such as "about one person in a small town", may be preferable. Population groups have been incorporated into a community risk scale (Table 11.5), which may be useful in setting probabilities in context.

Probabilities may also be given in relative terms (the chance has doubled) rather than absolute ones. This approach is sometimes used in discussion of the risk of

Table 11.6 Lifetime risks of death from various causes

Term for risk	Range of risks	Example causes	Risk estimate
Negligible	Less than 1:1 million	Point at which risk of cancer from a food additive is considered to be of concern	1:1 million
Minimal	Between 1:1 million and 1:100,000	Drowning in bath tub	1:600,000
		Killed by lightning	1:300,000
		Pregnancy for mother	1:170,000
Very low	Between 1:100,000 and 1:10,000	Anaesthesia (risk from single administration)	1:50,000
		Commercial aviation from 1000 miles jet travel per year	1:30,000
		Commuting 2 h per week by train or bus from 40–65 years	1:10,000
Low	Between 1:10,000 and 1:1000	Work in service industry	1:6000
		Murder	1:3000
		Work in manufacturing industry	1:2500
		Accident at work	1:2000
Moderate	Between 1:1000 and 1:100	Cycling for 300 miles per year for next 30 years (accident)	1:1000
		Additional risk of fatal cancer from work with ionising radiation 1 mSv $year^{-1}$ from 40–65 years	1:800
		Accident on the road	1:500
		Living in large city (air pollution)	1:160
High	Greater than 1:100	Lifetime exposure to background radiation (2.3 mSv $year^{-1}$)	1:100
		Pneumonia and influenza	1:30
		Excess risk of cancer in radiologists registered before 1920	1:7
		Smoking 10 cigarettes per day	1:5

Unless otherwise stated, the risks relate to an individual aged 40 years and to activities undertaken within the remainder of their life. Data have been derived for the UK population (National Radiological Protection Board, 1998), but have been supplemented with some data derived from the US population on specific risks. Where lifetime risks have not been available, annual risks have been multiplied by 35, assuming that on average a 40-year-old individual will live to 75 years of age.

childhood cancer following fetal exposure (Table 11.3), but is not applied to the overall risk of malignancy because of the high natural incidence.

Another way of communicating the level of risk is to compare it with that from a different source, such as smoking 10 cigarettes per day or driving a car (Table 11.6). Such comparisons help to calibrate perceptions of risk against real mortality statistics. However, the general public's perception of risk tends to be poor. The likelihood of death due to unusual or dramatic causes, such as plane crashes, is usually overestimated, as these events have a high profile in the press and are easily brought to mind. Thus an open discussion with the patient in which the risk is put into context in their framework is likely to be the best approach.

11.9 Summary

- Diagnostic medical exposures carry a small long-term risk of stochastic effects; cancer and hereditary disease.
- Risks of stochastic effects are greater for the developing embryo and fetus, so exposure of pregnant patients requires particular care in justification.
- The risk of short-term deterministic effects from radiology exposures is small and is limited to a risk of skin erythema for high dose interventional procedures.
- Following radiotherapy for treatment of cancer, deterministic effects may result from irradiation of tissues surrounding the target volume.
- Radiology examinations can involve risks from sources other than radiation, namely the use of contrast media or anaesthesia and the invasive nature of some procedures.
- All medical exposures must be justified for individual patients. This must be undertaken by an appropriately qualified practitioner.
- Medical exposures are optimised and techniques adapted to the clinical problem.
- Explanation of risks from radiation to patients must be undertaken with care, taking account of their own knowledge and perception of risk.

References and further reading

Administration of Radioactive Substances Advisory Committee. *Notes for guidance on the clinical administration of radiopharmaceuticals and use of sealed radioactive sources.* London, UK: Department of Health, 1998.

Hart D, Hillier MC, Wall BF, Shrimpton PC, Bungay D. *Doses to patients from medical X-ray examinations in the UK — 1995 Review*, NRPB Report R289. Chilton, Didcot, UK: National Radiological Protection Board, 1996.

Hart D, Wall BF. *Radiation exposure of the UK population from medical and dental X-ray examinations*, Report NRPB-W4. Chilton, Didcot, UK: National Radiological Protection Board, 2001.

International Commission on Radiological Protection. 1990 Recommendations of the International Commission on Radiological Protection, ICRP Publication 60. *Ann ICRP* 1991;21(1–3).

National Radiological Protection Board. *Living with radiation* (5th edn). Chilton, Didcot, UK: NRPB, 1998.

Sharp C, Shrimpton JA, Bury RF. *Diagnostic medical exposures. Advice on exposure to ionising radiation during pregnancy*. Chilton, Didcot, UK: National Radiological Protection Board, 1998.

United Nations Scientific Committee on the Effects of Atomic Radiation. *Sources and effects of ionising radiation, Vol. 1 Sources; Vol. II Effects*. New York, NY: United Nations, 2000.

Chapter 12

Principles of radiation protection and legislation

AG Brennan

The first part of this chapter summarises the three fundamental principles of radiation protection: justification, optimisation and dose limitation. The first two are the most important in medicine, since dose limitation does not apply for patients if the radiation exposure is clinically justified.

The second part of the chapter selects the most important aspects of the various items of legislation that are relevant to medical uses of ionising radiation.

12.1 Introduction

Ionising radiation must not be used indiscriminately because of the associated risks to health, therefore it is necessary to regulate all applications. The uses that are justified, the types of precautions that are required and the radiation level at which these should be implemented are all the subject of legislation. Radiation protection principles are remarkably consistent throughout the world and are standardised throughout the European Union (EU). They are based on an International Commission on Radiological Protection (ICRP) system of radiological protection for practices involving ionising radiation, together with ICRP and International Atomic Energy Agency (IAEA) recommendations. The ICRP (established in 1928) derives its authority from the scientific standing of its members and the merit of its recommendations. The European Commission has implemented the recommendations through binding Directives to:

- ensure a harmonised approach to radiological protection; and
- facilitate mobility of labour throughout the EU.

Principles of radiation protection for practices

- **Justification of a practice**
  No practice involving exposure to radiation shall be adopted unless it produces sufficient net benefit to the exposed individuals or to society to offset the radiation detriment it causes.
- **Optimisation of protection**
  In relation to any particular source of radiation within a practice, all reasonable steps should be taken to adjust the protection so as to maximise the net benefit, economic and social factors being taken into account.
- **Application of individual dose limits**
  Exposure of individuals resulting from all the practices to which they are exposed is subject to dose limits (other than exposure for medical purposes).

In the context of this book, the most important is Council Directive 97/43 Euratom of 30 June 1997, on health protection of individuals against the dangers of ionising radiation in relation to medical exposures. For more details on the Directive itself, see §15.9. As a result of these directives, a common approach to radiation protection has been implemented in legislation throughout the EU. This chapter deals with UK legislation.

12.2 Systems of radiological protection

The word "*practice*" is employed to describe any use, work activity or operation involving ionising radiation or radioactive material. The ICRP has established a system for such practices based on three principles; justification, optimisation and individual dose limits (see box on page 123).

Radiation exposures can be divided into three categories; occupational, medical and public.

- **Occupational exposures** are those incurred while at work as a result of practices that can be regarded as a responsibility of the employer.
- **Medical exposures** are those incurred by individuals as part of their diagnosis or treatment. These also include exposures incurred by patients or volunteers as part of a programme of biomedical research.
- **Public exposure** encompasses all exposures other than occupational and medical from sources under control.

The principles have been implemented in the following UK legislation:

- Ionising Radiations Regulations 1999 (IRR99) for occupational and public exposure.
- Ionising Radiation (Medical Exposure) Regulations 2000 (IR(ME)R 2000) for medical exposure.

Application of the principles of radiological protection is different for each type of exposure. For example, in the case of a patient undergoing a medical exposure, the individual exposure for that patient has to be justified based on the clinical problem. Optimisation of the exposure still applies in order to minimise the risk to the patient. However, dose limits do not apply as the patient will gain some net benefit from the exposure.

Insight: System of radiological protection for intervention

There are some situations where the radiation does not arise from a practice that is under the control of an individual or corporate body (§12.2), but it may nevertheless be necessary to intervene to reduce human exposure, e.g. after an accident that releases radioactive material to the environment. Intervention is used to describe actions that may be required either in a radiation emergency or to restrict exposure from a natural source (e.g. radon; §1.4.2). For these circumstances, the ICRP recommend a system of radiological protection based on somewhat different interpretations of justification and optimisation. Dose limits are now omitted. The principles of radiation protection for intervention are:

Justification for intervention
The proposed intervention should do more good than harm, i.e. the benefits resulting from the reduction in dose should be sufficient to justify the harm and costs, including social costs, of the intervention.
Optimisation for intervention
The form, scale and duration of the intervention should be optimised so that the net benefit of the reduction of dose, i.e. the benefit of the reduction less the cost of the intervention, should be maximised.

These principles have been implemented in planning for radiation emergencies in the Radiation (Emergency Preparedness and Public Information) Regulations 2001 (REPPIR 2001).

12.3 What do the principles mean?

12.3.1 Justification of practices

Although this may initially be seen as a simple and straightforward concept, it is very difficult to formalise in legislation because of the very wide range of practices that occur. Justification requires consideration of all the relevant benefits and detriments, including those to workers and the general public. Additionally, the detriment to be considered is not confined to that associated with the radiation. It must also include other detriments such as the cost of the practice. The statement clearly says that if there are other ways to achieve the same end, with or without radiation, it is important to analyse the costs and benefits of the alternatives before making a final decision.

Examples of practices in the past that have failed to satisfy the test of justification include the production of jewellery containing radioactive material (*e.g.* radium in luminous dials of watches) and security tags with radioactive sources.

As this is such a difficult concept to include in legislation, it has not been included in IRR99 but will be covered in other free-standing regulations. The concept of justification as applied to individual medical exposures is, however, easier to understand. This is commonly known as clinical justification and has been implemented in IR(ME)R 2000.

The requirement for justification of medical exposure is exercised at two levels, justification of a practice and clinical justification of the procedure for an individual patient. The first level is the use of radiation as a practice for a particular purpose, *e.g.* diagnosis, treatment or mass screening.

12.3.2 Clinical justification

The second level of justification is with respect to the individual patient, and is called "clinical justification". This is clearly a clinical decision involving consideration of:

> ### *Insight: Justification of medical exposure practices*
>
> #### *Example 1: Lumbar spine X-ray examinations for lower back pain*
> *In the past, an X-ray examination of the lumbar spine was relatively common for lower back pain. This practice has now been identified as untenable in many areas and consequently as a waste of resources. It is very useful for trauma patients, but it does not detect disc damage, spinal stenosis or soft tissue damage or injury. In fact, the report of a "normal" X-ray of the lumbar spine may be falsely reassuring, precluding further investigation and thereby inhibiting timely amelioration of the clinical problem.*
>
> *If conservative management of a lower back pain patient has failed, an MRI scan (or CT scan) of the area may demonstrate disc herniation, but it should be noted that approximately 10% of individuals have minor lumbosacral anomalies in the absence of associated symptoms.*
>
> #### *Example 2: Barium meal examinations for dyspepsia*
> *These examinations were relatively common in the past. Unfortunately, they do not detect subtle problems and are insensitive for demonstrating reflux, but they can detect hernias. It is now preferable to perform endoscopy on these patients as this will detect inflammation or ulceration and will allow a biopsy to be performed if required. Barium swallow examinations may still have a place in assessment for surgery.*

(a)   the clinical information supplied;
(b)   the specific objectives of the requested procedure and its relevance to the individual involved;
(c)   the potential benefit and detriment associated with the requested procedure; and
(d)   the efficacy, benefits and risks of suitable alternative techniques that are available and may or may not involve less ionising radiation exposure.

Clinical justification is discussed further in §12.5.

12.3.3 Optimisation of protection

This is commonly known as the *ALARA* principle (*i.e.* keeping doses *as low as reasonably achievable*) or, in the UK, *ALARP* (*as low as reasonably practicable*). In UK law, ALARP has a legal precedence whereas ALARA does not. Basically, this principle says that it is not sufficient merely to comply with dose limits. Since it is assumed that no radiation dose is entirely free from risk, it is important to pay attention to doses below the limit and to reduce them whenever it is reasonably achievable to do so. Optimisation of protection has been applied extensively in the last three decades and has reduced occupational exposure significantly.

For medical exposures, the concept of optimisation is enshrined in legislation and is now a legal requirement of each practical aspect of the exposure. This is achievable through training, good management and close supervision, together with the use of newer technology where appropriate.

12.3.4 Individual dose limits

Dose limits can be regarded as the final back-stop for radiation protection. Strict dose limits and dose constraints are imposed for workers and members of the public to ensure that individuals and their descendants are not exposed to an unacceptable degree of risk from exposure to radiation throughout their life.

The statutory whole-body dose limits (Table 12.1) are intended to control the incidence of serious long-term effects such as cancer and hereditary harm that involve some element of probability (stochastic effects) (see §10.3 and §11.2). Another set of limits protect the eyes, skin and extremities against short-term damage (deterministic effects) (see §10.2 and §11.3). These are noticeably higher due to the known threshold doses for damage to these organs and the relative absence of other radiosensitive organs.

> ### Insight: Some important points about dose limits
>
> ◊ *The dose limit does not mark an abrupt change between a safe and unsafe dose, as the risk of long-term effects is based on probability.*
> ◊ *There are different dose limits for workers and members of the public. This is because slightly higher risks are deemed more acceptable for workers, who receive a net benefit from their employment, than for members of the public whose risk is involuntary.*
> ◊ *It is not sufficient just to keep doses below the limit. The overriding requirement is to keep doses as low as reasonably practicable, the ALARP principle.*

Table 12.1 Annual dose limits for radiation workers and the public

	Dose limits (mSv year^{-1})		
	Employees (>18 years)	Trainees (<18 years)	Any other person
Whole body	20	6	1
Skin (averaged over 1 cm^2)	500	150	50
Extremities (hands, forearms, feet and ankles)	500	150	50
Eyes	150	50	15

12.4 Legislation: The Ionising Radiations Regulations 1999

The Ionising Radiations Regulations 1999 (IRR99) are specific regulations made under the Health and Safety at Work Act to minimise the radiation exposure of employees and members of the public. These regulations embody the three ICRP principles for radiation protection and contain legally prescribed dose limits. Unlike other health and safety legislation, which is by and large goal-setting, IRR99 builds a radiological protection framework around these dose limits. To conform to the wording of the Health and Safety at Work Act 1974 and all other UK safety legislation, reference is made to ALARP (§12.3.3). Certain regulations do not apply to persons undergoing medical exposures (*i.e.* dose limits do not apply) as this is covered in other legislation (IR(ME)R 2000, see §12.5).

The regulations impose a duty on employers to protect employees and other persons against risk arising from work with ionising radiation and they also impose a similar duty on employees, self-employed persons and trainees. Some explanations of the methods used are given in the insight boxes.

Equipment used for medical exposures

There are separate legal requirements for equipment used for medical exposures, specifically its commissioning, safety testing, maintenance and quality assurance throughout its life. Equipment maintenance and quality assurance programmes in radiology, radiotherapy and nuclear medicine are in place to fulfil these requirements. There is also a separate legal notification procedure required for exposures greater than intended owing to equipment malfunction or defect.

Insight: Methods for restricting exposure under IRR99

Prior risk assessment: *IRR99 requires the employer to have assessed the risks prior to starting work with ionising radiation. The employer should decide what measures are necessary to restrict exposure and in particular whether access to certain working areas needs to be restricted to ensure restriction of exposure. This risk assessment should cover both normal circumstances and potential accident situations.*

Restriction of exposure: *These regulations propose a framework for restriction of exposure using a hierarchy of controls. The regulations propose that doses should be restricted first by use of physical control measures (i.e. engineering means and shielding). Only after these have been applied should consideration be given to the use of supporting systems of work (i.e. procedures identifying "dos and don'ts" for employees). Lastly, the employer should provide **personal protective equipment** to further restrict exposure when this is reasonably practicable, e.g. lead/rubber aprons for X-ray staff.*

These regulations propose additional restrictions on exposure for pregnant and breast-feeding employees, and require an investigation to be performed when radiation doses reach a certain level (always less than the annual dose limit).

Radiation protection adviser (RPA): *The regulations require the employer to consult an RPA with specialist knowledge of the scientific aspects of radiation use and protection, and of radiation legislation, and propose a structure for recognition of RPAs. The RPA is usually a medical physicist conversant with the practices.*

Designation of areas: *Designated areas, called **controlled** or **supervised areas**, are those areas where some degree of control or supervision is required to ensure dose optimisation. For example, an X-ray room is likely to be a controlled area and there will be signs warning personnel of the hazard at the entrances. For controlled areas it is possible that an annual dose may be exceeded or there is potential for an accidental exposure. Consequently, entry into and work in these areas are controlled and special procedures must be followed to minimise the dose. For supervised areas some degree of supervision and review is required. Designated areas must be appropriately identified with trefoil warning signs and legends identifying the risk.*

Local rules: *Written local rules are key working instructions to restrict exposure to radiation in controlled and supervised areas. All employees must read the procedures and instructions in local rules and adhere to them whilst in the area. A **radiation protection supervisor** must be appointed by the employer to supervise the arrangements made to ensure compliance with the requirements of the local rules and IRR99 in the designated area.*

Insight: Requirements for dose limits and monitoring under IRR99

Dose limitation: *The regulations impose limits on the doses that employees and other persons may receive in any year (see Table 12.1). Dose limits do not apply to persons undergoing medical exposure or to people who "knowingly and willingly" incur a radiation exposure resulting from the support and comfort of another person undergoing a medical exposure.*

Classification and appointed doctors: *There is a specific requirement to classify persons who are likely to receive 3/10ths of any employee dose limit (Table 12.1) and to ensure adequate medical surveillance of these individuals. This medical surveillance is undertaken by an appointed doctor and comprises:*
◊ *medical examination before first being designated as a classified person;*
◊ *periodic reviews of health at least once a year;*
◊ *special medical surveillance when a relevant dose limit has been exceeded;*
◊ *determining whether special conditions are necessary;*
◊ *a review of health after cessation of work where necessary.*
"Notes of guidance for appointed doctors" under IRR99 is available from the Health and Safety Executive (HSE).

Monitoring of persons: *There are requirements for doses to employees to be monitored to confirm the dose levels to which they are exposed or to measure doses from any incidents in which they may be involved. There are additional requirements for investigations and notification of overexposures.*

12.5 Legislation: Ionising Radiation (Medical Exposure) Regulations 2000

Protection of the patient is provided by the Ionising Radiation (Medical Exposure) Regulations 2000 (IR(ME)R 2000). These regulations cover all medical exposure using ionising radiation in the UK including diagnostic radiology, nuclear medicine, radiotherapy, medicolegal and research exposures and all X-ray screening programmes. These regulations include the concepts of clinical justification and optimisation, which are legal requirements on the duty holders. The main legal duty however, rests with the employer who must have procedures in place for medical exposures.

Insight: Examples of the employer's IR(ME)R procedures

◊ *Identification procedures for the patient.*
◊ *Lists of referrers, practitioners and operators.*
◊ *Procedures for medicolegal exposures.*
◊ *Procedures to determine whether the patient is pregnant or breast-feeding.*
◊ *Quality assurance procedures.*
◊ *Patient dosimetry.*
◊ *Diagnostic reference levels.*
◊ *Procedures for research.*
◊ *Information on written instructions to patients.*
◊ *Report of outcome of the medical exposures.*
◊ *Incident reporting procedure for radiation incidents due to staff error.*

If the procedures are not followed, it is unlikely that best medical practice is being followed and the patient may not receive their medical exposure.

The main duty holders are the practitioner, operator(s) and medical physics expert. Most medical doctors and General Practitioners (GPs) are "referrers" under this legislation, referring the patient for a specialist medical opinion. Although they are not duty holders under IR(ME)R 2000, they must conform to the requirements of the employer's procedures (see Chapter 13).

Practitioner

The main function of the practitioner is to perform the clinical justification for the medical exposure as described in §12.3.2. The practitioner is a health care professional with specialist radiation training, who will most frequently be a radiologist or radiotherapist, but may be a radiographer or a cardiologist or other clinician with appropriate additional training. If the clinical information provided by the referrer is incomplete, the practitioner cannot justify the exposure and it should not be performed. Equally, although the request may have sufficient information for justification, the practitioner may decide that an investigation using ionising radiation is not appropriate and may use an alternative imaging technique involving less or no ionising radiation (*e.g.* ultrasound or MRI).

Operator

The main function of the operator is to optimise the practical aspects of the exposure such that the dose to the patient is minimised while still achieving the clinical objective. Additionally, the operator may authorise the exposure in the absence of the practitioner under a justification protocol agreed with the practitioner if the request conforms to the requirements of the protocol.

An example of the way in which organisational procedures might impact on a patient referred for a radiological examination by a GP is shown in the box.

The patient path

- **Step 1: The patient**
  The patient visits their GP with some clinical symptoms, which are confirmed upon examination. The GP decides that a radiological examination is appropriate.
- **Step 2: The referrer**
  The GP, as a referrer, refers the patient for a radiological investigation. The following information must be supplied: unique patient identification; specific details of the clinical problem to facilitate justification; if applicable, information on the patient's menstrual status; and a signature uniquely identifying the referrer. In addition, the referrer may indicate the examination that is thought to be appropriate.
- **Step 3: The practitioner**
  The practitioner in the radiology department (usually a radiologist or, for prescribed examinations, a radiographer) will review the request and, if it is clinically justified, will indicate the examination to be performed. This may be a different examination to that requested. If the practitioner believes the request contains insufficient information for clinical justification or that the information is incorrect, the examination will not be performed and the request will be returned to the referrer.
- **Step 4: The operator**
  The operator (usually a radiographer or radiologist) will perform the radiological examination as indicated by the practitioner if it has been justified. They will confirm the details on the request and then perform the examination to an agreed protocol, using their skills and training to optimise the exposure and minimising the dose to the patient.
- **Step 5: The report**
  The radiologist (or other trained health professional) will review the images or outcome of the radiological examination and issue a radiological report. This will be sent to the referrer.
- **Step 6: Clinical outcome**
  The referrer (GP) will review the clinical report from the radiologist and decide upon further clinical management of the patient.

Medical physics expert

The medical physics expert is required for consultation on scientific aspects involved in optimisation of the exposure. This includes:

- advice on and measurement of patient doses;
- measurement of equipment performance; and
- advice on medical exposures and associated radiation protection matters.

In some circumstances the relevant medical physics expert required by IR(ME)R 2000 may be the same person fulfilling the role of RPA under IRR99.

12.6 Legislation: Radioactive Substances Act 1993

The Radioactive Substances Act 1993 (RSA 1993) applies to nuclear medicine and radiotherapy. It controls the keeping and use of radioactive materials and the accumulation and disposal of radioactive waste, primarily to protect the public and the environment. All users of radioactive material should inform the Environment Agency, which is responsible for administration of the Act, and will have to register unless any of the various exemptions apply.

All disposals and accumulations of radioactive waste in hospitals have to be authorised except those covered by an exemption. These authorisations cover liquid, solid and gaseous disposals and require strict accounting systems for radionuclides and notifications of disposals to the statutory authorities. Environmental impact assessments are required for the accumulation and disposal of radioactive waste and strict limits apply on the amounts and types of radionuclides that can be held, on the disposal pathways and the amounts disposed. Usually the employer asks an RPA also to perform an advisory role to the employer for RSA 1993 issues.

12.7 Legislation: The Medicines (Administration of Radioactive Substances) Regulations 1978

These regulations (MARS 1978) prohibit administration of radioactive substances except by doctors or dentists holding a certificate issued by the Health Ministers for specified radioactive substances. These certificates are known as *ARSAC (Administration of Radioactive Substances Advisory Committee)* certificates. Certificates are normally only issued to senior staff of consultant status or equivalent. They have a time limit and are specific with respect to both radiopharmaceutical and hospital. It is acceptable that other persons acting on the ARSAC certificate holder's behalf or under their guidance may actually carry out the administration. This transfer of authorisation to administer should be set down in writing. Separate ARSAC certificates are required for research projects in addition to local research ethics committee approval. In fact, most ethics committees require an ARSAC certificate to accompany the application, or an undertaking that an application has been made to ARSAC (see Chapter 15).

12.8 Summary

- The three principles of radiation protection are justification of a practice, optimisation of protection and application of dose limits.
- Types of exposure covered by legislation are occupational, medical and public exposure.
- IRR99 covers the radiation protection of employees and members of the public.
- IR(ME)R 2000 covers the radiation protection of patients and volunteers involved in medical research.
- Separate legislation (REPPIR 2001) covers potential radiation emergencies.
- The main duty holders under IR(ME)R are the practitioner who justifies the exposure, the operator who carries out practical procedure and the medical physics expert who provides the scientific input.
- Duty holders under IR(ME)R must have appropriate training and experience relating to the function they perform.

- Under IR(ME)R, if a referral does not contain sufficient information or conform to the employer's procedures, it will be rejected and returned to the referrer.
- In nuclear medicine and radiotherapy, control of radioactive substances and administration of these substances to patients are governed by RSA 1993 and MARS 1978, respectively.

References and further reading

Administration of Radioactive Substances Advisory Committee (ARSAC). *Notes for guidance on the clinical administration of radiopharmaceuticals and use of sealed sources*. Chilton, Didcot, UK: National Radiological Protection Board, 1998.

European Communities. Council Directive 97/43/Euratom of 30 June 1997, on health protection of individuals against the dangers of ionising radiation in relation to medical exposure, and repealing Directive 84/466/Euratom. *Official Journal of the European Communities*, L180. Luxembourg: CEC, 1997.

Health and Safety Executive. *Work with ionising radiations: Approved code of practice and guidance* (Ref. L121). London, UK: HSE, 2000.

Health and Safety at Work etc Act 1974. London, UK: HMSO, 1974.

Institute of Physics and Engineering in Medicine. *Medical and dental guidance notes. A good practice guide to implementing ionising radiation legislation in the clinical environment*. York, UK: IPEM, 2002.

International Commission on Radiological Protection. 1990 Recommendations of the International Commission on Radiological Protection, ICRP Publication 60. *Annals of the ICRP* 1991;21(1–3).

Ionising Radiation (Medical Exposure) Regulations 2000 (Statutory Instrument 2000 No. 1059). London, UK: HMSO, 2000.

Ionising Radiations Regulations 1999 (Statutory Instrument 1999 No. 3232). London, UK: HMSO, 1999.

Medicines (Administration of Radioactive Substances) Regulations 1978 (Statutory Instrument 1978 No. 1006). London, UK: HMSO, 1978.

National Radiological Protection Board. *Guidance notes for dental practitioners on the safe use of X-ray equipment*. Chilton, Didcot, UK: NRPB, 2001.

Radiation (Emergency Preparedness and Public Information) Regulations 2001 (Statutory Instrument 2001 No. 2975). London, UK: HMSO, 2001.

Radioactive Substances Act 1993. London, UK: HMSO, 1993.

Chapter 13

Requesting an X-ray

RH Corbett

> In some respects this is the most important chapter in the book for doctors who are referring patients for diagnostic examinations. It deals with a number of very basic questions. Is a radiation examination appropriate? Which test is most suitable? How should the request form be written?

13.1 Introduction

Everything presented in the earlier chapters has been aimed at providing enough knowledge to enable the implications, both good and bad, of using ionising radiation to be understood. It is now time to apply that knowledge.

Patients may believe that "X-rays are good for you" as "they tell the doctor what is wrong". Certainly, if properly used, ionising radiation can be a very useful tool in the investigation, management and treatment of patients, but it will not necessarily give the information that is required or indeed give anything useful at all. The trick is to use ionising radiation only when it can be of benefit to the patient. Sometimes this is not easy. Unfortunately it is all too easy to request another test, perhaps involving X-rays, perhaps not. This may allow you to move on to another patient when you cannot think what else to do, but you only defer a decision that still has to be made and waste scarce health service resources into the bargain.

13.2 Deciding whether a radiation examination is appropriate

Medicine is sometimes said to be the art of interpretation of scientific information. When dealing with a patient, it is the aim of the clinician to reach a diagnosis, to instigate treatment and then to monitor that treatment. A working diagnosis is made for any patient after taking a careful history and making a thorough, appropriate physical examination. From your knowledge of and training in medicine, you will know the signs, symptoms, physical findings and progress of disease. To use tests properly, you have to turn this knowledge around and look at it from an alternative view. So with your working diagnosis, you have to select tests that are able, or are likely to be able, to confirm or refute the presence of some of the signs or symptoms to be expected if the working diagnosis is correct. This principle applies to all tests, not just to those that use ionising radiation.

> **Cochrane's Law**
>
> - Before you request a test, you should first ask yourself what you are going to do if the test is positive, then ask yourself what you are going to do if the test is negative.
> - If the answers are the same, do not do the test.

You should always ask the question "Will the test result affect *patient management*?" It may be that the health of a patient is such that a test is only being considered as just something to do, when a decision has already been taken on a course of action. The principle should be that if the outcome of a test will not affect your management, then the test is not required. This is known as Cochrane's Law.

13.3 What is the correct test to request?

Sometimes it is difficult to know what is the best test to request. In years gone by, it was traditional to start off with a "simple" test, *e.g.* a plain abdomen film, then to move on to a contrast examination and to tests of increasing complexity and radiation dose. This is no longer considered good practice. It is best to use the test that has the highest probability of delivering the most useful information. Such tests may have a high radiation dose. This does not matter, provided that the test is really justified, is carried out carefully and is performed only once. Then the use of the radiation is worthwhile. However, as part of the justification process, consideration will be given to the possible use of alternative tests that do not use ionising radiation. If you are not sure which test, if any, will help to reach a diagnosis, then go to the X-ray department and find a friendly radiologist with whom you can discuss your patient.

13.4 Referral guidelines

Recommendations in the RCR guidelines

Five categories have been specified

- Indicated
- Not indicated initially
- Indicated only in specific circumstances
- Not indicated
- Specialised investigation

Guidelines have been published by the Royal College of Radiologists (RCR) and the European Community, "Making the best use of a department of clinical radiology" and "Referral guidelines for imaging", respectively. The RCR guidelines are now in the 5th edition. Possession of a copy is essential for proper use of an X-ray department. Most hospitals will give a copy of "Making the best use of a department of clinical radiology" to new staff. The European Commission's version (based on the RCR's 4th edition) is also available on the Internet. These guidelines are used by X-ray departments to help in deciding whether or not a particular examination is appropriate.

Both versions are pocket sized and designed to be easy to use. They are laid out by system and clinical problem. The main investigations have been assessed and a best recommendation is provided, together with a comment on the status of the scientific evidence used to provide the recommendation. The evidence has been graded into three categories, A, B and C, where A is randomised controlled trials, meta-analyses or systematic reviews, B is robust experimental or observational studies and C is other evidence where the advice relies on expert opinion and has the endorsement of respected authorities.

A couple of examples from the guidelines are given in the box on page 135 for information.

13.5 The art of writing a request form

13.5.1 The purpose of a request

It is important to remember that a request form is actually a request for a consultation by another professional, usually another doctor, and usually a consultant. When you ask another doctor, albeit a physician or surgeon or whoever, to see your patient and advise, you will always give an indication of the problem, with relevant history, physical details and all other relevant information. The same must apply to the completion of any request form, *e.g.* Figure 13.1. After all, the form is merely a stylised version of a letter, aimed at obtaining all necessary information to carry out the correct test for the benefit of your patient. What is needed on the form is demographic information about the patient, their clinical history and practical information about the patient's needs.

13.5.2 Demographic information

Full name: "P Smith" is not good enough. The X-ray department is likely to have many "P Smiths" registered, so full name, please.

Insight: Examples from the RCR guidelines

Lumbar spine
Clinical problem 1: Chronic back pain with no pointers to infection or neoplasm
Possible investigation: Plain X-ray lumbar spine
Recommendation: Indicated only in specific circumstances
Scientific basis: Grade C
Comment: Degenerative change is common and non-specific. The main value is in younger patients, e.g. under 20 years, or in those over 55 years

Possible investigation: MRI
Recommendation: Specialised investigation, to be discussed with radiologist
Scientific basis: Grade C
Comment: MRI is considered the first-choice investigation, when symptoms persist, are severe or when management is difficult. Note that negative findings may be helpful

Clinical problem 2: Acute back pain, disc herniation; sciatica with no adverse features
Possible investigation: Plain X-ray lumbar spine
Recommendation: Indicated only in specific circumstances
Scientific basis: Grade C
Comment: Acute back pain is usually due to conditions that cannot be diagnosed on plain X-ray (osteoporotic collapse is an exception)

Possible investigation: MRI or CT
Recommendation: Specialised investigation
Scientific basis: Grade B
Comment: Demonstration of disc herniation requires MRI or CT and shoud be considered after failed conservative management. MRI preferred. Clinico-radiological correlation is important as a significant number of disc herniations are asymptomatic

Plain abdomen X-ray
Clinical problem: ? constipation
Possible investigation: Plain abdomen X-ray
Recommendation: Indicated only in specific circumstances
Scientific basis: Grade B
Comment: May be useful in geriatric and psychiatric specialties to show extent of fecal impaction

[Reproduced with permission from the Royal College of Radiologists]

Date of birth: This seems simple, but regularly there are problems with any given patient having two or more different dates of birth. Check the case records to see that there is only a single date of birth. Check also with the patient.

Address: Look in the case records of a few patients to see how often they change address. Some move accommodation every other month. Incredible, you may say, but very true. As the saying goes, "there is nowt so funny as folk". So check that the address you provide is current. If the patient has moved recently, give the old address as well.

HOSPITAL RADIOLOGY DEPARTMENT			

X-RAY No.

Hospital No.

Name:

Address:

D.O.B.

Tel no.   **Ward No.**

Consultant/
GP Stamp
(inc. tel no.)
Referring Clinician:

Status:

SIGNATURE:_____
Date   **Page/ext no.**

Transport (please tick)
Walking   Chair
Trolley   Ambulance

Justified by:
Prep: *Appoint:*

Operator:
Pat ID: *LMP*   *Ref Sig*

Essential info
Is patient diabetic
                    Yes / No
Treatment

Contrast Exams
Asthma   **Yes / No**
Hay fever **Yes / No**
Allergies **Yes / No**
Reactions **Yes / No**

LMP
To be completed for all
female patients between
the age of 12 to 55 years
Is Patient Pregnant
                    Yes / No
Date of LMP:

Observe pregnancy
rule?   **Yes / No**
Sign

MR Exams:
Pacemaker
                    Yes / No
Foreign
Bodies/Implant
                    Yes / No
Recent Surgery
                    Yes /No
(Detail Below)

EXAMINATION REQUESTED:

Clinical Information What question should this examination answer?

Figure 13.1 Example of an imaging department request card.

Patient location: Is the patient in a ward, if so, which ward, or is he/she attending from a clinic or as an outpatient?

Last menstrual period (LMP)/pregnancy: You must give the patient's date of last period if they are female between 12 years and 55 years of age. This allows the possibility of scheduling tests outside times of possible early pregnancy where the test involves exposure of the abdomen. If the patient is pregnant, alternative means of assessment may be required, *e.g.* ultrasound. It can be embarrassing enquiring about a patient's private life, but remember that a patient whose husband/partner has had a vasectomy may not be their only partner.

All this will help the X-ray department to identify the patient and to determine whether they have attended before. New reports and X-rays can then be amalgamated with older ones to provide a more complete record. It may be found that the very test that you have requested was carried out recently and the patient had not thought that it was important enough to tell you, thus leading to unnecessary repeated tests. Consideration of previous tests is part of the process of justification, which must be carried out for every request for a radiological procedure.

13.5.3 Clinical history

On every request card there is a space for clinical information. As a referrer, you are required legally to provide this information, but it must be pertinent. What is required is a brief synopsis of the current clinical problem, relevant previous history and what you hope to learn from the test. It is amazing how often a barium meal is requested following a gastrectomy without this information being given on the request form. As part of the justification process, this information will be assessed. If it is found wanting, the test will be refused. The refusal may happen in various ways. A standard form may be sent back to you or your consultant. This will lead to delays in the management of your patient, and probably much aggravation, most of which will fall on you. A radiographer may call you on the phone — further inconvenience and aggravation, especially at 3 a.m. A radiologist may call you. It is no use saying "I just did what my SHO told me". The radiologist will merely refuse the procedure and demand that your consultant calls. Why cause problems for yourself? Fill in the form properly every time. Remember, no patient history means no examination.

> **Essential clinical information on a properly completed request form**
>
> - Pertinent current clinical information
> - Pertinent past history
> - The question that needs to be answered
> - Doctor in charge of the patient
> - Referring doctor's contact details, *e.g.* bleep or GP practice number

Sometimes the radiologist will call to discuss your request. It is the radiologist's task to assess requests and to decide whether a test appears relevant and indeed necessary to the patient's management. Quite often the radiologist will ask further questions and may suggest an alternative test or course of action. This is part of the process of obtaining a useful radiological opinion. Often appearances on an X-ray film will have several possible causes. Good clinical information can go a long way to resolving ambiguities and to suggesting appropriate further tests.

Do not forget to provide the name of the doctor in charge of the patient, together with your name if different and contact details, *e.g.* bleep number. All this must be written legibly. If not, the card will be returned.

13.5.4 Practical information

What else is needed? Yes, there is more. The X-ray department will require practical information, which will enable the examination to be organised properly and will take account of the patient's needs.

- Is your patient able to walk? Is a wheel chair or trolley needed?
  Porters are great guys, but they get angry if they have to go and fetch a trolley when they came with a wheelchair. It also causes unnecessary delay.
- Is an ambulance needed to get the patient to hospital? If so who is to order it — the ward, GP or X-ray department?
- Is your patient in plaster?
  It is not easy to carry out a barium enema examination on a patient in a plaster jacket or with a leg in plaster. Yet this is a not infrequent request.
- **Sign the card**. No test will be done without a signed request card.

13.5.5 Other relevant patient information

There are sections on the request card that may seem irrelevant. But think, "Why are they there?"

Diabetes
Patients who are diabetic may be required to change their treatment regimen if they have to fast for a procedure. If they are taking Metformin, they may need to stop this before a test to avoid potential fatal interaction with contrast media.

Allergies and asthma
If a patient with these conditions is to have an injection of intravenous or even intra-arterial contrast medium, then they may require steroid cover to avoid possible contrast medium reactions.

Breast-feeding
Patients who are breast-feeding require special instructions when undergoing nuclear medicine examinations. (See §5.5 and §14.5.)

Reactions

If a patient has had a previous reaction to contrast media, you must give this information. Always remember to ask your patient.

MRI

Special information is needed for MRI requests. Does your patient have a pacemaker? Have they had a foreign body or implant? MRI can cause metallic objects inside a body to move, with potentially fatal results.

CT

Has your patient any implants, *e.g.* hip/knee implant, aneurysm clip. These can significantly degrade a CT scan (§4.7.3).

Finally, check that you have completed all sections of the request card, signed it and then send it to the X-ray department with appropriate priority.

13.6 Some problems

Problems will occur with inadequate demographic information. A simple but obvious problem occurs when patients are moved to another ward, or worse, discharged and the X-ray department is not informed. This leads to wasted appointments, patients being prepared and waiting patiently in one place while the department looks for them elsewhere or assumes that they have not turned up for their appointment. When eventually they are found or the ward calls to enquire, the radiologist may no longer be able to carry out the examination at that time.

Despite best endeavours, some patients have multiple registrations. The commonest cause is different dates of birth. Bad writing can lead to incorrect entering of the data in the X-ray department computer system. For example, a badly written 5 or an 8 can be misread as the other. This can mean that essential previous information is not available, either to the radiologist or the referring clinician.

Requests will be rejected with poor or inadequate history. There has to be a clear reason for the request, such as "poor air entry left lung" or maybe "creps at bases".

A request such as "No films at clinic — X-ray please" does not justify another examination. Although it might be inconvenient if films are not available, an X-ray must not be taken just because someone forgot to send for films for the clinic, even if they were obtained in a different hospital. This is inappropriate use of radiation. If you have a patient coming for review or referral from elsewhere, it is essential to insist that all previous relevant X-ray requests are indicated and the films/results provided in advance.

> **Examples of inadequate or inappropriate history**
>
> - Routine chest X-ray
> - Pre-op
> - Post-op
> - Films lost
> - Films elsewhere — please repeat
> - Medicolegal need only
> - Follow-up
> - ? fracture

13.7 Summary

- Only request a test involving ionising radiation if it will affect the management of the patient.
- Unnecessary requests give an avoidable radiation dose to the patient and waste scarce health service resources.
- Use the RCR guidelines to ensure that you are requesting the right test and discuss the patient with a radiologist if you are unsure.
- Include the patient's full name, date of birth and address clearly on the request.
- Include current pertinent clinical information and relevant clinical history.
- State the clinical question that needs to be answered.
- For female patients aged 12–55 years, check whether they could be pregnant and write the date of their LMP on the request.

- Provide practical information about the patient's mobility, transport requirements and physical condition, which may be needed for organising the test.
- Fill in all the parts of the request form regarding diabetes, allergies and reactions.
- Information on breast-feeding will be required for nuclear medicine examinations and on any metallic implants for MRI.
- Give the name of the doctor in charge of the patient and your own contact details.
- Sign the request.

References

European Commission. *Referral guidelines for imaging*, Radiation Protection 118. Luxembourg: European Commission, 2000.

Royal College of Radiologists. *Making the best use of a department of clinical radiology* (5th edn). London, UK: RCR, 2003.

Chapter 14

Personal protection

DG Sutton

This chapter contains practical guidance on ways to protect both patients and staff from unnecessary radiation exposure. It is aimed at those who may be involved in any use of ionising radiation, even if this only extends to being present in a theatre when a mobile image intensifier is operated or working in a ward to which patients return after nuclear medicine scans.

14.1   **The hazard from radiation**
14.2   **Time, distance and shielding**
14.3   **Protection of the patient in radiology**
14.4   **Staff protection in radiology**
14.5   **Patient protection in nuclear medicine**
14.6   **Staff protection in nuclear medicine**
14.7   **Summary**

14.1 The hazard from radiation

Ionising radiation is hazardous whether it arises from a source outside the body, when it is called external radiation, or from radioactive material inside the body, when it is called internal radiation. In radiology, the hazard is from external radiation. The patient is exposed to a beam of X-rays, called the primary beam, and receives a radiation dose from both this radiation and from radiation scattered inside the body. Most of the dose to the patient arises from the primary beam. Staff, on the other hand, should only be exposed to radiation that is scattered from the patient. They should never be exposed to the primary beam.

The situation is different in nuclear medicine where a radiopharmaceutical is injected directly into the patient (see Chapter 5). The radiation dose to the patient arises from radioactivity accumulating in internal organs (internal radiation), whilst staff can receive an external radiation dose from the patient who is to all intents and purposes a radioactive source. There are other possible causes of staff exposure. Needle stick injury during or after the injection will result in internal radioactive contamination of the staff member. There is potential for internal exposure arising from airborne contaminants from ventilation scans. Any radioactivity spilt onto surfaces such as benches (contamination), if not identified and removed, can easily be ingested either through the skin or by hand to mouth contact — this is the most likely cause of internal exposure. Contact with patients' bodily fluids during nursing procedures can also result in contamination of the skin. Points to remember are given in the box.

External and internal radiation

- In radiology, the hazard is from external radiation only.
- In nuclear medicine, the hazard can arise from both internal and external radiation.

14.2 Time, distance and shielding

14.2.1 Time

It stands to reason that the longer someone is exposed to radiation, the greater the dose they will receive. Points to remember are given in the box.

Minimise the time that you (and the patient) are exposed to radiation

- In radiology this means: the beam should be on for as short a time as possible. Do not enter the room unless absolutely necessary for the procedure.
- In nuclear medicine this means: remember that the patients are radioactive. Don't practice your bedside manner with them. No long chats etc. — but do not keep away from them either. Patient care should not be compromised. Remember that the radionuclide used is usually ^{99m}Tc, which has a 6 h physical half-life and an effective half-life that is usually much less owing to excretion of the radiopharmaceutical.

14.2.2 Distance

The further one is away from a source of radiation, the lower the radiation dose rate from the source. In most cases it is reasonable to assume that the inverse-square law applies, that is the dose rate (and hence the dose in any given time period) varies inversely with the square of the distance from the source. Thus, at 2 m it is one-quarter of that at 1 m, at 3 m it is one-ninth, at 4 m it is one-sixteenth, and so on. Points to remember are given in the box.

Keep your distance

- You should be present during a radiology procedure only if required.
- The dose rate from radioactivity inside a nuclear medicine patient will be lower at the bottom of the bed than at the patient's side.
- In the case of mobile radiography on a ward, you should stay at least 2 m away from the X-ray machine whilst the radiographer is performing the procedure. If your presence is required any closer, you should wear a lead apron.

14.2.3 Shielding

X- and γ-rays are attenuated by dense materials (§1.3.2). The denser the material, the greater the amount of attenuation. For example, X-ray rooms are often constructed of high density concrete or have lead sheet in the walls so that the doses outside the room comply with legal requirements. If one were to rely on distance alone, such rooms would have to be very large. Similarly, operators' consoles are shielded to protect staff, and image intensifier units are often surrounded by lead curtains to enable the radiologist to work close to the patient. In radiology, *lead/rubber aprons* and *thyroid shields* (Figure 14.1) are often used to reduce the radiation dose to staff from scattered radiation.

This is not the case in nuclear medicine. Because of the way that the shielding provided by a material decreases with the energy of the radiation, a lead apron designed to protect against the 140 keV γ-rays from ^{99m}Tc would be so heavy that you could not wear it! However, the patients themselves absorb some of the radiation and so will

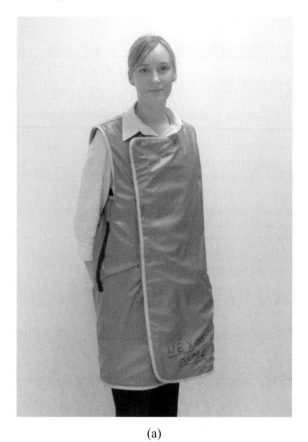

(a)

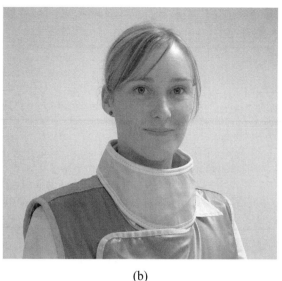

(b)

Figure 14.1 Lead rubber protection used in radiology to protect against scattered radiation: (a) apron to protect the body and (b) thyroid shield (reproduced with permission of G Phanco and L Lindsay).

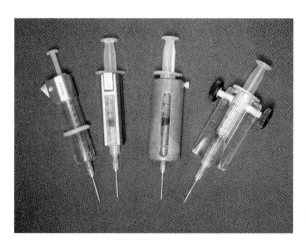

Figure 14.2 Syringe shields of various types. The right-hand shield is made of Perspex for shielding against β-radiation; the others incorporate lead or tungsten to protect against γ-rays (reproduced with permission of G Phanco).

provide a certain degree of shielding. As a result, provided that reasonable adherence is paid to the principles of distance and time, personal protective shielding is not required when attending to and nursing patients who have had diagnostic nuclear medicine examinations. However, *lead pots* or shielded boxes are used to transport and store radiopharmaceuticals, and *syringe shields* made of lead or tungsten should be used to protect the fingers of the operator whilst injections are being performed (Figure 14.2).

Points to remember are given in the box.

Use shielding when available

- The use of shielding can reduce the radiation dose and dose rate to members of staff and the public to acceptable levels in radiology.
- The thickness of shielding materials required in nuclear medicine applications means that in many cases it is not practicable to use it for personal protection from patients.
- Shielding should not just be thought of in terms of lead. In nuclear medicine, simple barrier techniques, such as the wearing of latex gloves whilst injecting patients and the use of face masks during lung ventilation examinations, can be thought of as the application of shielding against internal contamination.

14.3 Protection of the patient in radiology

14.3.1 Procedural approach

Protection of the patient in radiology involves not only the application of technology or indeed the principles of time, distance and shielding. These are all, of course, important, but equally relevant are what might be termed procedural measures. Those that are the responsibility of the referrer are discussed in Chapter 13, but others relate to the practitioner and operator. If not carried out, they can all result in unnecessary radiation being

---

Insight: Uses of equipment and technology in reducing patient dose

Pulsed fluoroscopy: In the most elementary form of fluoroscopy equipment (§3.3.2) the radiation is on continuously and images are displayed on a television screen at 25 frames per second. Modern equipment allows the radiation to be pulsed and this can give a lower dose without any loss of diagnostic information. For example, if the radiation is pulsed 12.5 times per second and every second frame is repeated on the TV screen, it is unlikely that an observer would notice any difference in image quality, yet less radiation would be delivered to the patient. In some applications, pulse rates as low as three frames per second are adequate.

The last image hold facility: Modern image intensification equipment holds the last image on the television screen when the operator takes his or her foot off the foot switch. Thus, it is not necessary to expose the patient continuously to radiation to identify essential landmarks.

X-ray beam filtration: X-ray beams contain a lot of low energy photons when they are generated. Most of these would interact in the skin of the patient to give a high skin dose and would be unlikely to contribute to the X-ray image. Aluminium filters are therefore used in all X-ray equipment to remove most of these photons (see §1.3.2).

Additional beam filtration: In some procedures, for example cardiac angiography, the skin dose accumulated over the length of the examination may be so high that there is a risk of inducing deterministic effects (§10.2). A greater proportion of the lower energy photons can be removed and the patient's skin dose can be reduced significantly by adding special copper foil filters. Many modern image intensifier units allow the user to add extra copper filters. These will slightly reduce image quality, and the degree of trade off between image quality and dose that is acceptable will depend on the application.

Gonad shields: Gonad shields, which are just shaped pieces of lead, are used to reduce the radiation dose to radiosensitive organs.

---

delivered to a patient. Some reminders and examples are given here.

- Fill in the request card appropriately.
- Only request a CT of the relevant area.
- X-ray the right patient.
- X-ray the patient only when the examination is justified.
- Do not X-ray the same patient twice for the same reason.
- If appropriate, determine whether the patient is, or might be, pregnant.

14.3.2 Technology/equipment

Choice and use of X-ray equipment will inevitably affect the radiation dose delivered to the patient. These matters are not exclusively the realm of the specialist in radiology, because other medical staff may have responsibilities involving the use of fluoroscopic X-ray equipment for procedures such as pacemaker insertions, cardiac angiography, and orthopaedic and urological procedures. If you are involved in investigations using fluoroscopic equipment, you need to be aware of the technological factors that affect patient dose and some of these are considered in the Insight box on page 144.

14.3.3 Technique

Radiological technique plays a large part in reducing doses both to patients and staff. Many techniques that result in a reduced dose to the patient will also give a lower dose to staff who are present. Some measures that can be taken are explained in the Insight box below.

Insight: Methods of minimising patient dose in radiology

*Use the tightest collimation possible. The area of the X-ray beam is restricted by **collimators**. Use of a beam tightly collimated to the region being investigated will irradiate a smaller volume of the patient's tissues and hence give a lower dose.*

Use the highest kV and lowest mA that will give an acceptable image. The X-ray tube output is determined both by the tube voltage (kV) and by the current flowing through it (mA). The higher the kV the lower the entrance skin dose, as a higher proportion of the X-ray photons will pass through the patient to form the image. However, since there will be less contrast at higher kVs (§3.2), the overall image quality will be poorer. The kV and mA for fluoroscopy are usually controlled according to predetermined relationships. There are often a number of different options that can be used and it is important to select the correct one for the procedure being performed to minimise the dose to the patient whilst obtaining an adequate level of image quality.

Choice of projection: In some cases it is possible to choose projections so that radiosensitive organs are distant from the surface on which the X-ray beam is incident. An example is the use of the posteroanterior (PA) chest examination, which results in a reduced radiation dose to the breasts compared with the anteroposterior (AP) projection.

In fluoroscopy, position the image intensifier as near to the patient as possible and the X-ray tube as far away as you can. The further the X-ray tube is from the patient, the lower the skin entrance dose.

In fluoroscopy, only use X-rays when you have to. Keep your foot on the pedal for as short a time as possible. Use the last image hold facility whenever possible.

The dose rate to the skin will be greater for large patients. This is because a smaller proportion of the radiation will pass through a heavy patient and so a higher radiation intensity will be required to form an image. As a result, deterministic effects can occur more readily if exposure times are long.

14.3.4 Patient dose audit

Audit of radiation doses plays an important part in patient protection since it provides an important feedback mechanism and a link to clinical governance. Audit can be performed using a variety of patient dose related elements such as skin entrance dose, dose–area product or screening time. Regulations governing the use of ionising radiation in medicine explicitly require that patient doses are measured for a representative sample of examinations on a regular basis and compared with nationally recommended diagnostic reference levels.

Insight: Diagnostic reference levels

Diagnostic reference levels (DRLs) provide guidance on the dose levels that should not normally be exceeded for an average patient undergoing a diagnostic examination.

In diagnostic radiology, DRLs are set in terms of practical dose measurement quantities (see box on page 110) and values established from surveys of dose levels in UK hospitals. DRLs provide a practical tool to assist in identification of poor practice and so aid in optimisation.

14.4 Staff protection in radiology

Employers have a duty to ensure that employees receive radiation doses that are as low as reasonably practicable (ALARP — see §12.3.3). Employees share in that duty and are required to use any protective equipment provided by the employer, to wear personal dosimeters provided by the employer and to exercise due care whilst using

---

Insight: Factors affecting staff doses in radiology

***Lead aprons** do not provide adequate protection against the primary beam, they only protect against scattered radiation. Since radiation scatters in all directions, aprons should wrap around the body to provide protection on all sides (Figure 14.1a).*

Up to 100 kV, an apron containing 0.25 mm thick lead is sufficient, above this you should wear a 0.35 mm lead apron. In general, a 0.25 mm apron is sufficient for theatre work. Wearing a much thicker lead apron is not particularly efficient, causing only a small reduction in the effective dose. Ask your radiation protection adviser for advice on wearing a thyroid collar if you perform a lot of procedures during which you need to stand near to the X-ray tube (Figure 14.1b).

***Personal dosimeters** do not provide any protection against X-rays. They are worn to check after the event that you have been following the correct procedures and that you have not exceeded any dose limit (Figure 14.3). If you are issued with a dosimeter, it must be worn.*

Wear your dosimeter under your lead apron, as this is standard practice in the UK. If the dosimeter is worn above the apron, it provides misleading information about the radiation dose you have received.

***The X-ray beam**: Always collimate the X-ray beam to the area of interest — the amount of scattered radiation to which you are exposed is directly related to the volume of the patient that is irradiated.*

Never put your hand in the X-ray beam. This is an obvious statement, but nevertheless some procedures (in orthopaedics for example) require special care to be taken as manipulations can be performed very close to the primary beam.

***Undercouch X-ray tubes**: If possible, use a geometry in which the X-ray tube is under the table and the intensifier is above it. Provided that the intensifier is close to the patient and the tube as far away as possible, this will result in lower doses to both patient and staff. There will be more scattered radiation to your upper body, head and eyes with the X-ray tube above the table.*

Complex fluoroscopic units used for higher dose procedures such as interventional radiology or cardiology will have additional protection such as lead/rubber drapes attached to the couch and lead/glass screens to protect the eyes and thyroid (Figure 14.4).

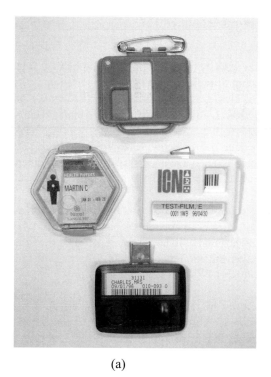

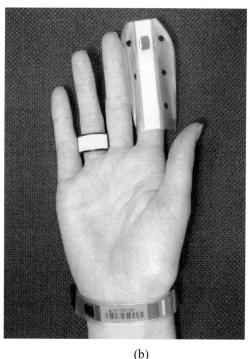

(a)   (b)

Figure 14.3 Examples of personal dosemeters used for (a) body monitoring and (b) measuring the dose on different parts of the hand (reproduced with permission of G Phanco and L Lindsay). Several examples of each are shown, although normally only one would be worn. The type of monitor and the position chosen would depend on the application and would be determined with advice from the Radiation Protection Advisor.

radiation to ensure that the ALARP principle is adhered to. Some factors that are important are discussed in the Insight box. One thing to remember is that in many cases a lower dose to the patient will result in a reduced dose to the members of staff who are present.

Pregnant staff

If you are pregnant and may be exposed to radiation, you should inform your employer that you are pregnant. There are special arrangements for pregnant staff that the employer must put into place, but only when he/she is informed of the fact.

Members of the public

In general, members of the public should not be present during radiological examinations to minimise their potential exposure to radiation. There are, however, some exceptions, such as in the case of paediatric investigations when parents or guardians (provided they are suitably instructed) can be considered to have the status of "*comforters and carers*". This is a class of person with slightly relaxed radiation dose limits over members of the general public because of the direct assistance they are giving to the patient.

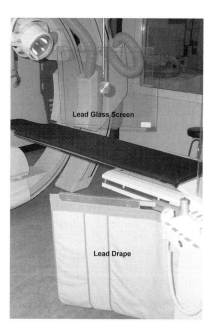

Figure 14.4 A complex fluoroscopic unit showing lead/rubber drapes to protect the legs and a lead/glass screen to protect the eyes and thyroid.

14.5 Patient protection in nuclear medicine

The radiation dose to the patient will be determined by the activity (in MBq) of the radiopharmaceutical used in the diagnostic study or therapeutic procedure. The amount of radioactivity that can be used in a diagnostic procedure is strictly regulated — in the UK, maximum activities (limits) for tests are specified by the Administration of Radioactive Substances Advisory Committee (ARSAC) of the Department of Health. The ARSAC limit for any investigation is considered to be the diagnostic reference level for that investigation. The ARSAC limits are published and are widely available. Similarly, therapeutic interventions require much higher activities and, as well as delivering a higher dose to the patient, which is of course necessary to achieve the therapeutic result, have the potential to deliver considerably higher doses to personnel and members of the public who come into contact with the patient.

As with diagnostic radiology, it is imperative that all procedures are justified, that the correct patient is examined, that examinations are not unnecessarily repeated and that special attention is paid to patients who are or might be pregnant. The nuclear medicine department in any hospital will have a list of referral criteria that will be available to all who are entitled to refer a patient for an investigation involving radiopharmaceuticals.

Points to note are:

- **Doses to patients having imaging examinations will not be trivial**. In general, the effective dose to a patient from a nuclear medicine imaging study will be considerably greater than that to a patient undergoing a plain film X-ray. In fact, it is more likely to be comparable with more complex radiological procedures such as barium and CT examinations (see Table 11.2). Non-imaging tests such as carbon-14 breath tests (effective dose 0.003 mSv) require far lower activities and result in much smaller doses.
- **Protection of other organs**: Radiopharmaceuticals may accumulate in organs other than those being investigated and techniques used to protect organs at risk are: (i) administering thyroid blocking agents when radio-iodine-labelled compounds are used to investigate parts of the body other than the thyroid; and (ii) encouraging patients to drink after a procedure is completed and to empty their bladder frequently to reduce doses to the bladder and surrounding organs.
- **Paediatric patients**: Special care must be taken with paediatric patients. Even when an examination is justified, the amount of radiopharmaceutical used will need to be modified to reflect the smaller size of the patient.
- **Pregnant patients**: Administration of a radiopharmaceutical to a pregnant woman will inevitably result in exposure of the fetus to radiation (§11.4.1). Consequently, any nuclear medicine examination of a pregnant woman will require particular justification (§11.6.3) since there will be no benefit to the unborn child whatsoever.
- **Breast-feeding patients**: When a radiopharmaceutical is administered to a breast-feeding mother, radioactivity will be secreted in her milk and her infant will suffer internal exposure from the radiation emitted by the ingested radioactivity. If the effective dose to the infant from breast-feeding is likely to be too high, then it should be reduced to an acceptable level by an interruption in feeding. It may be possible to express breast milk before the radiopharmaceutical is administered and give this to the baby for their next feed. If the radionuclide has a relatively slow rate of clearance, it may be necessary to stop breast-feeding altogether. Advice on this will be provided by the nuclear medicine department.

14.6 Staff protection in nuclear medicine

Radiation is much easier to control in the radiology environment than in nuclear medicine. In nuclear medicine, the patient is a mobile radioactive source, there is a potential dose rate from unused activity and there is a risk of internal and external dose arising from contamination, which can have a variety of sources. Radioactivity cannot be turned off like an X-ray beam, so staff protection is a complex problem. Some of the more important issues are outlined in the box on page 149.

Insight: Protection of staff dealing with diagnostic nuclear medicine patients

Lead protection: *A patient who is to have an imaging examination will usually be injected with several hundred MBq of ^{99m}Tc, which has a 6 h physical half-life. As already mentioned, lead aprons are of little use in a nuclear medicine environment. Free-standing lead shields are sometimes provided, but in general time and distance should be used to reduce radiation dose to the body.*

Syringe shields: *The radiation dose at the surface of a syringe used to inject the patient will be very high. As a result these syringes are encased in a tungsten or lead shield, which is intended to protect the operator's hand (Figure 14.2). At no time should the syringe shield be removed. The shield only surrounds the body of the syringe and there will be a measurable radiation dose rate at the plunger. Injections should therefore be performed quickly. Used syringes will contain a residue of radioactive material and must be disposed of as radioactive waste.*

On the ward: *It is important to remember that the patient will act as a radioactive source. The biological half-life governing removal of the radiopharmaceutical from the patient will usually be considerably less than 6 h, so the risk will decrease rapidly with time. In general, by the time the patient returns to the ward the risk is minimal and the advice given at the beginning of this chapter, i.e. to minimise the time spent near a patient whilst not compromising their care in any way, is probably the best available. It is prudent not to site two nuclear medicine patients in adjacent beds and it may be wise to store soiled linen for a day before consigning it to the laundry. Special care will need to be taken with incontinent patients. Many nuclear medicine departments provide information leaflets specifically aimed at ward staff.*

Outpatients *returning home or visiting their GP after a nuclear medicine imaging or laboratory investigation do not pose a significant risk to those around them.*

Radionuclide therapy patients

The situation is somewhat different for therapy patients who present their own particular problems. The most common nuclear medicine therapy, in which orally administered ^{131}I is used to treat hyperthyroidism, is usually carried out on an outpatient basis. Patients are provided with instruction leaflets telling them how long to stay off work, to avoid close contact with adults and children and if necessary other restrictions. Older patients who may reside in nursing homes can cause some logistical problems.

The same radionuclide, ^{131}I, can be used in considerably larger quantities to treat thyroid cancer and in this case the patient remains in hospital until the activity has reduced to levels that will allow them to be discharged. Specialised nursing is provided and the patient is always located in their own shielded room. Although dose rates from these patients can be quite high, many hospitals allow them to have visitors under controlled conditions using the relaxations allowed for comforters and carers. Written instructions issued to the patient by the hospital will outline the arrangements for visitors.

Other therapies, using β^--particle emitters such as ^{89}Sr, result in negligible radiation protection problems post administration owing to the nature of the radionuclide.

Pregnant staff

As is the case in diagnostic radiology, members of staff who become pregnant and who work with radioactivity should inform their employer of the fact. As well as the external hazard, there is the increased risk of internal contamination.

Contamination monitoring

Contamination monitoring is an essential aspect of all work with unsealed radionuclides. Sensitive instruments are used that can detect small amounts of radioactive material. Monitoring serves two purposes: the first is to demonstrate that there is no contamination present and the second is to show that the control measures that will have been put into place to prevent contamination actually work. It is important that contamination monitoring is carried out wherever there is work with radionuclides. Contamination monitoring can be of the hands or body or of the workplace. Monitoring should be performed in accordance with the written instructions issued by the Radiation Protection Supervisor.

14.7 Summary

- In radiology, the hazard is from external radiation.
- In nuclear medicine, the patient contains radioactivity. Hazard can arise from external radiation emitted from the patient and from radioactive contamination that can be taken into the body and give an internal hazard.
- Minimise the time that you are exposed to radiation.
- Use distance — the further you are from the radiation source, the lower the dose rate. You should not be present during an X-ray examination if you are not required.
- Use shielding devices provided for the task, *e.g.* lead/glass screens, lead aprons and thyroid collars for radiology, and syringe shields for injecting radiopharmaceuticals.
- Always wear any personal dose monitors provided by your employer.
- If you are involved in fluoroscopic examinations, be aware of radiology techniques and equipment features such as pulsed fluoroscopy, last image hold and added filtration that can reduce the dose to the patient.
- A lower radiation dose to the patient will usually give a lower dose to staff as well.
- Be aware of specific requirements for radiation examinations involving paediatric patients, pregnant patients or nuclear medicine patients who are breast-feeding.

Further reading

Martin CJ, Sutton DG. *Practical radiation protection in healthcare.* Oxford, UK: Oxford University Press, 2002.

Perkins AC. *Nuclear medicine: science and safety.* London, UK: Libby, 1995.

Chapter 15

Research projects involving radiation

K Goldstone

This chapter is more specialised, but it is very important for doctors who are planning research projects involving ionising radiation with either patients or volunteers.

The chapter considers all aspects of the problem and concludes with an essential checklist of issues that must be addressed before the project is submitted to an ethics committee.

15.1 Introduction

All research projects involving human subjects must be submitted for approval to an ethics committee. The committee is set up according to national laws and regulations and this committee ultimately decides whether the benefits of the research outweigh the risks to the individuals exposed in the project. Doctors who are planning to get involved in research will be quickly appraised by their peers of the requirements and constraints imposed by the ethics committee.

However, even experienced clinicians frequently overlook the fact that their project involves the use of ionising radiation, either directly or indirectly, and are not aware of the additional requirements that this imposes on the planning process.

One may ask why a research project involving the exposure of patients and volunteers to ionising radiation is different from any other research project. The reason is that if human beings are exposed to various drugs or physiological effects, there is a safe "threshold dose". However, in the case of stochastic effects of ionising radiation, e.g. cancer (see §10.3), the risk is assumed to be linearly related to dose, with no threshold. Therefore the lower the dose, the lower the risk, but the risk can never be considered zero. This means that not only the basic principles of research, but also the basic principles of radiation protection, must be applied.

If you plan to do a project that you think may use ionising radiation, it is important to discuss the project with radiation experts at an early stage to establish that ionising radiation is necessary. This is the start of the "justification" process. You will need to talk both to clinicians and to medical physics experts (MPEs) in the appropriate field, e.g. nuclear medicine. You will also need to discuss the project with the radiation protection adviser (RPA). These persons will be able to help you to calculate the radiation dose and to estimate the radiation risk, and to advise you of the legal requirements.

This chapter will give an overview of what is involved, looking at the principles of research that are affected by radiation protection considerations, calculating the radiation dose, estimating the risk, complying with legal requirements and submitting an application to the appropriate ethics committee.

15.2 Principles of medical research

The basic principles of medical research are set out in the Declaration of Helsinki adopted by the World Medical Assembly in Helsinki in June 1964, and subsequently amended — most recently in Edinburgh in October 2000 (with further clarification in Washington in 2002).

Table 15.1 Categories of risk and corresponding levels of benefit

Level of risk	Risk category (total risk)[a]	Corresponding effective dose range (adults) (mSv)	Level of societal benefit
Trivial	Category I ($\sim 10^{-6}$ or less)	<0.1	Minor
Minor to intermediate	Category II:		
	IIa ($\sim 10^{-5}$)	0.1–1	Intermediate to moderate
	IIb ($\sim 10^{-4}$)	1–10	
Moderate	Category III ($\sim 10^{-3}$ or more)	>10[b]	Substantial

[a]The risk as specified in the table takes into account fatal and non-fatal cancer risks and serious hereditary effects. For children, the detriment per dose is 2 to 3 times higher, and for adults over 50 years it is 5 to 10 times lower.

[b]To be kept below deterministic thresholds except for therapeutic experiments.

Note that these risk factors are average values, and age and sex may modify the risk factor. In young persons the risk may be a few times higher, and after the age of 50 years the risk decreases, being a factor of 5–10 lower at the age of 70–80 years (see §10.7).

Hereditary effects are of concern if the irradiated subjects are likely to have children. Therefore, unless specifically required for the study, younger persons are excluded. Also, by suitable selection of volunteers, the possibility of irradiating a fetus can be minimised.

In some circumstances individuals may wish to volunteer for multiple projects. Investigators should be aware of this possibility and take steps to minimise the chance of this occurring. Likewise, those already receiving a dose of ionising radiation as a result of their employment should not usually volunteer for research projects that subject them to additional dose, and classified workers (see §12.4) should definitely not participate.

15.6 Research with radionuclides

When unsealed radionuclides are involved there are two cases to consider, one where materials and techniques used for normal clinical procedures are employed, the other where novel radiopharmaceuticals are used. In the first case the radiopharmaceutical will have known dosimetry, and effective doses in terms of dose per unit of administered activity will be available in the literature, *e.g.* ICRP Publication 80. Where new radiopharmaceuticals are involved, special calculations will be needed to determine the dose. These will almost certainly be based on pharmacokinetic behaviour in animal experiments, which will give the relative uptakes in different organs and the change in activity in a specific organ with time. The MPE and the supplier of the radiopharmaceutical should be able to help with the dose calculation.

If new radiopharmaceuticals are required for therapeutic purposes, it would be normal practice for experimental animal data first to be extrapolated to human volunteers at a low administered activity (doses well below threshold doses) before being used at therapeutic activities.

If the project involves radioactive material, a licence will be required to administer the material for research purposes. In the UK an application has to be made to the Administration of Radioactive Substances Advisory Committee (ARSAC) for a licence. The radiopharmacist, the MPE in nuclear medicine and the RPA all have to sign the application form to confirm that facilities to carry out the project are adequate. The licence is valid for 2 years and is project- and hospital-specific. Only a person experienced in administration of radionuclides would be granted an ARSAC licence for a research project.

In addition, the researcher will need to confirm, usually with the RPA, that the radionuclide can be accommodated within the overall site licence for holding and, if using unsealed radioactive material, disposing of this specific radionuclide. If this is not the case a delay will almost certainly result while Registration and Authorisation for Disposal under the Radioactive Substances Act is arranged (see §12.6). A further complication may arise if the material is to be administered or used in a location where radioactive materials are not usually present, *e.g.* an operating theatre. In such circumstances risk assessments will be required to determine the precautions that need to be taken, including the level of training required for staff involved and the content of local rules.

15.7 Dose constraints and target doses

Where there is no direct medical benefit expected to the individual from an exposure, the researcher should establish a *dose constraint*. A dose constraint is defined in the Euratom Directive on Health Protection of Individuals against the Dangers of Ionising Radiation in relation to Medical Exposure (97/43 Euratom) as: "a restriction on the prospective doses to individuals which may result from a defined source, for use at the planning stage in radiation protection whenever optimisation is involved." The dose constraint should be set in consultation with an MPE (in the appropriate field) or the RPA. At worst, the constraint should be set at the limit of the risk/benefit band into which the project falls. However, a better approach, more in keeping with the principle of optimisation, is to consider the likely dose from the procedure and to allow some small leeway as a contingency, should it be necessary to repeat the study, *e.g.* a volunteer moves during a study; a poor injection is given and most of the radioactivity goes into adjacent tissue.

If there is expected to be some benefit for the individual, a *target dose* must be specified and individually planned for each participant in the project. This is likely to be the case in exposures undertaken for treatment purposes.

To show that there is compliance with the dose constraint or target dose, the researcher needs to consider how and where the dose information will be recorded. This is especially important if exposures are to take place in a department other than that in which the researcher works, exposures are going to take place in more than one location, or there will be serial exposures.

15.8 Selection of subjects and information for volunteers

The factors discussed result in the general considerations in selecting subjects for research shown in the box.

Insight: Summary of criteria for selection of volunteers

◊ *Age range: Wherever possible >50 years. Only if exceptional circumstances apply <18 years*
◊ *Numbers: Minimum necessary to obtain the information. Statistical analysis will be needed to establish this number; the study should not proceed if the anticipated numbers required to achieve a statistically significant result are unrealistically high*
◊ *Females: Pregnant and breast-feeding (if unsealed radionuclides are used) persons excluded unless that is the subject of the research*
◊ *Multiple studies: Annual dose constraint of 10 mSv for all research exposures. Previous exposure history should be considered*
◊ *Occupationally exposed workers: Must be aware of additional risks*
◊ *Classified workers: Should normally be excluded*

If the study includes the use of ionising radiation, this must be made clear in the information for volunteers. Many patients are not aware that, say, mammography, a scan or bone densitometry may involve the use of X-rays. To describe X-rays as "like light" may be true in the strict physics sense but it is misleading for the average patient.

The patient information sheet must include adequate detail on the radiation risk. For example, it may be entirely reasonable to state that the risk from an X-ray examination is extremely small. It is misleading to say there is no risk. Comparisons in everyday terms are often useful. You may wish to compare the dose with that from a single chest X-ray (approximately 20 µSv). Reference to natural background radiation is sometimes helpful. This is approximately 2.3 mSv per annum (6 µSv per day). Thus, a single chest X-ray carries approximately the same risk as 4 days background radiation. For further discussion of the perception of risk see §11.8.

Chapter 16

Radiation protection implications of screening

K Faulkner and J Law

Asymptomatic screening has an increasingly important role in modern medicine but there are special problems when it involves the use of ionising radiation.

Mammography is currently the most well established technique in this category and it is used here to illustrate how the benefit must exceed the risk by a fairly significant factor if screening is to be justified.

16.1 Introduction

The aim of screening is to detect the presence of disease in symptom-free persons by use of a simple medical procedure. For benefit to result, the disease in question must have a better prognosis when detected early, or before symptoms appear, than if it is left until symptoms cause the patient to seek medical advice. Screening is normally directed at a defined population, *e.g.* all persons (or those of one sex) in a specified age range, or those in a defined subgroup deemed to be at greater risk than others. Those who are screened are assumed to be healthy and are not patients at the time of initial screening, although they may become patients before more detailed investigations arising from screening are completed.

Before any screening programme is established, it is important to predict its likely impact. The general principles of screening are summarised in the box. Each potential screening programme should be tested against each criterion on this list. It is essential in any screening programme that the benefits justify the costs involved and that the benefits outweigh the risks.

General principles of screening (as outlined by the World Health Organisation)

- The condition screened for should pose an important health problem.
- The natural history of the condition should be well understood.
- There should be a recognisable latent or early stage.
- Treatment of disease at an early stage should be of more benefit than treatment started at a later stage.
- There should be a suitable test or examination.
- The examination should be acceptable to the population.
- For diseases of an insidious onset, screening should be repeated at intervals determined by the natural history of the disease.
- There should be adequate facilities available for the diagnosis and treatment of any abnormalities detected.
- The chance of physical or psychological harm should be less than the chance of benefit.
- The cost of funding (including diagnosis and subsequent treatment) should be economically balanced against the benefit it provides.

Insight: The balance of benefit and risk for breast screening

To assess the balance of benefit and risk, we must consider:
  (A) the cancer detection rate;
  (B) the X-ray dose to glandular tissues in the breast; and
  (C) the cancer induction risk factor (per unit radiation dose).

The number of cancers induced is given by (B) × (C) and may be compared with (A). The cancer detection rate (A) is well established for the NHSBSP. Typical breast cancer detection rates are around 5 per 1000 for women aged 50–64 years and detection rates increase with age. Future rates can be predicted to ±20% or better. The mean glandular dose (B) is known as a population average to ±2% or better. For a typical woman having two-view mammography, the glandular tissue receives an absorbed dose of 4.5 mGy. The cancer induction factor (C) for the screened age group is approximately 1 per 100,000 per mGy. It is known at best to within about a factor of 2. Combining (B) and (C), the rate of potential breast cancer induction is of the order of 5 per 100,000 women aged 50–70 years, and this decreases with age.

Normally (A) exceeds (B) × (C) by a factor of around 100 for women aged 50–70 years receiving 3-yearly screening, as in the NHSBSP, but the factor will be much lower for younger women and for annual screening. The balance of benefit and risk improves considerably as women get older. The ratio of cancers detected/induced may not be a strict estimate of benefit/risk; the latter will be less than the former, but they are unlikely to be very different.

These ratios are influenced by various factors, some of which are under our control while others are not. Cancer detection rates are certainly influenced by image quality in the X-ray film, e.g. by contrast and resolution or sharpness. Measures taken to improve image quality also tend generally to increase X-ray dose, e.g. high resolution or fine grain films and screens require a higher radiation dose (see §3.3.1). In addition, increasing the tube potential (kV) increases beam penetration, which in turn reduces both contrast (i.e. the ability to distinguish tissues with similar composition) and dose (see §3.2). Successful mammography depends not only on highly trained, experienced staff to position the women and to read the films, but also on the very best possible imaging techniques and equipment, all of which must be subject to strict quality control and peer review.

There are problems in establishing a quantitative relationship between cancer detections/inductions and benefit/risk. Not only is the radiation induction risk estimate uncertain by a factor of two, but there are problems in quantifying benefit owing to uncertainties in treatment outcome. For example, unlike many other forms of cancer, 5-year survival is not a very good index of "cure" for breast cancer; even 20-year survival is held by some to be insufficient. Also, because there is about a 10-year interval between radiation exposure and appearance of the first cancers that may result, most of those induced by the NHSBSP will arise after age 70 years when they may not be detected by screening. This is because there is a 10-year time interval after X-ray exposure before the first cancer induced by that exposure begins to appear. This makes it difficult to estimate the outcome of these potentially induced cancers.

The balance of benefit and risk is certainly affected by screening frequency and by the age of the women. If screening is performed annually instead of 3 yearly, the dose per screening round remains the same while the detection rate falls to about one-third of its previous value, although this fall is slightly reduced by a reduction in interval cancers. (Interval cancers are those that appear between screening rounds and are detected symptomatically.) Although annual screening of women aged 40–49 years may be acceptable from a radiation protection standpoint, such frequent screening may be inadvisable for women below 35 years without a family history of the disease. For those with such a family history, screening from a slightly lower age may be acceptable. This point remains under investigation and further advice should be sought if necessary. Screening of younger women, especially those with family history, requires many factors to be considered. Radiation risk is only one of these, but it must never be ignored or overlooked.

The balance between risk and benefit for breast screening

- Neither benefit nor risk can be precisely quantified but both can be estimated.
- Women with thicker or larger breasts receive higher doses, but benefit still exceeds risk for virtually every individual aged 50–70 years.
- This balance becomes increasingly favourable with age. Annual screening of women aged below 35–40 years (no family history) or aged below 30–35 years (with family history) may be inadvisable.
- In most situations the benefit/risk ratio will be less than but comparable with the ratio of cancer detection/induction..
- Careful consideration of many aspects is needed in determining policy on breast screening, but radiation risk must always be one of these.

Because of the geometry of mammography, with a collimated beam directed across the breast, there is negligible risk to other organs or to any fetus that might be present. The amount of scattered radiation is very small, which also means that mammography radiographers making hundreds of exposures per week will normally record no exposure on their dose monitors provided they remain behind the protective screens provided.

Radiation risks and benefits of any X-ray screening programme should be regularly monitored and assessed. They should also be included when considering changes to such programmes.

16.4 Bone mineral densitometry

Low bone density or osteoporosis is a condition that affects many post-menopausal women and some men. It results in a loss of mechanical strength in bone and gives the individual a predisposition to fractures. Bone mineralisation correlates with bone strength to some degree. Osteoporosis may be suspected if a patient has unremitting back pain after minor trauma, but the reader is directed to the Royal College of Radiologists' guidelines for further information (reference §13.4).

Bone mineral densitometry is now used extensively in situations where osteoporosis is suspected. General measures for treatment of osteoporosis include ensuring that the patient takes regular exercise and has an adequate calcium intake, together with medication. Since such treatment is more effective when given at an early stage, there are reasons for considering whether high-risk groups should be screened, but this is not yet established. There are various

---

Insight: Groups at risk of osteoporosis

Primary osteoporosis is found in patients who have:
◊ *pituitary disease or tumour, Cushing's syndrome, Turner's syndrome, microprolactinoma, Crohn's disease, coeliac colitis and any other malabsorption-related conditions;*
◊ *cystic fibrosis (excessive mucous from pancreas stops absorption);*
◊ *hyperparathyroidism, thyroid disease;*
◊ *hypogonadism;*
◊ *anorexia.*

Secondary osteoporosis, which is induced by side effects of treatment of other conditions, is also found in patients with:
◊ *asthma and other respiratory conditions (steroid treated);*
◊ *temporal arteritis (steroids);*
◊ *epilepsy (anticonvulsants);*
◊ *rheumatoid arthritis (steroids and immobility);*
◊ *Grave's disease;*
◊ *amenorrhoea.*

---

reasons for this. For example, reverting to the general principles of screening, not every woman with a low bone density will be at risk of a fracture. Furthermore, the treatment is not always effective.

The underlying principle of bone mineral densitometry is measurement of the attenuation of X-rays passing through the body. The technique uses measurements for two different X-ray beam energies and employs

Chapter 17

Overall diagnostic strategy and conclusions

AK Dixon

This final chapter draws together many of the issues that have been considered earlier in the book. These include the choice and sequence of investigations, good clinical practice, and risks relating to the use of ionising radiations. It also points out that all the above must be achieved within a framework of increasingly scarce resources.

17.1 Introduction

It is no easy task to emphasise the increasing importance of radiation issues to the wide range of medical doctors and other health workers who may now refer patients for imaging. Many of these issues have now been formalised into legislation, as discussed in Chapter 12. All doctors, young and old, now have to be aware of the technical aspects and risk issues of the various imaging techniques, especially now that patients are becoming better and better informed. It is hoped that the day will never come when a patient claims that a cancer in later life was caused by inappropriate radiation-intense diagnostic procedures in earlier years, but such potential issues are worth considering when choosing imaging procedures. All doctors have a duty to choose the most effective investigation (or investigation strategy), having carefully weighed up diagnostic accuracy, cost and risk. A blanket approach of requesting all possible relevant investigations must be discouraged — on the grounds of cost, potential risk and lost opportunity for other patients.

Throughout this chapter the word radiological request is used (advisedly). A clinician does not (theoretically) order a radiological investigation. A request for a radiological investigation is a request for a radiological opinion. Where an appropriate investigation is requested, this will be performed and a report issued. However, where the investigation requested is inappropriate, the radiologist has good grounds to refuse to perform it if it involves ionising radiation and offers no health gain; an example might include: "15-year-old girl — slipped on ice — X-ray sacrum/coccyx — ?fracture". Such radiology involves a moderate dose of radiation to the pelvic organs (*e.g.* ovaries), offers no therapeutic gain and should be discouraged.

For the above reasons the radiological team will frequently contact the referring clinician and suggest a more appropriate investigation with a lower radiation dose. For example, ultrasound or magnetic resonance imaging (MRI) of the pelvis would generally be preferred over computed tomography (CT) in most paediatric settings. To help with such decisions, national and European guidelines for making the best use of a department of clinical radiology (§13.4) have been prepared and most hospitals make these readily available to all doctors (increasingly accessible via Internet-based technology). Some of these aspects were considered in Chapter 13.

This chapter will attempt to bring the contents of the book into clinical focus by way of some specific clinical examples. In particular the following aspects will be considered:

- The choice of investigations and evidence of effectiveness.
- The sequence of investigations.

- Good clinical practice.
- Radiation issues.
- Making good use of scarce resources.

17.2 The choice of investigations and evidence of effectiveness

Doctors and other health professionals get somewhat baffled by the array of possible investigations on offer. New investigations emerge all the time. For example, when investigating certain hepatobiliary problems, any of the following investigations may be indicated: chest X-ray (CXR), abdominal X-ray (AXR), abdominal ultrasound, CT, endoscopic retrograde cholangiopancreatography (ERCP), MRI including magnetic resonance cholangiopancreatography (MRCP), barium studies, nuclear medicine studies including positron emission tomography (PET), and interventional studies including angiography. Clinical radiologists have the unique training and experience to provide help through this maze, increasingly so following discussion at multidisciplinary clinicoradiological meetings (Leung and Dixon, 1992).

Certain clinical set pieces (*e.g.* investigation of pulmonary embolus) have been subjected to meta-analysis and detailed cost effectiveness (Van Beek et al, 2001; Safriel and Zinn, 2002). However, in most available guidelines (§13.4) the majority of recommendations are still based on intermediate level evidence or even clinical consensus. This is largely because it is extremely difficult to obtain evidence about the effectiveness of radiological investigations (Mackenzie and Dixon, 1995), which can be broken down into five hierarchical levels: technical efficiency; diagnostic efficiency; diagnostic impact; therapeutic impact; and impact on health.

Most papers reporting new radiological advances are concerned about technical efficiency (*e.g.* 1.0 T *vs* 1.5 T MRI) or diagnostic efficacy (accuracy, sensitivity, specificity, predictive values of positive and negative results, etc). Only rarely do scientists examine whether the new investigation carries high diagnostic or therapeutic impact. Even less frequently is the effect of diagnostic imaging related to the outcome for the patient; screening mammography is one obvious exception. More often the influence of the investigation becomes overshadowed by the overall management of the patient (*e.g.* the poor overall progress in carcinoma of pancreas).

Even if there is little to choose between two investigations, other factors correctly play a part. In a landmark paper comparing CT with MRI in patients with possible posterior fossa lesions (Teasdale et al, 1989) there was no significant difference in the quality of life of patients offered one test rather than the other. However, clinicians much prefer the information provided by MRI (Southern et al, 1991) and this investigation does not use ionising radiation. Thus MRI is increasingly used. Maybe the patient should choose. Few patients with spinal disorders would wish for myelography in the era of MRI. But the replacement of an invasive investigation (myelography) with a non-invasive one (MRI) invariably means that many more patients are referred for sophisticated spinal imaging than in the past. This factor contributes to the ever increasing pressure on MRI and the development of long waiting lists (see §17.6).

The choice of investigations is also influenced by locally available expertise and the age/habitus of the patient. In my own institution we have extremely skilled ultrasound personnel in the department who have developed, amongst other things, ultrasound of the male urethra. However, this technique is not widely available and most institutions rely on ascending urethrography (embarrassing, invasive and radiation intense). By the same token, not all radiologists are confident about excluding appendicitis by ultrasound, hence the increasing use of CT. The patient's habitus also comes into the equation: ultrasound gives much better information in thin patients and this technique may become impossible in the obese. Conversely, CT is easier in patients with moderate fat stores. Happily most children are thin and thus ultrasound may often solve intra-abdominal problems thereby avoiding ionising radiation.

17.3 The sequence of investigations

Quite apart from the perceived effectiveness of the various investigations, the sequence in which they are performed may have considerable bearing on the way in which a diagnosis is established. Investigation of a patient with possible pulmonary embolus (PE) provides an interesting example where the sequence and range of investigations vary extensively from hospital to hospital and from country to country.

There have probably been more papers analysing effectiveness and cost effectiveness for investigation of PE than for any other clinical condition (*e.g.* Van Beek et al, 2001). Nevertheless, considerable controversy reigns, not least because of the speed with which new investigations emerge (CT pulmonary angiography (CTPA), MR pulmonary angiography (MRPA), D-dimer testing, etc). A protocol that is widely adopted in many hospitals in the UK broadly divides patients into two groups: those with a normal CXR proceed to ventilation/perfusion (VQ) scintigraphy; those with an abnormal CXR undergo spiral CTPA (Cross et al, 1998). Patients with indeterminate results may proceed to the alternate investigation. Only a very small minority proceed to formal pulmonary angiography even though this is still regarded (by some) as the definitive investigation. There is increasing demand for CT in all patients as, with new multidetector CT, the cause of the chest pain or dyspnoea should be apparent in all patients with significant disease. This may, in time, lead to a reduction in the use of VQ scintigraphy.

Sometimes the sequence of investigations must proceed along certain lines. For example, CT of the abdomen should generally precede barium studies because the barium residue will cause artefacts on subsequent CT images (§4.7.3). Conventional diagnostic angiography (less often requested now in the era of CT/MRI) should precede CT, as bowel opacification on CT may obscure some angiographic detail. Such technique-specific sequencing of investigations may contradict the usual tendency to start with simple investigations and work towards more complex ones. But such thinking may not always be correct. It is increasingly argued that a single, comprehensive, sophisticated (albeit expensive) investigation at the outset may yield the correct diagnosis more quickly with savings in inpatient stay and morbidity. Use of CTPA for possible PE has already been alluded to; this investigation can be extended to include a venous phase study of the abdomen, pelvis and thighs, which may confirm pelvic thrombus and even demonstrate the silent intra-abdominal neoplasm that promoted thrombo-embolism. Another example would be the increasing use of CT for acute abdominal problems: patients with a normal CT could be discharged; those with clear evidence of appendicitis can be quickly scheduled for appropriate surgery (Rao et al, 1998).

17.4 Good clinical practice

The art of requesting radiographic examinations is a matter of fine judgement. It is all too easy to err on the side of caution and over-investigate, even though this wastes scarce resources (see §17.6). It is also tempting to be cavalier and only investigate selectively. The first group of patients may suffer harm because of false positive results. Inevitably the second group may suffer through a missed diagnosis. Two examples will be considered.

A relatively well woman aged 40 years experiences minor right hypochondrial intermittent pain. An ultrasound examination is requested; some small gall stones are seen, which probably account for the symptoms. However, the ultrasound also shows a solitary, tiny 10 mm echogenic structure in the liver; liver function tests and other blood tests are normal. Nevertheless the clinician decides to investigate the lesion by CT. This cannot determine the nature of the lesion. The patient becomes anxious. The clinician requests an ultrasound-guided liver biopsy. The patient undergoes the biopsy as a day case. She has an anxious wait for the biopsy result (a benign lesion). The likelihood of this small solitary liver lesion being something sinister was around 1 in 100.

The other scenario is a man aged 40 years with non-specific back pain. The general practitioner correctly checks for worrying features; blood tests reveal normal findings, including white cell count and erythrocyte sedimentation rate. The back pain is deemed to be due to early degenerative changes and it is considered that a radiograph would be non-contributory; in any event it would impart a modest radiation dose. 6 months later the patient re-presents with new neurological symptoms in the leg. MRI now reveals evidence of a slow growing (fortunately benign) neurofibroma in one of the lumbar spine exit foramina. The likelihood that this type of patient had something serious in the lumbar spine at outset was much less than 1 in 100.

These two clinical histories highlight the difficulty faced by the clinician. In the light of current publicity given by the media to medical cases, the clinician may feel that he is "damned if he does, and damned if he doesn't!" Hence the comfort of well designed and evidence-based guidelines. The general practitioner in the second case had correctly made attempts (by blood tests) to exclude infection and disseminated malignancy and could easily resist any potential litigation.

Even with established guidelines, practising clinicians tend to cluster into two groups; those that generally over-investigate and those that investigate more selectively. The latter group tend to be the more experienced clinicians who place considerable value on the clinical history and physical examination — both time consuming. Clinicians in the former group may not spend so much time with the patient at presentation but may consider all the results in detail at follow-up. There is no right or wrong here, merely differences in philosophy. Medical students and junior doctors may observe a wide range of referral practices and will, over the years, establish their own pattern of practice.

17.5 Radiation issues

These have been dealt with in detail by experts in other sections of the book. But, under the Ionising Radiation (Medical Exposure) Regulations (IRMER), radiation exposure must always be considered as part of the overall diagnostic strategy.

When deciding upon investigative strategies, paediatric clinical problems pose particular difficulties. It is all too easy to apply similar strategies in children as used in adults. However, CT should be avoided wherever possible in children. Thus, should the child with equivocal right iliac fossa signs be investigated by CT for possible appendicitis? In the ideal world there would be an ultrasound expert readily available 24 h a day for just this sort of problem. But relatively few ultrasonographers have the necessary skills to allow confident *exclusion* of appendicitis. So does the clinician rely on clinical signs and risk missing a perforated appendix, or is CT justified despite its radiation dose? Again there is no correct answer — much may depend on the individual case. Nevertheless, it is likely that over the coming years there will be increasing levels of discussion, especially regarding the justification of radiation-intense procedures in children (Golding and Shrimpton, 2002).

Even in somewhat later life these issues are important. A man aged 30 years with testicular teratoma undergoes staging CT of the chest, abdomen and pelvis at presentation. If a surveillance policy is adopted following orchiectomy, conventional policy is to use repeated CT as a means of follow-up. But this essentially fit patient could receive a considerable radiation dose over the next 5 years, especially if the pelvis is examined at each visit. Recent work has shown that CT of the pelvis might be safely omitted at follow-up in most patients. A more innovative approach might be to replace CT by MRI, if capacity permits (see §17.6).

Obviously the concerns about radiation become less significant as the patient becomes older or when there is established advanced malignancy.

Despite concerns about radiation dose — and some clinicians still question the concept that the *diagnostic* use of radiation is linked to subsequent cancer (see Figure 10.4) — it is worth remembering that no appropriate investigation should be withheld on radiation grounds alone. It may very well be necessary to perform CT on a young child with unexplained abdominal symptoms, but the decision should be made at a senior level after detailed clinicoradiological discussion. Furthermore, such investigations should not be repeated unless absolutely necessary.

17.6 Making the best use of scarce resources

The relative cost of health care continues to increase exponentially and so too does the cost of imaging. It is a matter for taxpayers, insurers and individuals to decide whether this can go on indefinitely. In the UK there are significant capacity restraints in terms of equipment, staffing and finance. Few hospitals have as much modern equipment as they would like. There are several significant deficiencies: some district general hospitals still have no MRI system on site; there is a dire shortage of PET facilities in the UK.

The next problem is that there is a worldwide shortage of radiologists and radiographers despite heroic efforts to train more. This in part reflects the considerable success of modern radiology: the nationwide adoption of screening mammography required significant extra manpower; advances such as MRI have also consumed trained (and re-trained) staff.

Even in an institution that has good equipment and adequate staffing, it is unlikely that the hospital budget could afford unlimited expansion of the workload (*e.g.* by running MRI 24 h a day, 7 days a week). Any increase in costs would probably have to be capped at around 5–10% growth per annum.

All these factors mean that most radiology departments have to keep the overall workload close to the out-turn of the previous year (perhaps 5–10% increase). Even in more affluent countries (*e.g.* USA) care is being "managed" so that the number of examinations are controlled — a far cry from the "fee for service" models of old.

Hence the development of guidelines and general education about referrals (see §13.4). In broad terms, if a clinician obtains one unnecessary examination, it may be at the expense of an important investigation on his next patient or that of a colleague. This "lost opportunity" is being seen as an important concept in health economics.

These factors highlight the relevance of the personal philosophy outlined in §17.4 — good clinical practice. Some clinicians tend to be over-investigators; others may make requests more frugally. It could be argued that over-investigators are "poaching" imaging slots that might be available for patients from the under-investigators. Some radiology departments publish league tables showing the number of requests made by various clinicians, firms or departments and let others decide whether any particular group is being particularly profligate. What is always upsetting for all clinicians (and radiology staff) is when it proves difficult to schedule a really important investigation because all appointments have been filled with others that are likely to offer limited diagnostic and therapeutic impact. An example of a really important procedure would be a CT-guided biopsy of a young patient with a para-aortic mass shown by ultrasound — the likely diagnosis is non-Hodgkin's lymphoma, a haematological malignancy with reasonable prognosis. However, the CT capacity over the next few days might be congested with referrals at the margins of appropriateness, *e.g.* investigation of the colon in a frail 95-year-old patient with mild iron deficiency anaemia. Similarly, it can be very difficult to obtain urgent MRI examinations in many units. This causes frustration for junior hospital doctors who have to "negotiate" with radiology staff who get equally frustrated that they cannot offer a prompt appointment for urgent cases. Many radiology departments reserve several appointments per week for "emergencies" that they know will occur. But this delays the routine referrals. Sometimes an urgent appointment can only be accommodated by postponing another appointment; the clinician may be asked "is this examination more urgent than the one scheduled for your other patient this afternoon?"

In the ideal world, radiology departments would only book at 90% capacity to allow prompt appointments for the inevitable emergency work. In practice the referrals escalate to fill any void. This is particularly true for non-invasive procedures that have replaced invasive ones. For example, referrals for MRCP (Lomas et al, 1999) are increasing rapidly, overcoming the potential morbidity of ERCP studies.

For all the above reasons, waiting lists develop and emergency work is increasingly performed out of hours. At least no one can say that radiology is not in demand!

17.7 Conclusions

The purpose of this book has been to draw together related themes. On the one hand it provides an up-to-date review of the diagnostic imaging modalities currently available. Chapters are devoted to conventional radiology, CT, nuclear medicine, ultrasound and MRI.

Several of these investigations make increasing use of ionising radiation. Therefore, the second objective has been to review the evidence that X-rays and radioactive materials can cause harm. Chapters on basic radiobiology and risk assessment show how the risks from a particular examination can be estimated and explain why the ALARP principle (as low as reasonably practicable) (§12.3.3) is adopted as a conservative approach to radiation protection. The diagnostic use of X-rays is now more formally regulated. So, in this context, the book is meant to provide a guide through the maze of legislation, pointing out the rules that apply for doctors in training, doctors starting on the wards or beginning to use fluoroscopic techniques and senior members of the profession who wish to brush up on these matters.

Subsequent chapters discuss the importance of striking the correct balance between clinical benefit and radiation damage or risk in a wide range of situations including adult and paediatric radiology, screening techniques, research projects and radiotherapy. Radiotherapy is an extreme case where some normal tissue damage is accepted as an unavoidable consequence of attacking the tumour. In diagnostic procedures the long-term risk is more theoretical, never having been demonstrated in patients, but must always be considerably less than the clinical benefit.

The range of techniques available for imaging often provides a number of possible options for assessing any particular patient. Collective experience has established which are the most suitable to use for different types of investigation. For some organs, one particular imaging investigation may be obviously superior and provide all the clinical information that is required for assessment of a certain type of disease. For other organs, different techniques may give complementary evidence and all contribute to the final diagnosis.

The recommended methods for investigating particular organs and diseases often change with time as new techniques appear. It is important that those responsible for medical exposures keep up-to-date with current trends to ensure that each patient receives the best diagnosis and treatment available at the time, with the lowest risk.

This final chapter has considered many of the important features of these twin themes and has tried to put them into a wider clinical and practical context to show how radiation and legislation might be managed in a busy NHS hospital.

It is inevitable that there will be increasing scrutiny of radiology departments in the coming years in all parts of the world. In many ways the UK and the European Union lead in these matters. Radiation from diagnostic procedures is taken more seriously in the UK than in many countries. Radiographers are, quite rightly, trained to question inappropriate referrals, and radiologists are expected to contact clinicians and discuss alternative (less radiation intense) imaging strategies. Such dialogue is time consuming and may tend to disrupt professional relationships. Indeed some radiologists may be regarded as being "difficult" about certain requests. Others may flinch from such confrontation. However, increasing inspections from various statutory bodies — often with little or no warning — make it imperative that radiation issues are well policed and kept well at the forefront of radiology departmental strategy. Thus, radiation doses must be properly documented, the ALARP principle applied and requests properly vetted and audited. Staff must constantly seek methods of lowering dose whenever possible. Woe betide any department or NHS Trust without proper documentation. The Manager, Clinical Director and other personnel would have a very rocky ride in these days of clinical governance!

By way of concluding this discussion, it is worth rehearsing the three distinct groups of personnel responsible for diagnostic procedures involving ionising radiation.

- *The referrer*: often a clinician who is duty bound to provide sufficient clinical information to justify the exposure. Increasing delegation tends to reduce the clinical information supplied.
- *The operator*: usually a radiographer who performs the examination in accordance with the ALARP principles.
- *The practitioner*: usually a radiologist who takes overall responsibility for the work generated by the above two groups.

Ultimately, the practitioner's employer carries the final responsibility for ensuring the quality of the imaging service.

It is hoped that you, as a responsible clinician, armed with the material in this book will be able to make effective use of the facilities provided by the imaging departments in your local hospitals. If you consider the interests of your patient and the needs of the imaging department when making any request, you should avoid any serious problems!

References and further reading

Cross JJL, Kemp PM, Walsh CG, Flower CDR, Dixon AK. A randomized trial of spiral CT and ventilation perfusion scintigraphy for the diagnosis of pulmonary embolism. *Clin Radiol* 1998;53:177–82.

Golding SJ, Shrimpton PC. Radiation dose in CT: are we meeting the challenge? *Br J Radiol* 2002;75:1–4.

Leung DPY, Dixon AK. Clinicoradiological meetings: are they worthwhile? *Clin Radiol* 1992;46:279–80.

Lomas DJ, Bearcroft PWP, Gimson AE. MR cholangiopancreatography: prospective comparison of a breath-hold 2D projection technique with diagnostic ERCP. *Eur Radiol* 1999; 9:1411–7.

Mackenzie R, Dixon AK. Measuring the effects of imaging: an evaluative framework. *Clin Radiol* 1995;50:137–43.

Rao PM, Rhea JT, Novelline RA, Mostafavi AA, McCabe CJ. Effect of computed tomography of the appendix on treatment of patients and use of hospital resources. *N Engl J Med* 1998;338:141–6.

Safriel Y, Zinn H. CT pulmonary angiography in the detection of pulmonary emboli: a meta-analysis of sensitivities and specificities. *Clin Imaging* 2002;26:101–5.

Southern JP, Teale A, Dixon AK, et al. An audit of the clinical use of magnetic resonance imaging of the head and spine. *Health Trends* 1991;23:75–9.

Teasdale GM, Hadley DM, Lawrence A, et al. Comparison of magnetic resonance imaging and computed tomography in suspected lesions in the posterior cranial fossa. *BMJ* 1989;299:349–55.

Van Beek EJ, Brouwers EM, Song B, Bongaerts AH, Oudkerk M. Lung scintigraphy and helical computed tomography for the diagnosis of pulmonary embolism: a meta-analysis. *Clin Appl Thromb Hemost* 2001;7:87–92.

Index